access to history

War and Peace: International Relations

1890–1941

DAVID G. WILLIAMSON

FOURTH EDITION

HODDER
EDUCATION
AN HACHETTE UK COMPANY

To Saul, Luca and Marco

The Publishers would like to thank Nicholas Fellows and David Ferriby for their contribution to the Study Guide.

The Publishers would like to thank the following for permission to reproduce copyright material:

Photo credits: p2 Hulton-Deutsch Collection/Corbis; **p4** Library of Congress, LC-DIG-ggbain-16825; **p15** Library of Congress, LC-USZ62-122505; **p25** "1890 Bismarcks Ruecktritt". Licensed under Public domain via Wikimedia Commons; **p30** Library of Congress, LC-USZ62-89797; **p37** Bildagentur für Kunst, Kultur und Geschichte; **p49** Bettmann/Corbis; **p66** Bettmann/Corbis; **p67** Corbis; **p68** Library of Congress, LC-USZ62-111781; **p71** Hulton Archive/Getty Images; **p74** Bettmann/Corbis; **p78** Bettmann/Corbis; **p99** Bettmann/Corbis; **p120** Hulton-Deutsch Collection/Corbis; **p128** Hulton-Deutsch Collection/Corbis; **p134** Library of Congress; **p145** Popperfoto/Getty Images; **p146** Library of Congress, LC-USZ62-48839; **p154** Library of Congress, LC-USZ62-32833; **p158** Hulton-Deutsch Collection/Corbis; **p172** Parliamentary information licensed under the Open Parliament Licence v3.0; **p185** Hulton-Deutsch Collection/Corbis; **p188** Bettmann/Corbis; **p203** Corbis; **p207** Library of Congress, LC-USZ62-104778.

Acknowledgements: are listed on page 244.

Every effort has been made to trace all copyright holders, but if any have been inadvertently overlooked the Publishers will be pleased to make the necessary arrangements at the first opportunity.

Although every effort has been made to ensure that website addresses are correct at time of going to press, Hodder Education cannot be held responsible for the content of any website mentioned in this book. It is sometimes possible to find a relocated web page by typing in the address of the home page for a website in the URL window of your browser.

Hachette UK's policy is to use papers that are natural, renewable and recyclable products and made from wood grown in sustainable forests. The logging and manufacturing processes are expected to conform to the environmental regulations of the country of origin.

Orders: please contact Bookpoint Ltd, 130 Milton Park, Abingdon, Oxon OX14 4SE. Telephone: +44 (0)1235 827720. Fax: +44 (0)1235 400454. Lines are open 9.00a.m.–5.00p.m., Monday to Saturday, with a 24-hour message answering service. Visit our website at www.hoddereducation.co.uk

© David G. Williamson
Fourth edition © David G. Williamson 2015

First published in 1994 by
Hodder Education
An Hachette UK Company
Carmelite House, 50 Victoria Embankment
London EC4Y 0DZ

Impression number   10 9 8 7 6 5 4 3
Year   2019 2018 2017

Cover image: The Trail of War, 1919 (depicting destroyed Turkish aircraft) (oil on canvas) by Sydney Carline (1888–1929), © York Museums Trust (York Art Gallery), UK/Bridgeman Images
Produced, illustrated and typeset in Palatino LT Std by Gray Publishing, Tunbridge Wells
Printed and bound by CPI Group (UK) Ltd, Croydon CR0 4YY

A catalogue record for this title is available from the British Library

ISBN 978 1471838286

Contents

Dedication

Keith Randell (1943–2002)

The *Access to History* series was conceived and developed by Keith, who created a series to 'cater for students as they are, not as we might wish them to be'. He leaves a living legacy of a series that for over 20 years has provided a trusted, stimulating and well-loved accompaniment to post-16 study. Our aim with these new editions is to continue to offer students the best possible support for their studies.

CHAPTER 1

International relations 1879–1945: an introduction

The purpose of this introductory chapter is to help you to understand the overall pattern of events before studying the complexity of international relations during the period 1890–1945 in greater detail. It sets the scene by examining:

★ The ideological background

★ The Great Powers 1890–1945

Key dates

1879		Austro-German Alliance	
1894		Franco-Russian Alliance	
1904		Anglo-French *entente*	
1914	**Aug.**	Outbreak of First World War	
1917		USA declared war on Germany	
	Oct.	Bolshevik revolution in Russia	
1918		Defeat of the Central Powers	
1919		Treaty of Versailles	
1929–33		Great Depression	

1933		Hitler appointed chancellor of Germany
1939	**Sept. 3**	Britain and France declared war on Germany
1941	**June 22**	Germany attacked USSR
	Dec. 7–8	Japan attacked Pearl Harbor
1945	**May 9**	Unconditional surrender of Germany
	Aug. 15	Unconditional surrender of Japan

1   The ideological background

▶ *To what extent were imperialism, nationalism and militarism major causes of the First World War?*

▶ *Why did Fascism and National Socialism develop into mass movements after the end of the First World War?*

The late nineteenth and the early years of the twentieth century were a period of peace and growing **economic integration**, but at the same time public opinion was becoming increasingly nationalist and imperialist. The emergence of the popular press, cheap newspapers with a wide circulation and the extension of the franchise all ensured that public opinion increasingly influenced

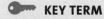 **KEY TERM**

Economic integration
Mutual dependence and the coming together of national economies.

foreign policy. **Imperialism**, **nationalism** and **militarism** were the prevalent national ideologies in the two decades before 1914 and intensified the divisions and tensions between the Great Powers who, in the words of the historian F.S. Northedge, surveyed 'each other through their visors like medieval knights in the jousting field'.

Imperialism

European imperialism and the expansion of European power into Africa and Asia in the final two decades of the nineteenth century were caused by several factors. Businessmen and industrialists put pressure on their governments to annex areas where they had important economic interests. Strategy also played a key role. Britain, for instance, occupied Egypt in order to safeguard the Suez Canal and the route to India. Increasingly, the governments of the Great Powers, urged on by public opinion, began to believe that they could only remain powerful as long as they had colonial empires which could provide trade, access to raw materials and opportunities for settlement.

Statesmen and political thinkers became affected by **social Darwinism** and were convinced that international life was a struggle for survival where only the strongest nations would survive. The French economist Paul Leroy-Beaulieu (1843–1916), for example, stressed that it was 'a matter for life and death' for France to become a 'great African nation or in a century or two she will be no more than a secondary European power, and will count in the world as much as Greece or Romania'.

KEY TERMS

Imperialism The policy of acquiring and controlling dependent territories carried out by a state.

Nationalism A patriotic belief by a people in the virtues and power of their nation.

Militarism Excessive emphasis on military ideals and strength. The supremacy of military values such as discipline, obedience and courage in a society.

Social Darwinism The application of Darwin's theory of the survival of the fittest to international relations, justifying the absorption of smaller, weaker states by more powerful ones.

SOURCE A

? Study Source A. Is this photograph evidence of German militarism or just love of tradition?

Kaiser Wilhelm at a German army review in Berlin in 1912. Wilhelm (in the centre on horseback) is surrounded by imperial footguards whose uniforms hark back to King Frederick of Prussia (1740–86).

Nationalism

Imperialism went hand in hand with nationalism. Earlier in the nineteenth century nationalism in Italy and Germany had been essentially a **liberal ideology** aimed at achieving national unification and establishing a constitutional government. The main aim of nationalists was to unite their countries. Once this was achieved, the emphasis of nationalism gradually shifted to asserting the power of a nation on the global stage. To unify their countries and overcome class or regional differences, governments frequently exploited nationalism by pursuing a policy that later historians have called **social imperialism**.

Militarism

The nationalist and imperialist rivalries of the Great Powers inevitably encouraged militarism. The armed forces were the key instruments, not only in defence, but also in carving out empires and projecting national strength. In Germany, particularly, the army enjoyed huge prestige and was independent of parliamentary control, while in Britain public opinion played a key role in forcing the government to accelerate the construction of modern battleships, the **Dreadnoughts**, in 1908 (see page 38). In Germany and Britain, **pressure groups** were formed to force the government to accelerate the build-up of the armed forces. In both countries, for example, Navy Leagues played a key role in the development of large navies. The acceptance of military values by large sections of people in all the great European states undoubtedly contributed to the mood which made war possible and to the enthusiasm with which the outbreak of war in 1914 was greeted in every belligerent state.

Fascism and National Socialism

Extreme nationalism, imperialism and militarism were all important components of **Fascism** and **National Socialism**, which became major movements after the end of the First World War. However, even before 1914 in Italy and France extreme nationalist groups were already attempting to fuse nationalism with **socialism** to create a more socially united and therefore stronger national state. One French nationalist, Charles Maurras (1868–1952), wrote in 1899 that there existed 'a form of socialism which when stripped of its democratic and cosmopolitan accretions [additions] would fit with nationalism just as a well-made glove fits a beautiful hand'. This was initially the driving force behind both Fascism and National Socialism. For Hitler, however, anti-Semitism and the desire to make Germany a 'racially pure state' rapidly became the dominant factor in National Socialism.

It was the impact and consequences of the First World War that enabled Fascism and Nazism to become mass movements. In Italy, economic crises, a sense of being cheated at the Paris Peace Conference in 1919 of its just rewards as a member of the victorious coalition (see page 103), and above all the fear of a

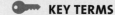

KEY TERMS

Liberal ideology Belief in constitutional government and individual and economic freedom.

Social imperialism A policy aimed at uniting all social classes behind plans for creating and expanding an empire.

Dreadnought A class of battleship of 17,900 tons compared to the conventional size of 16,000, its speed was 21 knots rather than 16, and it was much better armed than its predecessors.

Pressure group An association formed to promote a particular interest by influencing government policy.

Fascism The Fascist Party was formed in Italy by Mussolini in 1919. Its programme combined social reforms and a tax on war profits with an intensely nationalist foreign policy.

National Socialism German National Socialism had many similarities with Fascism, but its driving force was race, and in particular anti-Semitism.

Socialism A belief that the community as a whole rather than individuals should control the economy.

SOURCE B

Study Source B. In what way did the construction of Dreadnoughts revolutionise battleship construction?

HMS *Colossus*, one of the new Dreadnought-class of battleships was launched in 1910, and in August 1914 eventually became the flagship of the Royal Navy's First Battle Squadron.

🔑 KEY TERM

Great Depression The world economic slump from 1929 to 1933.

Bolshevik revolution, created the context in which Benito Mussolini, the leader of the Italian Fascist Party, gained power in 1922 (see page 134). In Germany it took another ten years and the impact of the **Great Depression** (see page 144) before Hitler (see page 149) and German National Socialism could come to power.

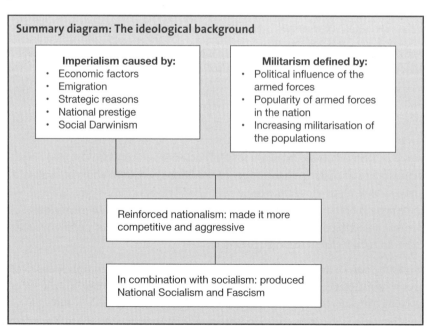

Summary diagram: The ideological background

Imperialism caused by:
- Economic factors
- Emigration
- Strategic reasons
- National prestige
- Social Darwinism

Militarism defined by:
- Political influence of the armed forces
- Popularity of armed forces in the nation
- Increasing militarisation of the populations

Reinforced nationalism: made it more competitive and aggressive

In combination with socialism: produced National Socialism and Fascism

2 The Great Powers 1890–1945

▶ *To what extent were the tensions, which led to the two world wars of 1914–18 and 1939–45, already visible by 1900?*

▶ *Why was the acquisition and possession of colonies considered so vital to the Great Powers during this period?*

In 1890 the European Great Powers still dominated the world. Britain and France each had large colonial empires in Africa and Asia, while Russia seemed poised to expand into China. Germany and Italy were recently established states which had only achieved unity in the decade 1860–70. German unity, which was achieved by the defeat of France, was dramatically to alter the balance of power in Europe. Austria-Hungary and the Turkish Empire were both described in the First World War by a German general as 'rotting corpses', as they were both empires in decline, although in 1890 they still possessed reserves of power and influence. Outside Europe, both the USA and Japan were emerging as formidable powers, while China seemed on the verge of disintegration.

Germany

Germany's economy was the strongest in Europe, its population growth was outstripping Britain and France and it had the most formidable army, which had defeated France in 1870–1. Yet, looking at the British and French Empires, it perceived itself to be excluded from global power and feared that ultimately it might be strangled by the great imperial powers. In short, it considered itself a 'have-not nation'. Consequently, one of the main themes of German foreign policy from 1890 to 1914 was **Weltpolitik**, which aimed at acquiring colonies, particularly in Africa. When faced with superior British sea power in the First World War and the loss of its few possessions in Africa and Asia, Germany sought compensation in Europe and particularly Russia by creating a German-dominated **Mitteleuropa**, which would compensate for its lack of a colonial empire. By November 1918, German troops controlled almost as much of western Russia as Hitler did in the summer of 1942.

This prize was snatched away by defeat on the Western Front in 1918. The Treaty of Versailles stripped Germany of all its wartime gains, global investments and colonies, and in the eyes of the German people confirmed its status as a 'have-not nation', even though its potential strength remained unimpaired. The collapse of Austria-Hungary, the creation of a weak Polish state and Russia's loss of the western Ukraine left Germany in a potentially strong position.

The key question was, how would Germany exploit its latent strength? Would Germany use it, as its foreign minister Gustav Stresemann (see page 117) did between 1924 and 1929, to co-operate with Britain and France in the peaceful reconstruction of a Europe which Germany through its natural strength would

 **KEY TERMS**

Weltpolitik Literally 'world policy' or a policy that attempted to make Germany a global power.

Mitteleuropa A German-controlled central Europe.

KEY TERMS

Lebensraum Literally 'living space', which Hitler hoped to acquire in Russia for German settlement.

Reich The German Empire or state.

Central Powers The wartime alliance of Germany, Austria, Turkey and Bulgaria.

Mutilated victory A victory which was scarred by the refusal of the Allies to give Italy what it had been promised.

Prussia An independent state until German unification in 1871.

come to dominate, or would it use force? Once Hitler was swept into power by the Great Depression, it became increasingly clear which option Germany was going to take. Hitler was determined to colonise western Russia and thereby create **Lebensraum** for the German people and finally free Germany from its dependence on the Western powers. Germany's defeat in 1945 put an end to these plans and resulted in 1945–9 in the division of the German **Reich** into two separate states, which were only reunified in 1990.

Italy

Italy had been unified in the same decade as Germany, and liked to see itself as a Great Power in the traditions of Ancient Rome. In reality, Italy was one of the weakest of the European powers both economically and militarily. In 1896 its attempt to annex Abyssinia ended with a humiliating defeat at Adowa.

Italian foreign policy right up to 1943 was essentially opportunistic and aimed at securing influence and territory in the Mediterranean. Italy could gain most when Europe was divided into rival alliances, which attempted to outbid each other for its favours. Thus, in May 1915 Italy was bribed by the Treaty of London with promises of territory in north Africa and along the Dalmatian coast to join Britain and France rather than the **Central Powers**.

Although Italy emerged from the war strengthened by the collapse of Austria-Hungary, the failure of the Allies to honour the promises made at the Treaty of London (see page 64) left it embittered, and even more determined to assert its power in the Mediterranean and northern Africa. Indeed, what was called the **mutilated victory** of 1918 was one of the causes of Fascism's growing popularity and Mussolini's coming to power in 1922.

In the 1930s Mussolini initially hoped to benefit from Hitler's seizure of power to extract concessions from Britain and France, but their failure to agree to the Italian occupation of Abyssinia gave Mussolini little option but to gravitate towards Nazi Germany. In May 1939 he signed the Pact of Steel with Germany, but did not declare war on Britain and France until June 1940, when he was convinced that with the fall of France Hitler had already won the war. Mussolini was overthrown by the Italians themselves in 1943. The new government then negotiated an armistice with Britain and France, but the Germans occupied much of Italy until their defeat in 1945.

France

France had been defeated by **Prussia** in 1871, and both economically and in terms of population size it had been overtaken by Germany and Britain. France's industrial base was small and its coal deposits were a fraction of those of Britain and Germany. France had nevertheless managed to rebuild and re-equip its army and compensate for the relative smallness of population by building up a large north African empire, which would provide men in time of war.

The key to France's survival as an independent power, however, lay in its ability to forge a strong alliance system to contain Germany. The crucial move in this direction was the alliance with Russia in 1894. Worried about the ultimate effectiveness of the Russian Alliance, the French tried to underpin it by bringing years of Anglo-French friction and rivalry to an end through the negotiation of the 1904 colonial agreement and *entente* with London. Germany's and Austria's isolation in Europe by 1914 is striking evidence of the success of French policy in breaking out of the isolation in which Bismarck had initially so successfully confined it for almost 20 years after its defeat.

With British and later US help, France was able to defeat the Central Powers in 1918, but it was a **pyrrhic victory**. France emerged in 1919 as an exhausted power. It had failed to weaken Germany permanently through the Treaty of Versailles, and largely, as a result of the Depression, its attempts to integrate Germany peacefully into Europe also came to nothing. With the Nazi seizure of power and Italy's realignment with Germany after 1936, France increasingly became dependent on Britain, and in September 1939 went to war with Germany as Britain's junior partner. France was defeated by Germany in a brief campaign in June 1940. It was liberated in 1944 and played a relatively minor role in the invasion of Germany in 1945.

Great Britain

A Chinese statesman observed to the British prime minister, Lord Salisbury (1830–1903), in the 1890s that Britain and China 'were two empires on the decline'. Although Britain was enormously wealthy in 1914, the foundations of its power were being eroded. Britain had built up its wealth on the basis of domination of the world's trade, underpinned by control of the seas. By 1900 this had been dangerously weakened. France, Russia, Germany and even Italy were all capable of playing a global role and moving into areas such as China, where previously Britain had enjoyed a virtual **trade monopoly**.

Economically, Britain was being overtaken by Germany and the USA and its absolute control of the seas was threatened by the construction of the German fleet. Through its sheer size, the British Empire became an unwieldy and vulnerable giant. Consequently, Britain attempted to defuse challenges to its position by a policy of compromise and **appeasement**, which enabled the successful negotiations of the Anglo-French and Anglo-Russian colonial agreements of 1904 and 1907. Britain was ready to appease Germany, too, but only at the cost of Germany abandoning its naval challenge. It was primarily this challenge that led to Britain entering the war in 1914.

Superficially, Britain emerged from the war in 1919 as a clear winner. All its war aims had been fulfilled, but the war had also gravely weakened the British Empire financially and encouraged the growth of nationalism in India, Ireland and Egypt. Britain's decline was masked by US isolationism and the weakness

> ### 🔑 KEY TERMS
>
> **Entente** A friendly understanding between states, rather than a formal alliance.
>
> **Pyrrhic victory** A victory won at such a high cost that it damages the victor.
>
> **Trade monopoly** Exclusive control of trade.
>
> **Appeasement** The conciliation of a potential enemy by making concessions. The term is particularly applied to Neville Chamberlain's policy towards Nazi Germany.

of the USSR and France. As before 1914, Britain tried to safeguard its position through avoiding entanglements and appeasing potential enemies. Only when it became clear that a settlement with Nazi Germany was impossible did Britain take the radical step of guaranteeing Poland. Ultimately, Britain went to war in 1939, as in 1914, to stop the German domination of Europe. By the autumn of 1940, Britain had escaped immediate defeat by Nazi Germany, but to continue fighting, it had increasingly to become financially and militarily dependent on US aid. It also benefited from the USSR's destruction of the bulk of the Nazi army in western Russia during 1942–4. In 1945 Britain was one of the victorious powers, but greatly overshadowed by both the USSR and USA.

Russia

By 1914 Russia had a population that was double the size of Germany's and an economy that was developing rapidly. Nevertheless, the effective deployment of this massive strength was always threatened by domestic instability, which had already boiled over into open revolt in 1905. By 1914, foreign observers were unanimous that Russia was sitting on 'the edge of a volcano'.

In 1917 that volcano erupted. After three years of **total war**, Russia was engulfed by revolution. With the victory of the **Red Army** in the Russian Civil War in 1920, the European powers were confronted with **Bolshevism** in power in Russia. Briefly, with the Soviet invasion of Poland in 1920, it seemed as if the Red Army would drive deep into Europe, but it was defeated outside Warsaw and forced to retreat. The creation of a Polish state embracing much of the western Ukraine ensured that the **USSR** was physically cut off from central Europe until the partition of Poland with Nazi Germany in September 1939 (see page 182).

With the coming to power of the Nazis in 1933, however, the USSR joined the League of Nations, and in 1935 signed a pact with France. At this point it seemed as if the pre-1914 Franco-Russian Alliance had been restored, but Britain's and France's appeasement of Nazi Germany in 1938 during the Sudeten crisis (see pages 176–8) and their deep distrust of Bolshevism ultimately persuaded Stalin to sign the Nazi–Soviet Pact with Hitler in August 1939. In the short term this agreement gave the USSR greater security and kept it out of the war. Stalin assumed that Britain, France and Germany would exhaust themselves fighting in western Europe. Instead, France was defeated in June 1940 and the British were expelled from the Continent. In June 1941 Hitler invaded the USSR. His ultimate defeat in 1945 opened the way up to the USSR becoming a **superpower** and controlling eastern and central Europe until 1989.

⚷ KEY TERMS

Total war A war waged by a state in which the whole population is involved and every resource is used to further the war.

Red Army The Soviet army.

Bolshevism The ideology of the Russian Communist (Bolshevik) Party. It was based on the theories of Karl Marx and Lenin, which predicted the overthrow of capitalism and the creation of socialism.

USSR The Union of Soviet Socialist Republics. The new Bolshevik name for Russia and its satellite states.

Superpower A state much larger in size and possessing much larger armed forces than most of the other powers.

Austria-Hungary

In 1867, after its defeat by Prussia, Austria became two virtually independent states – Austria and Hungary – which shared a common crown and operated a joint foreign policy. (Officially Austria was now known as Austria-Hungary, but the former name of Austria was still commonly used.)

The Hungarians strengthened the anti-Russian tendency of Austrian foreign policy as they feared the impact of Russia's sympathy for the Balkan **Slavs** on their own large Slav population. Austria-Hungary contained within its frontiers some eleven different nationalities which were to present the peacemakers of 1919 with insuperable problems when they came to draw up the frontiers of the new small states that replaced the empire.

Austria-Hungary's fate was perceived by contemporaries to be linked with the Ottoman Empire. Vienna feared that the Balkan states, which had virtually driven the Turks out of the Balkans by 1912, would eventually also destroy the Austrian Empire. Above all, the Empire felt itself threatened by the emergence of a strong independent Serbia, which it was convinced enjoyed the backing of Russia and was aiming to liberate the Serbs in the Austrian province of Bosnia. The Empire's main defence against Russia remained the Austro-German Alliance of 1879. Through this alliance the German problem became linked with the Balkan, or eastern, question, with potentially lethal consequences for the peace of Europe, as Berlin's support for Austria began to be regarded by France and Russia as a camouflage for German expansion into south-eastern Europe (see the map on page 14). It was the perceived threat from Serbia and Russia to Austria-Hungary that led to the German declaration of war on Russia that triggered the First World War. Defeat led to the break-up of Austria-Hungary. In 1938, the small state of Austria was annexed by Nazi Germany, but in 1945 it was occupied by the victorious powers and only regained its independence in 1955.

The Turkish Empire

In 1914 the Turkish Empire was in a more advanced stage of decay than Austria, but even before 1914 there had been hints of the remarkable revival of energy that was to galvanise the Turks under Mustapha Kemal (see page 106) into forcing the British and French in 1922–3 to renegotiate the punitive peace treaty of Sèvres.

In 1908 the **Young Turk Movement**, in a desperate attempt to prevent the disintegration of the Turkish Empire, seized power and began the process of modernising Turkey. Turkey was then drawn increasingly into the German orbit. In 1913 the German government was invited to send a military mission to Constantinople to help modernise and re-equip the Turkish army, and in October 1914 Turkey declared war on Britain and France.

Turkey's defeat in 1918 led to the loss of its empire in the Middle East to Britain and France. In the Second World War Turkey remained neutral.

KEY TERMS

Slavs An ethnic group in central and eastern Europe, of which the Russians are the largest component.

Young Turk Movement The name given to a reform movement in the Turkish Empire. Its members were originally exiles in western Europe.

United States of America

The USA for most of the nineteenth century had been shielded from any danger of Continental European intervention by Britain's undisputed supremacy of the seas. The USA had consequently been able to enjoy the benefits of neutrality and isolation in complete security. However, the formidable challenge to the Royal Navy launched by Germany did open up the disturbing prospect of a German naval presence in the Atlantic, and by 1914 the USA had taken the precaution of building up the third largest navy in the world.

Like Japan, the USA also became an imperial power. In the colonial war against Spain in 1898 US forces had seized Cuba and Puerto Rico in the Caribbean and the Philippines and Hawaii in the Far East. Although US public opinion was still isolationist, the USA's extensive financial and economic interests in both Europe and the Far East made it increasingly difficult for it to keep out of world affairs. This was clearly seen in April 1917 when in response to Germany's determination to sink all neutral ships trading with Britain, of which the largest percentage were American, the USA declared war on Germany.

By 1919 the USA had already emerged as a potential superpower, but far from playing a world role it retreated into isolation when **Congress** effectively vetoed membership of the League of Nations (see page 100). Yet even then the USA could not turn its back on the European economy and between 1924 and 1929 played a key role in formulating the Dawes and Young Plans, which did much economically to stabilise post-war Europe. In the late 1920s there was even speculation that the USA would join the League of Nations.

The impact of the Great Depression, however, drove the USA back into isolation. Despite the coming to power of Hitler, Congress was determined to keep the USA out of another world war. Although the USA was ready to supply Britain with money and war supplies in 1940, it was only the Japanese attack on the naval base at Pearl Harbor and Hitler's declaration of war on the USA that finally brought it into the Second World War. It emerged in 1945 as the dominant global power and played the main part in blocking the expansion of Soviet power and influence into western Europe after 1945.

Japan

In 1914, Japan was a formidable regional power with a population of some 46 million. Japan had initially, in 1858, been compelled to grant Western nations considerable economic privileges and rights when it opened up its ports to trade with the West, but thanks to a policy of rapid modernisation, Japan had managed to avoid becoming dependent on any one European power. By 1899 Japan had not only regained its economic freedom, but also embarked on a period of territorial expansion that ended with defeat in 1945 (see page 35).

Lacking the strength to operate in isolation and foreseeing confrontation with Russia in Manchuria, Japan negotiated an alliance with Britain in 1902 which

KEY TERM

Congress The US parliament.

enabled it to defeat Russia in 1905 and strengthen its position in Korea and southern Manchuria (see page 35). Driven on by the intense nationalism of its army officers and the various patriotic societies, both of which were to exercise a powerful influence on foreign policy up to 1945, the Japanese government attempted to exploit the mounting chaos in China caused by the overthrow in 1912 of the Chinese imperial government by internal revolution. For the next 30 years the main aim of Japanese foreign policy was directed towards exploiting the ever-deepening chaos in China in order to build up its own economically self-sufficient empire, the **Greater Asia Co-Prosperity Sphere**. In 1941 this was to bring Japan into direct conflict with the USA, leading to its defeat in 1945.

 **KEY TERM**

Greater Asia Co-Prosperity Sphere
A bloc of territory dominated and exploited by Japan which embraced Manchuria, China and parts of South-east Asia. Japan's aim was to create a self-sufficient bloc free of the Western powers and under its own control.

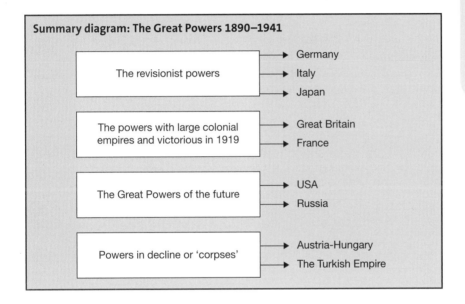

Summary diagram: The Great Powers 1890–1941

The revisionist powers	→ Germany → Italy → Japan
The powers with large colonial empires and victorious in 1919	→ Great Britain → France
The Great Powers of the future	→ USA → Russia
Powers in decline or 'corpses'	→ Austria-Hungary → The Turkish Empire

Chapter summary

By 1890 the most popular ideologies in Europe were imperialism, nationalism and militarism. The emergence of the new popular press spread these ideas and ensured that public opinion increasingly influenced the formulation of foreign policy. The popularity of these ideologies helped to produce an atmosphere of mutual suspicion between the Great Powers and encouraged a race for colonies and accelerating armaments programmes, which were major causes of the First World War. They were, too, components of Fascism and Nazism, which were to plunge Europe into war again in 1939. In 1890 Europe was dominated by six Great Powers: Germany, Austria, Russia, France, Britain and Italy. Outside Europe only the USA and Japan were in a position to compete with them. Over the next 55 years two world wars would dramatically alter the global balance of power and ensure that only the USA and the USSR emerged as superpowers.

Refresher questions

Use these questions to remind yourself of the key material covered in this chapter.

1 Why was imperialism such an influential ideology before 1914?

2 What was militarism?

3 Why did Fascism and National Socialism develop into major political movements after the First World War?

4 With what justification did German nationalists and imperialists consider Germany to be a 'have-not nation'?

5 Why was Italian policy essentially opportunist?

6 Did Japan remain purely a regional power throughout the period 1900–41?

7 To what extent was Britain 'a giant with feet of clay' during the period 1871–1941?

8 What prevented Russia from effectively deploying its potential strength in Europe from 1905 to 1941?

9 What role did the USA play in world politics from 1900 to 1941?

10 Why did Austria fear the nationalism of the Balkan states?

11 To what extent was the Turkish Empire in decline?

CHAPTER 2

Growing international tension 1878–90

The defeat of France by Prussia led to the creation of the German Empire and a major shift in the balance of power in Europe. At the same time, the decline of the Turkish Empire caused increasing tension between the Austrian and Russian Empires in the Balkans. This chapter analyses the consequences of these events under the following headings:

★ The unification of Germany and its consequences

★ The Balkans and the League of the Three Emperors

★ Bismarck's web of alliances 1879–83

★ The Anglo-French quarrel over Egypt and its consequences

★ The Bulgarian crisis 1885–7

Key dates

1871	Treaty of Frankfurt: war ended between France and Germany	1882	Triple Alliance British forces landed in Egypt
1873	League of the Three Emperors created	1884–5	Foundations of the German colonial empire laid
1878	Congress of Berlin		
1879	Austro-German Alliance	1887	Reinsurance Treaty
1881	Three Emperors' Alliance	1890	Bismarck dismissed

1 The unification of Germany and its consequences

▶ *Why did German unification mark a major shift in power in Europe?*

The defeat of first Austria in 1866 and then France in 1871 by Prussia was to have a profound effect on international relations. Before 1867 Germany as a unified state had not existed. Instead, there was a loose **confederation** of 39 German states, which was dominated by Prussia and Austria. Rivalry between these two states erupted into war in 1866 and led to the creation of the North German Confederation. Unlike the former German Confederation this was essentially a powerful new German state dominated by Prussia with the potential to change the balance of power in Europe. France was therefore

 **KEY TERM**

Confederation A grouping of states in which each state retains its sovereignty.

determined to veto any move to complete German unification by Prussia and in 1870 declared war. French defeat in 1871 led to the creation of the German Empire, whose birth, to the utter humiliation of France, was proclaimed in the Hall of Mirrors in the Palace of Versailles on 30 January. In May the war was ended with the Treaty of Frankfurt by which France ceded the provinces of Alsace and Lorraine to Germany and an indemnity was to be paid after which the Prussian army of occupation would be withdrawn from northern France.

? To what extent does this map show how the newly united Germany changed the balance of power in central and eastern Europe?

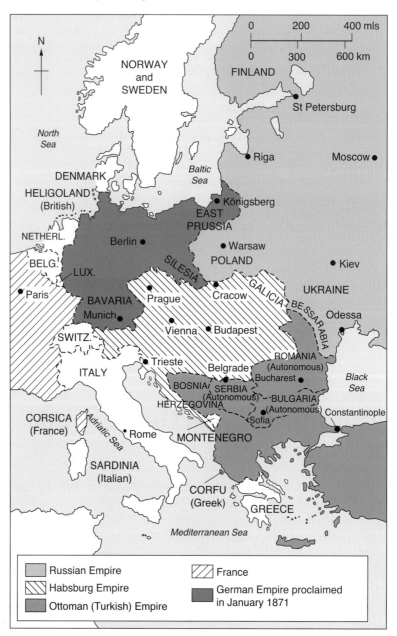

Central and eastern Europe in 1871.

Otto von Bismarck

1815	Born in Schönhausen
1848	Supported the Prussian Crown during the revolts of 1848–9
1851–8	Prussian ambassador in Frankfurt
1859–61	Prussian ambassador in St Petersburg and Paris
1862	Appointed chief minister of Prussia
1866	Established North German Confederation after the defeat of Austria
1871–90	Chancellor of the German Empire
1890	Dismissed by Kaiser Wilhelm II
1898	Died

Bismarck was born into an old, established, landed family in Prussia. He entered politics in 1847 and made a reputation for himself as an extreme **counter-revolutionary** when he supported the Prussian king during the revolutionary turmoil of the years 1848–9. As a reward he was appointed Prussian ambassador to the German Confederation in 1851. He rapidly became critical of Austria's attempt to dominate the Confederation and at every opportunity urged Prussia to seize the leadership of Germany. He became the prime minister of Prussia in 1862 and, after the defeat of both Austria and France, created the German Empire in 1871. Up to 1871 he was intent on challenging the existing order, but once Germany was unified he was anxious to avoid any further changes which might destroy what he had created.

The creation of the German Empire marked a real shift in the balance of power in Europe. **Disraeli**, the leader of the Conservative Party in Britain, went so far as to argue in the House of Commons that it was a revolution (see Source A).

SOURCE A

From a speech to the House of Commons in 1871 by Benjamin Disraeli, quoted in L. Gall, *Bismarck: The White Revolutionary*, Allen & Unwin, 1986, pp. 40–1.

This war represents the German revolution, a greater political event than the French revolution of the last century … You have a new world, new influences at work, new and unknown objects and dangers with which to cope … The balance of power has been entirely destroyed …

The new Germany possessed the most formidable and experienced military force in Europe, based on a growing economic strength. It had abundant supplies of coal and iron ore in the Ruhr and Upper Silesia and, thanks to the growth of the railways, an integrated economy. Already by the early 1870s many of the great firms, such as Krupp and Thyssen, which were to become world leaders some 30 years later, were established.

Of course, economically the Germany of the 1870s was not yet as strong as the Germany of 1913, but even so its unique combination of military and economic strength had its own dangers. Sooner or later France would recover and would seek to reverse its defeat of 1871. If Germany used power unwisely and inspired fear, it would be all the easier for France to gain allies and encircle Germany with a hostile alliance, as indeed was to happen by 1914. Bismarck was all too aware of this danger. He sought therefore to isolate France and reassure Britain, Austria and Russia that Germany was a 'satiated' state.

 **KEY TERM**

Counter-revolutionary
Person who opposes a revolution and wants to reverse its results.

?

Study Source A. Why does Disraeli refer to the result of the Franco-Prussian war as 'the German revolution'?

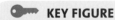 **KEY FIGURE**

Benjamin Disraeli (1804–81)

Tory leader in the House of Commons for twenty years, British prime minister 1868 and 1874–80. He was an ardent imperialist who believed that patriotism and nationalism could overcome class divisions.

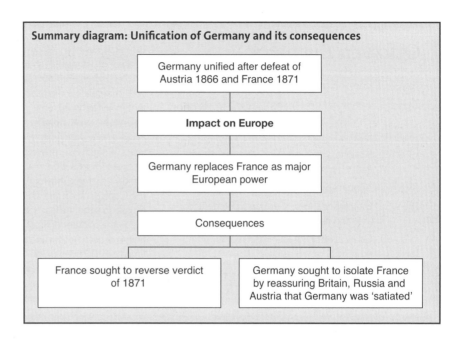

Summary diagram: Unification of Germany and its consequences

Germany unified after defeat of Austria 1866 and France 1871

↓

Impact on Europe

↓

Germany replaces France as major European power

↓

Consequences

France sought to reverse verdict of 1871

Germany sought to isolate France by reassuring Britain, Russia and Austria that Germany was 'satiated'

2 The Balkans and the League of the Three Emperors

▶ *Why were the Balkans an area of potential international conflict?*

For Bismarck there was also the danger that Germany might become involved in an Austro-Russian war over the future of the Balkans. The accelerating decline of Turkish power (see the map on page 45) opened up the prospect that Turkish rule in the Balkans might collapse. For both Russia and Austria, the Balkans were of great strategic importance. Russia could not allow a hostile power to control the western shores of the Black Sea and the straits of the Bosphorus and Dardanelles, which were the main access to the Mediterranean. Similarly, Austria did not want the emergence of an independent group of Balkan states which would block any future extension of its influence into the Balkans, and also attract the support of the Slavs within its own empire, particularly within Hungary. Britain too was concerned about the Russian threat to its position in both the Mediterranean and India, and did not want to see Russia fill the **vacuum of power** left by the decline of Turkey.

Both Russia and Austria attempted to enlist Germany as a future ally, but initially Bismarck was able to avoid any unilateral commitment by proposing that the three powers form the League of the Three Emperors, in 1873. In the event of a crisis they would consult only with each other before deciding what action to take.

🔑 KEY TERM

Vacuum of power
Territories left undominated by another state after the withdrawal or collapse of the original ruling power.

The Eastern crisis of 1875–8

The advantage for Germany of the League of the Three Emperors was that it isolated France and enabled Germany to avoid making a choice between Russia and Austria. It was in many ways the model for German foreign policy until Bismarck's dismissal in 1890. However, the eruption of the great Eastern crisis ultimately forced Bismarck to make a choice between Russia and Austria, even though he spent the next decade attempting to bring these powers together again.

The crisis began in July 1875 with a revolt against Turkish rule in Bosnia and Herzegovina. Within a year it had spread to Bulgaria, and Serbia and Montenegro declared war on Turkey. Briefly, it looked as if the whole Turkish Empire in Europe would collapse, but contrary to expectation the Turks defeated the Serbs and stabilised the situation.

The Eastern crisis now entered a new and dangerous phase as the Russian government was not ready to sit back and tolerate Turkey re-establishing itself in the Balkans. Initially, Russia did obtain Austrian consent to drive the Turks out of the Balkans, provided it did not set up a large pro-Russian Bulgaria and allowed Austria to occupy Bosnia and Herzegovina. Russian troops advanced on Constantinople. Turkey held out until January 1878, but was then forced to agree to a peace that, contrary to all assurances, set up a large and apparently pro-Russian Bulgaria. Inevitably, this triggered a major international crisis which could have resulted in war between Russia and Austria which would be backed by Britain. It opened up the scenario that Bismarck dreaded: France would be able to offer assistance to one or other of the belligerents in return for a promise to revise the Treaty of Frankfurt.

The Berlin Congress

Faced with the Eastern crisis it is not surprising that Bismarck agreed to hosting, at Austria's suggestion, a congress at Berlin. Bismarck in his role as **honest broker** dominated the negotiations. Yet however hard he tried to be neutral, the very fact that he presided over a congress that stripped Russia of many of its gains from the Turkish war made the Russians bitterly resentful of Germany's 'false friendship'.

Under Bismarck's skilful chairmanship the congress managed to find at least temporary solutions to some of the intractable problems of the Balkans:

- Bulgaria was broken up into three parts. The largest of these sections was the core state of Bulgaria, which officially became a **self-governing principality** ultimately under Turkish control. The Russians were to control its administration for nine months until a new government could be formed.
- The three Balkan states of Serbia, Montenegro and Romania gained complete independence.
- Austria was given the right to occupy, but not annex, Bosnia and Herzegovina (see the map on page 14).

 **KEY TERMS**

Honest broker Impartial mediator.

Self-governing principality A semi-independent state ruled by a prince.

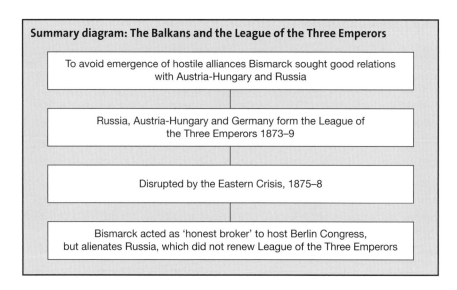

Summary diagram: The Balkans and the League of the Three Emperors

To avoid emergence of hostile alliances Bismarck sought good relations with Austria-Hungary and Russia

Russia, Austria-Hungary and Germany form the League of the Three Emperors 1873–9

Disrupted by the Eastern Crisis, 1875–8

Bismarck acted as 'honest broker' to host Berlin Congress, but alienates Russia, which did not renew League of the Three Emperors

③ Bismarck's web of alliances 1879–83

▶ *What pressures forced Bismarck to negotiate the web of alliances 1879–83?*

The Austro-German Dual Alliance 1879

A major consequence of the Berlin Congress was the deterioration in relations between Germany and Russia and the collapse of the Three Emperors' league. The crisis had convinced Bismarck that Germany could not tolerate the defeat of Austria by Russia as this would immeasurably strengthen Russia and directly threaten Germany's future security. Consequently, on 7 October 1879, the Austro-German Dual Alliance was signed. Its terms were as follows:

- Should one power be attacked by Russia, the other would come to its rescue with 'the whole war strength' of its empire.
- If one of the two empires were attacked by any other power, its ally would adopt a neutral but friendly attitude.
- The treaty was in the first instance to last five years but could be renewed.
- It was secret, but in the event of Russian threats its gist would be leaked to the tsar to deter him from taking any further action.

The Dual Alliance gave Germany considerable influence over Austrian foreign policy, and Bismarck was to exploit this to ensure that Vienna did not provoke an unnecessary war with Russia. He also hoped that the mere existence of the treaty, even if its details were secret, would force Russia back into negotiations with Austria and Germany.

The Alliance of the Three Emperors

Bismarck's calculations proved correct. Although the **Pan Slav** nationalists urged Tsar Alexander II to ally with France and attack Austria, the Russian foreign office doubted whether France would be able to offer much assistance in the Balkans and managed to persuade the tsar to agree to open negotiations with Germany.

Talks began with Bismarck in January 1880. The Russians wanted an agreement that would recognise their gains in the Balkans and close the straits of the Bosphorus and the Dardanelles to the British navy. Bismarck was not ready to sign a treaty with Russia unless Austria was also involved. At first Austria still pinned hopes on co-operation with Britain against Russia, but with the defeat of Disraeli in the general election of 1880, British foreign policy became markedly less hostile to Russia. Under German pressure, Vienna therefore agreed somewhat reluctantly to accept a new version of the Three Emperors' League. The Three Emperors' Alliance was signed with Russia on 18 June 1881. Its main terms were:

- Austria-Hungary and Germany agreed that the Straits should be closed to the warships of all nations. This stopped the threat of Britain sending its navy into the Black Sea and greatly strengthened Russia's position.
- Austria conceded the eventual reunification of Bulgaria, while Russia agreed that at some time in the future Austria would be able to annex Bosnia and Herzegovina.
- If a member of the League found itself at war with a fourth power, unless it was Turkey, the other two powers would remain neutral.
- There were to be no further territorial changes in the Turkish Empire without the consent of the three empires.
- The treaty was in the first instance to last three years.

The treaty did not provide any long-term solution to Austro-Russian rivalry in the Balkans, but it did temporarily reduce the friction between Austria and Russia.

The Triple Alliance 1882

Despite the Three Emperors' Alliance, Russian policy in the Balkans remained unpredictable. The new tsar, Alexander III, continued to consult the Pan Slav leaders who had established contacts with Russian sympathisers in the French army and media. Bismarck's response was to strengthen the Austro-German Dual Alliance. First he expanded it in 1882 into a Triple Alliance with Italy. Since Austria had controlled much of northern Italy, and in 1859 and again in 1866 had fought to prevent its unification, the Italian government had understandably seen Austria as a hostile power. It also had claims to the Italian-speaking Tyrol and Trieste, which were still controlled by Austria. However, the French occupation of Tunis in 1881, which the Italians regarded as their own sphere of

KEY TERM

Pan Slavs Russian nationalists who believed that the Slavs in central and south-eastern Europe should be liberated by their fellow Slavs in Russia.

interest, caused Italy to propose an alliance with Austria. Bismarck immediately suggested extending it into a Triple Alliance. The key clauses of the treaty were as follows:

- Both the Central Powers were now committed to support Italy in the unlikely chance of an attack from France.
- Italy, in turn, would help them only if they were attacked by two other powers (say, France and Russia).

The real gain for Germany was that if war broke out with Russia, Austria would now no longer have to keep troops on its Italian frontier just in case Italy might be tempted to make a surprise attack to the rear.

Austria's position was then further strengthened by an alliance with Serbia in June 1882 and with Romania in 1883, which Germany joined and turned into a **defensive alliance** against Russia. Simultaneously, Bismarck also successfully strengthened the influence of the pro-German ministers in the Russian government by both refusing demands at home for further rises in **tariffs**,

---

KEY TERMS

Defensive alliance An agreement between two states whereby each will come to the defence of the other if attacked.

Tariffs Taxes placed on imported goods to protect the home economy.

SOURCE B

? Study Source B. To what extent was Bismarck really the 'ringmaster' controlling the Triple Alliance in the interest of Germany?

A French cartoonist's view of the Triple Alliance. This 1889 cartoon shows Bismarck as the ringmaster conducting the Triple Alliance of Germany, Austria and Italy.

which would damage Russian trade, and encouraging German banks to finance Russian loans. As a result, in 1884 the tsar agreed to renew the Three Emperors' Treaty.

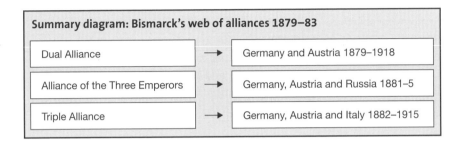

Summary diagram: Bismarck's web of alliances 1879–83

Dual Alliance →	Germany and Austria 1879–1918
Alliance of the Three Emperors →	Germany, Austria and Russia 1881–5
Triple Alliance →	Germany, Austria and Italy 1882–1915

4 The Anglo-French quarrel over Egypt and its consequences

▶ *Why was Franco-German co-operation so short lived?*

Anglo-French involvement in Egypt

Egypt was a self-governing territory within the Turkish Empire which was ruled by the **Khedive**. The Suez Canal, which was opened in 1869, was built by a French company and rapidly became a key link in Britain's communications with India. In April 1876, Egypt went bankrupt and could no longer pay the interest on the money lent by European investors. Britain, which was the majority shareholder in the Suez Canal Company, and France consequently took over joint control of Egypt's finances. In 1881 both powers were challenged by a nationalist uprising led by officers in the Egyptian army. As the French parliament vetoed the dispatch of French troops, it was left to the British to defeat the uprising. The British now became the masters of Egypt, and despite repeated assurances that they would leave as soon as order had been restored, they did not do so. Inevitably, this infuriated the French and made any co-operation with Britain virtually impossible for more than twenty years.

Germany's exploitation of the Anglo-French quarrel

Bismarck had made no secret of the fact that he wished to encourage France to seek compensation for the loss of Alsace-Lorraine by building up a colonial empire in Africa. In 1880 he told the French ambassador: 'I want you to take your eyes from Metz and Strasbourg by helping you find satisfaction elsewhere.' This would both distract France from seeking revenge against Germany and create tension with the other colonial powers, particularly Britain, thereby giving Germany an opportunity to co-operate with France outside Europe.

KEY TERM

Khedive The title used by the governor and ruler of Egypt and the Sudan.

The creation of the German colonial empire

In 1884 the German government, in order to protect German trading interests and forestall British claims, annexed territory in South West Africa, the Cameroons, Togoland and New Guinea. In the following year, Germany and France were able to co-operate and override British objections to calling an international conference in Berlin to decide on the future of a huge belt of central African territory stretching from the Atlantic to the Indian Ocean. Franco-German relations improved dramatically, and the French prime minister, **Jules Ferry**, commented that France was no longer 'the Cinderella of European politics'.

The end of Franco-German co-operation

Franco-German co-operation was short lived. In 1885 a new French government led by Louis Freycinet (1828–1923) was forced to adopt a more anti-German policy when the **charismatic** and fiercely nationalistic General **Boulanger**, who believed that his mission was to prepare for war against Germany, joined the cabinet as minister for war. He rapidly became a cult figure for the extreme nationalist **League of Patriots**, and for a time it seemed, much to the alarm of Bismarck, that he might even seize power and become a dictator. The German army was confident that it could again defeat the French, but it was doubtful whether France could now be dealt with in isolation. French attempts to establish closer relations with Russia were powerfully helped by the eruption of the Bulgarian crisis (see page 23), and in the autumn of 1886 for a brief period of time it looked as if a Franco-Russian Alliance directed against Germany might be possible.

(see page 23)

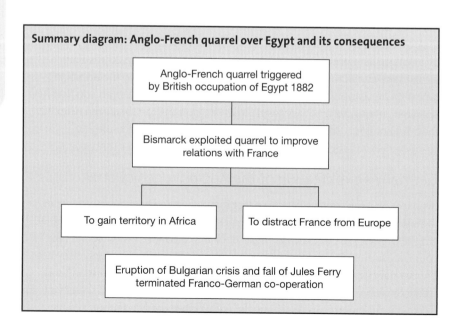

Summary diagram: Anglo-French quarrel over Egypt and its consequences

- Anglo-French quarrel triggered by British occupation of Egypt 1882
- Bismarck exploited quarrel to improve relations with France
  - To gain territory in Africa
  - To distract France from Europe
- Eruption of Bulgarian crisis and fall of Jules Ferry terminated Franco-German co-operation

5 # The Bulgarian crisis 1885–7

▶ *How did Bismarck seek to avoid an Austro-Russian war breaking out over the Bulgarian crisis?*

At the Berlin Congress it had been agreed that **rump Bulgaria** would be administered by an elected ruler, who would administer it within the Turkish Empire (see page 17). In April 1879 Prince Alexander of Battenberg, the Russian tsar's nephew, was elected, but when he refused to become a puppet, the Russian government had him kidnapped and forced him to abdicate. Inevitably, this revived British and Austrian fears of Russia's intention of taking over Bulgaria. Russia brushed aside Austrian objections and privately in Berlin the Russian ambassador told Bismarck that 'It is absolutely necessary that we should make Austria disappear from the map of Europe.'

The League of the Three Emperors had disintegrated. War between Russia and Austria now seemed possible, and Austria and Britain both looked to Berlin to take the lead against Russia, but Bismarck was determined not to be pushed into confrontation, especially at the very time that Boulanger was urging a war of revenge against Germany. He attempted to restrain both Austria and Russia, which he described as 'two savage dogs'. Bismarck again made very clear to his Austrian allies that Germany would not be dragged into war against Russia. On the other hand, he was not prepared to stand back and see Austria defeated by Russia. To reconcile these two often conflicting objectives he pursued his traditional policy of strengthening Austria while at the same time attempting to reassure Russia of Germany's peaceful intentions.

The Mediterranean Agreement, February 1887

Bismarck aimed to deter Russian expansion into the Balkans by encouraging Britain, Italy and Austria-Hungary to negotiate the First Mediterranean Agreement in February 1887. This provided for the maintenance of the *status quo* in the Mediterranean, including the Adriatic and Aegean seas. He hoped that the agreement would encourage these three powers to stand up to Russia and convince Tsar Alexander III that only through negotiations with Berlin could a compromise over Bulgaria be arranged.

The Reinsurance Treaty, 18 June 1887

Any improvement in Germany's relations with Russia was dependent on the outcome of the struggle to influence the tsar, which was bitterly waged between the Pan Slavs and the traditionally pro-German officials of the Russian foreign office. In March 1887, Tsar Alexander III finally became impatient with the increasingly more outspoken attempts of the Pan Slavs to influence his foreign policy and rejected their demands for a break with Germany. While refusing to renew the Three Emperors' Treaty of 1881, he agreed to negotiate a secret

KEY TERMS

Rump Bulgaria What was left of Bulgaria after its partition at the Berlin Congress.

Status quo A Latin term to denote the state of affairs as it exists at the moment.

agreement with Germany, the Reinsurance Treaty, which was signed on 18 June 1887. Its terms were as follows:

- Both empires were pledged to be neutral in a war fought against a third power unless Germany attacked France, Russia or Austria.
- Germany recognised the rights 'historically acquired' by Russia in the Balkans, particularly in Bulgaria and Eastern Roumelia.
- Turkey was not to open the Straits to the navy of a power hostile to Russia – this essentially meant Britain. If the Straits were opened, Germany and Russia would regard it as a hostile act towards themselves.

In his attempt to reconcile Austria and Russia, Bismarck had effectively created two contradictory diplomatic systems. On the one hand, the Reinsurance Treaty promised Russia German backing at the Straits and in Bulgaria, while the Mediterranean Agreement, the negotiation of which was encouraged by Bismarck, supported Austria by encouraging the territorial *status quo*.

The aftermath of the Bulgarian crisis

The Reinsurance Treaty did not immediately calm the tension in the Balkans. The election of a new ruler to the Bulgarian throne, Prince Ferdinand of Coburg, in July 1887 was regarded by the Russians as an Austrian conspiracy. Once again the Pan Slavs whipped up a press campaign against Germany, which was accused of secretly supporting Austria, and by the autumn it looked as if the Russians were on the verge of invading Bulgaria. To stop this, the German government ordered the **Reichsbank** in November not to accept Russian **bonds** as **collateral security** for loans raised in Germany. This had very serious economic consequences for the Russians as Germany was the source of most of its foreign loans. Russia was plunged into financial chaos which effectively prevented it from occupying Bulgaria or risking war with Austria. In December, Bismarck, again quite contrary to the spirit of the Reinsurance Treaty, further strengthened the position of Austria by persuading Britain and Italy to conclude with it a second Mediterranean Agreement aimed at keeping Russia out of Bulgaria and Turkey. These measures successfully deterred the Russians from invading Bulgaria, but also caused them to turn to France for the loans which the Germans were no longer ready to finance. Inevitably, this was to strengthen Franco-Russian relations.

Bismarck's dismissal

When William II came to the German throne in June 1888, and began to urge on Bismarck a British alliance, the tsar rapidly became more appreciative of Bismarck's policy and offered to renew the Reinsurance Treaty permanently. Bismarck, however, was dismissed in March 1890 before negotiations could begin, and his successor, General von Caprivi (1831–99), convinced that it

KEY TERMS

Reichsbank The national bank of Germany.

Bonds Certificates issued by a government or large company promising to repay borrowed money at a fixed rate of interest by a specified date.

Collateral security Bonds or property pledged as a guarantee for the repayment of a loan.

contradicted the Triple Alliance and would complicate Germany's relations with Britain, did not renew it. In retrospect, this was a dangerous step, which was to encourage Russia to draw closer to France.

SOURCE C

Study Source C. How successful had Bismarck been as a 'pilot' of Germany's foreign policy?

'Dropping the Pilot.' The satirical magazine *Punch*'s view in 1890 on Bismarck's departure. Its message is that the statesman who had unified Germany and then it guided through many crises over the years 1871–90 was now rashly being dropped by the Kaiser.

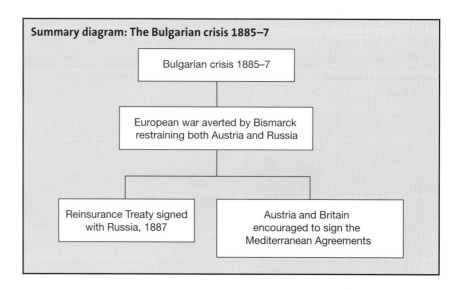

Summary diagram: The Bulgarian crisis 1885–7

Bulgarian crisis 1885–7

European war averted by Bismarck restraining both Austria and Russia

Reinsurance Treaty signed with Russia, 1887

Austria and Britain encouraged to sign the Mediterranean Agreements

Chapter summary

German unification in 1871, after the defeat of France, created a strong power with immense economic and military potential in the middle of Europe. Bismarck's aim until his resignation was to isolate France and reassure the European powers that Germany was a 'satiated nation'. Above all, he wanted to avoid the outbreak of a major war on the continent of Europe. As long as Austria and Russia enjoyed good diplomatic relations, there was little danger from France. In 1884–5 France and Germany were able to co-operate briefly in

Africa. It was the Balkans that were the real threat to peace. The accelerating decline in Turkish power left a vacuum which neither Russia nor Austria could allow the other to fill. This nearly led to war in 1878 and again in 1885–7. An Austro-Russian war might quickly escalate into a European war and give France a chance to regain the territory and power it lost in 1871. Thus, in order to safeguard Germany from encirclement and to preserve the peace between Austria and Russia, Bismarck constructed a web of sometimes contradictory alliances: the Dual Alliance, the Treaty of the Three Emperors, the Triple Alliance and finally the Reinsurance Treaty. Up to a point, these worked and ensured a fragile peace.

Refresher questions

Use these questions to remind yourself of the key material covered in this chapter.

1 Why did a united Germany change the balance of power in Europe?

2 Why were the Balkans an area of potential international crisis?

3 What international problems did the Eastern crisis of 1875–8 cause?

4 What decisions were taken at the Berlin Congress?

5 What was the significance of the Dual Alliance?

6 What was the aim of the Three Emperors' Alliance of 1881?

7 How did Bismarck strengthen Austria against Russia?

8 What were the consequences of the Anglo-French quarrel over Egypt?

9 Why did the Russians want to remove Prince Alexander, the ruler of Bulgaria?

10 How did Bismarck keep the peace between Austria and Russia during the Bulgarian crisis?

11 What was the role of the Reinsurance Treaty in Bismarck's alliance system?

12 What were the consequences of the Bulgarian crisis?

13 What immediate impact did Bismarck's dismissal have on German-Russian relations?

 Question practice

ESSAY QUESTIONS

1 'Between 1871 and 1890 Germany was forced into pursuing a European rather than a German foreign policy out of self-preservation.' Assess the validity of this view.

2 'Bismarck successfully dealt with the consequences of Austro-Russian hostility in the Balkans.' How far do you agree?

3 Assess the consequences of a united Germany for Europe during the period 1871–90.

4 'A European war caused by Austro-Russian rivalry in the Balkans seemed increasingly likely by 1889.' Explain why you agree or disagree with this view.

INTERPRETATION QUESTION

1 Read the interpretation and answer the question that follows. '[Apart from Bismarck] no other statesman ... had ever before shown the same great moderation and sound political sense of the possible and desirable' (from W. Langer, *European Alliances and Alignments*, 1951). Evaluate the strengths and limitations of this interpretation, making reference to other interpretations you have studied.

CHAPTER 3

The origins of the First World War

In 1914 Europe was plunged into a terrible and costly war. The empires of France, Russia and Britain on the one side, and Germany, Austria and Turkey on the other, fought a brutal war of attrition which was to last four years and cost, at a conservative estimate, some 12 million casualties. The war impoverished Germany, bled France white, and shattered the Austrian and Turkish empires. It also led to the triumph of Bolshevism in Russia and Fascism in Italy. By inflicting serious and long-term damage on the European economies, it also ultimately led to Hitler coming to power in 1933 in Germany. Understandably, then, the causes of the First World War constitute one of the most hotly debated issues in modern history. The events leading up to the outbreak of the First World War are examined under the following headings:

★ The 'New Course' in German foreign policy and its consequences

★ Nationalism and worldwide imperial rivalries

★ Making of the Triple *Entente*

★ The second Moroccan crisis 1911 and its consequences

★ The Balkans and the Great Powers 1906–1914

★ Outbreak of the First World War 1914

The key debate on *page 53* of this chapter asks the question: Can it be argued that no one power alone bears the chief responsibility for the causes of the First World War?

Key dates

1894	Franco-Russian Alliance signed	1914	June 28	Sarajevo incident
1898	Fashoda crisis		July 28	Austria declared war on Serbia
1902	Anglo-Japanese Treaty		Aug. 1	Germany declared war on Russia
1904	Anglo-French *Entente*			
1906	First Moroccan crisis		Aug. 3	Germany declared war on France
1907	Anglo-Russian Agreement			
1908	Bosnia and Herzegovina annexed by Austria		Aug. 4	German troops invaded Belgium
1911	Second Moroccan crisis			Britain declared war on Germany
1912–13	First and Second Balkan Wars			

The 'New Course' in German foreign policy and its consequences

▶ *To what extent can the 'New Course' in German foreign policy be considered a failure?*

The end of the Reinsurance Treaty

Once Bismarck had been dismissed by Kaiser Wilhelm II, German foreign office officials advised his successor, General Leo von Caprivi, not to renew the Reinsurance Treaty with Russia. They argued with some justification that it conflicted with the Dual Alliance of 1879 and the Mediterranean Agreements of 1887 (see pages 18 and 23–4). Instead, they decided to work for a new alliance system or 'New Course', which would associate Britain with Germany's two allies, Italy and Austria, and so hold in check both Russia and France. It was felt that Germany was now strong enough to give up Bismarck's complicated system of checks and balances and should ally with states with which it had apparently a common interest.

Britain's refusal to join the Triple Alliance

The problem for the Germans was that, while the British government was ready to settle colonial disputes with them, as eventually it also did with France and Russia, it was not prepared to negotiate binding alliances. Berlin refused to believe this, and remained convinced that sooner or later French and Russian pressure on Britain's large and vulnerable empire would end in war and force Britain to turn to Germany for help. 'For us', as Caprivi remarked in 1893, 'the best opening of the next great war is for the first shot to be fired from a British ship. Then we can be certain of expanding the Triple into a **Quadruple Alliance**.' Ultimately, however, this was wishful thinking, and the British were determined not to join the Triple Alliance, because, as Lord Salisbury (1830–1903), the British prime minister, observed, the 'liability of having to defend the German and Austrian frontiers against Russia is greater than that of having to defend the British Isles against France'.

Having failed to secure a British alliance, Germany now became increasingly dependent on Austria as its key ally, and consequently the Austrians were in a position to put pressure on the Germans to back them against Russia when the next major Balkans crisis erupted. It also accelerated the negotiation of the Franco-Russian Dual Alliance.

 **KEY TERM**

Quadruple alliance
An alliance of four powers.

Kaiser Wilhelm II

1859	Born: his mother was British Queen Victoria's eldest daughter
1888	Ascended the throne
1890	Dismissed Bismarck
1896	Sent 'Kruger telegram'
1905	Visited Tangier
1914	Gave Austria unconditional support against Serbia
1916	Sidelined by Generals Hindenburg and Ludendorff
1918	Abdicated
1919–41	Lived in exile in the Netherlands
1941	Died in German-occupied Netherlands

Wilhelm was an unstable and neurotic figure, who suffered from rapid mood swings and may even have been mentally ill. His complex love–hate relationship with his English mother and Britain created considerable political problems in the years 1890–1914. When he came to the throne in 1888, he was determined to rule Germany himself. By 1897 he had greatly increased his own power at the expense of excluding genuinely independent-minded men from office.

In 1908 Wilhelm gave an interview to the *Daily Telegraph* which made him the laughing stock of Germany and effectively led to the end of his period of personal rule, although he still continued to intervene directly in military and foreign affairs until 1916. He was forced to abdicate in November 1918 and fled to the Netherlands. He was wanted as a war criminal by the Allies in 1918, but the Dutch refused to hand him over.

France and Russia draw together

KEY TERM

State visit Ceremonial visit by a head of state.

The Kaiser's **state visit** to London in July 1891 convinced the Russians – wrongly of course – that Britain and Germany had signed a secret alliance. Nikolay Giers (1820–1895), the Russian foreign minister, therefore suggested to the French that the two states should begin to negotiate an *entente*. Talks began almost immediately, and the French fleet visited the Russian base of Kronstadt as a symbolic act of friendship. Within a month the two states had already agreed 'to take counsel together upon every question of a nature to jeopardise the general peace'.

A year later this was backed up with a secret defensive military agreement which was approved by both governments in January 1894 (see Source A on page 31).

The treaty marked the end of France's isolation in Europe and, even though its precise terms were secret, fuelled German fears that in any future war France and Russia would be allies.

The potentially dangerous situation in which Germany now found itself was partly obscured by the shift of European rivalries in the 1890s from Europe and the Balkans to Africa and China. Outside Europe, Germany, France and Russia were able often to co-operate at the cost of the British Empire. For a time Germany still remained confident that Britain, whose huge and vulnerable empire was coming under intense pressure, would be forced into an agreement on Germany's terms with the Triple Alliance, but this, as we have seen, was a miscalculation.

SOURCE A

From the Franco-Russian Treaty 1892, quoted in Yale Law School, The Avalon Project, Documents in Law, History and Diplomacy,
http://avalon.law.yale.edu/19th_century/frrumil.asp

1. If France is attacked by Germany, or by Italy supported by Germany, Russia shall employ all her available forces to attack Germany. If Russia is attacked by Germany, or by Austria supported by Germany, France shall employ all her available forces to attack Germany.

2. In case the forces of the Triple Alliance, or of any one of the Powers belonging to it, should be mobilized, France and Russia, at the first news of this event and without previous agreement being necessary, shall mobilize immediately and simultaneously the whole of their forces, and shall transport them as far as possible to their frontiers.

3. The available forces to be employed against Germany shall be, on the part of France, 1,300,000 men, on the part of Russia, 700,000 or 800,000 men.

Study Source A. What were the terms of the Franco-Russian Alliance?

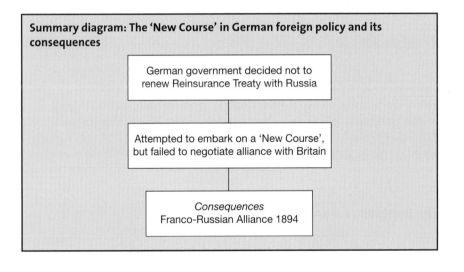

Summary diagram: The 'New Course' in German foreign policy and its consequences

German government decided not to renew Reinsurance Treaty with Russia

Attempted to embark on a 'New Course', but failed to negotiate alliance with Britain

Consequences
Franco-Russian Alliance 1894

2 Nationalism and worldwide imperial rivalries

▶ *Why did imperial rivalries in Africa and China not lead to a major war between the Great Powers?*

The 1890s witnessed a renewed scramble for territory and influence in Africa and Asia by the Great Powers, joined by Japan. However, contrary to expectations, imperial rivalries in Africa and China did not lead to the outbreak of a major war between the European powers, but they did encourage the growth of nationalism, imperialism and militarism in each European country (see pages 2–4).

The struggle for empire was at its most intense in the following regions:

- the Upper Nile
- South Africa
- China.

The Upper Nile and Fashoda crisis

The French, bitterly resentful of Britain's dominant position in Egypt, which it had acquired in 1882, intended to seize a wide strip of territory right across central Africa from the Indian Ocean to the Atlantic. Both Britain and France raced to control the territories of the Upper Nile. In September 1898 a small French force reached the Upper Nile first and hoisted the French flag at Fashoda, but was confronted a few days later by an army under General Kitchener (1850–1916), which had just defeated the Sudanese forces at Omdurman. An armed clash that could have led to war was avoided when Kitchener decided not use force to eject the French. Instead, it was left to the two governments to find a diplomatic solution. France, lacking any support from the other powers, had little option but to concede totally to British demands in the Sudan.

Fashoda has been called by the historian J.V. Keiger, 'the worst crisis in Franco-British relations since **Waterloo**'. Yet, paradoxically, it also led to an improvement in Anglo-French affairs, as influential voices in Paris began to argue that France should cut its losses, write off Egypt and gain British backing for the annexation of Morocco.

South Africa

The Jameson raid and the Kaiser's response

Here the British faced similar threats to their colonial ambitions but this time from the Germans, who they feared would try to extend their power eastwards from German South West Africa to the borders of the **Transvaal**. This would effectively block any northward British expansion. The economic significance of the Transvaal had been transformed by the discovery of gold there in 1886, and by 1894 its economy was dominated by the Germans. German bankers controlled the Transvaal's National Bank and some 20 per cent of the foreign investment in the state came from Germany.

The independence of the **Boers** in the Transvaal was, however, threatened by the large number of British prospectors and adventurers who poured in. When Cecil Rhodes, the prime minister of Britain's Cape Colony, illegally launched a badly planned and unsuccessful attempt to overthrow the Boer government, the so-called **Jameson raid**, in 1895, the Germans could hardly remain indifferent to it. The Kaiser at first wanted to declare the Transvaal a German protectorate,

KEY TERMS

Waterloo In 1815 the British defeated Napoleon in the Battle of Waterloo.

Transvaal This was an independent state, although by agreement with the British in 1884 it could not conclude treaties with foreign powers without their agreement.

Boers Descendants of Dutch settlers who had originally colonised South Africa.

Jameson raid Armed intervention in the Transvaal led by the British politician in Cape Colony, Leander Starr Jameson, over the New Year weekend of 1895–6.

send military aid to Paulus Kruger, the president of Transvaal, and then summon a congress in Berlin, which would redraw the map of South Africa, but in the end he was persuaded by his own diplomats that because of British sea power, these were just empty threats. Instead, he sent a telegram to Kruger congratulating him on preserving the independence of his country against attack.

This caused intense resentment in Britain as it was perceived to be Germany meddling in the private affairs of the British Empire. Windows belonging to German-owned shops were smashed and for the first time popular anti-German feeling became widespread and intense.

The Boer War and the absence of a Continental League

Four years later Kruger, who had rebuilt the Boer army and equipped it with modern German artillery, declared war on Britain, believing that France, Germany and Russia would intervene and force Britain to make concessions. 'There could never be', as the historian A.J.P. Taylor observed, 'a more favourable opportunity, in theory, for the Continental Powers to exploit British difficulties.' Yet nothing happened both because British control of the seas made military intervention physically impossible and because neither France, Russia nor Germany could in the final analysis agree to co-operate. Britain was therefore able to defeat the Boers in a long, drawn-out war, which ended only in 1902.

SOURCE B

From a speech by the British prime minister, Lord Salisbury, on 4 May 1898 to the Primrose League at the Albert Hall, London, quoted in J. Joll, editor, *Britain and Europe*, Oxford University Press, 1967, pp. 192–4. The League was part of the Conservative Party.

*You may roughly divide the nations of the world as the living and the dying. On the one side you have great countries of enormous power growing in power, every year, growing in wealth, growing in dominion, growing in the perfection of their organisation. … By the side of these splendid organisations there are a number of communities, which I can only describe as dying. For one reason or another – from the necessities of politics or under the pretence of **philanthropy** – the living nations will gradually encroach on the territory of the dying, and the seeds and causes of conflict among civilised nations will speedily appear … These things may introduce causes of fatal difference between the great nations whose mighty armies stand opposite threatening each other … .*

Study Source B. What is Lord Salisbury's assessment of the global situation?

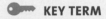 **KEY TERM**

Philanthropy The desire to help humanity.

China

As in Africa, Great Power rivalry in China was determined by a mixture of political, economic and strategic factors. Up to the 1890s Britain had been able to dominate China's foreign trade and, through its superior sea power, block any attempts by other powers to divide up the Chinese Empire; but the construction

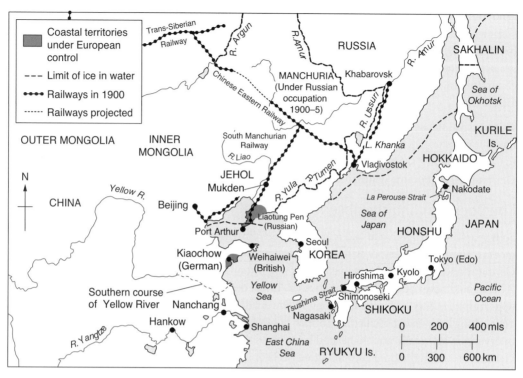

Map of northern China, Manchuria and Japan, showing the growth of the railways by 1900.

KEY TERM

Ice-free port A seaport that can be used throughout the year.

of the trans-Siberian railway by Russia, which commenced in 1891, completely changed the situation as Russia would now be able to deploy troops to back up its demands. Russia's main aim in China was to annex Manchuria and gain an **ice-free port** in Korea. In China, unlike Africa, Britain now faced the prospect of a challenge to its commercial position from a major power, which could deploy troops to assert its aims. Russia could usually rely on the backing of France and Germany in China, while Britain's only potential ally was Japan, which saw Russian expansion into Korea and Manchuria as a threat to its own security.

The Anglo-Japanese Treaty of 1902

To protect their interests, Japan and Britain negotiated a defensive alliance. Japan recognised Britain's interests in China, while Britain accepted that Japan was 'in a peculiar degree politically as well as commercially and industrially' interested in Korea. Both powers then went on to agree in January 1902 that if these interests were threatened, each power should be free to take the necessary action to protect them. In the event of war between Japan and another country, Britain would remain neutral unless a third power came to Russia's assistance. Similarly, if Britain were involved in a conflict in the Far East, Japan would only intervene if a third power declared war against Britain.

China and Japan: two contrasting histories

Both empires were in 1800 **isolationist** and hostile to Western contacts, but Japan adapted to Westernisation and emerged as an important regional power by 1900, while China seemed to be on the verge, like Africa, of being divided up between the Great Powers. A major step in opening up China to Western influence was the Treaty of Nanking of August 1842. The British forced the Chinese not only to import opium from India, but also to cede them the island of Hong Kong and to open up five coastal cities to foreign traders. Over the next 50 years further concessions were forced out of the Chinese.

Japan's isolation ended when the USA sent a fleet in 1854 and persuaded its government to open up two ports for trade and the use of the US navy. In 1868 a political revolution took place in Japan, the so-called Meiji Restoration, which gave greater power to the emperor. He then rapidly transformed Japan into a modern state.

 **KEY TERM**

Isolationist Remaining aloof from international politics.

The Russo-Japanese War 1904–5

When it became clear by 1904 that Russia would not withdraw troops from Manchuria and cede to Japan a dominant position in Korea, the Anglo-Japanese Treaty enabled Japan to launch a surprise attack on Port Arthur. The subsequent Russo-Japanese War was fought in isolation. Neither France, which had just signed a colonial agreement with Britain, 'the *Entente*' (see page 39), nor Germany wanted to fight Britain, and each feared that its involvement in a Far Eastern war would make it vulnerable to an attack in Europe. After the defeat of their fleet at Tsushima and of their army at Mukden, the Russians, paralysed by revolution at home (see page 8), agreed to mediation by the US president in August 1905. By the terms of the Treaty of Portsmouth (New Hampshire), Russia ceased to be an immediate threat to either Britain or Japan in the Far East and withdrew from Korea and Manchuria.

Summary diagram: Nationalism and worldwide imperial rivalries	
Africa	Anglo-French rivalry in Egypt and the Sudan came to a head at Fashoda 1898
	Anglo-German rivalry fuelled by German support for Kruger 1896
	Yet neither France nor Germany was able to organise a Continental League during the Boer War 1899–1902
China	Construction of trans-Siberian railway opened up northern China to Russian influence
	This challenged Britain's monopoly of trade and Japan's influence in Manchuria and Korea
Russo-Japanese War	Japan and Britain signed a defensive alliance 1902
	In 1905 this enabled Japan to defeat Russia and halt Russian expansion in China

3 Making of the Triple *Entente*

▶ *To what extent did the Triple* Entente *mark a 'diplomatic revolution'?*

▶ *Why was the Anglo-French* Entente *agreement negotiated?*

At the end of the nineteenth century it was the British Empire that was under pressure and a war between Britain and Russia over China seemed imminent. Although Germany faced a potentially hostile Franco-Russian Alliance in Europe, in Africa and the Far East it was often able to co-operate with these two powers against Britain. By 1907, however, the international situation had dramatically changed. It was Germany that was isolated and Britain had settled its most acute disagreements with both Russia and France. Anglo-German relations had sharply deteriorated to a point where war between these powers was a distinct possibility. In any war between the Dual Alliance and the Triple Alliance, it was safe to predict that by 1907 Britain would join France and Russia. The main causes of this dramatic change, which some historians call a **diplomatic revolution**, are as follows:

- There was growing Anglo-German commercial rivalry.
- The construction of the German fleet combined with an aggressive or clumsy *Weltpolitik,* which forced Britain into taking action to preserve its position as a Great Power.
- The Anglo-Japanese Alliance of 1902 made Britain independent of Germany in the Far East.
- The Franco-British Agreement of April 1904 at last marked the end of Anglo-French hostility over Egypt.
- Germany's violent reaction to French claims to Morocco in 1905 only cemented the Franco-British *Entente* even more.
- Russia's defeat by Japan in 1905 made Russia less of a threat to British interests in China and made possible the Anglo-Russian Agreement of 1907.

Anglo-German economic rivalry

Between 1900 and 1914 Germany became an economic giant. The German steel and iron industries, protected from foreign competition by tariffs, could undercut rivals abroad by selling at some 40 per cent below the current price. Germany had also made startling progress in developing chemical, electrical and engineering industries which were in the forefront of the **second industrial revolution**. By 1910 Germany also possessed the second largest merchant fleet in the world (second only to Britain) and after Britain and France was the third largest **creditor nation**. German exports dominated the Middle Eastern, South American and South African markets and had largely displaced British goods there.

KEY TERMS

Diplomatic revolution A complete change in alliances and relations between states.

Second industrial revolution The development of electrical, chemical and engineering industries beginning at the end of the nineteenth century.

Creditor nation A state which lends or invests surplus capital abroad.

Inevitably, the German 'economic miracle' was a challenge to Britain's long commercial and industrial supremacy and caused considerable anxiety and hostility. A popular book by E.E. Williams, *Made in Germany* (1896), argued with considerable exaggeration that 'on all hands England's industrial supremacy is tottering to its fall, and this result is largely German work'. In retaliation against German imports there were growing demands in Britain for the end of **free trade** and the introduction of tariffs. This in turn led to German fears that their exports were about to be shut out of British markets and to increased demands for the acquisition of a larger German colonial empire.

SOURCE C

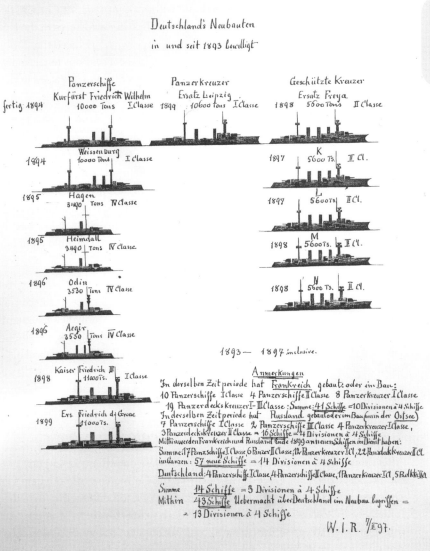

Study Source C. What does this illustration show about Kaiser Wilhelm's thinking on the question of sea power?

A naval chart drawn in 1897 by Kaiser Wilhelm. He heads the chart with 'Germany's new ships [planned and] approved since 1893'. Below in the right-hand corner he notes how many ships France ('Frankreich') and Russia ('Russland') had built during the same period.

Anglo-German naval rivalry

It was above all the Anglo-German naval arms race that inflamed public opinion in both countries. The launching of the German naval programme in 1897 alarmed Britain, and led to an escalating arms race between the two states, which by 1912 – in the words of the Austrian foreign minister – had become the 'dominant element of the international situation'. The construction of the German navy struck at the core of British power: in order to preserve its empire, Britain had to retain control of the seas. As long as Germany continued to build up its navy, Britain would therefore ultimately be numbered among Germany's enemies.

The German government intended to build within twenty years a German fleet of 60 battleships, which was to be aimed against British naval bases in the North Sea. Admiral **Tirpitz**, the head of the German navy, was convinced that this would ultimately force Britain to make major colonial concessions to Germany. This programme was also genuinely popular in Germany and appealed to the new German nationalism.

The British government responded to the challenge by modernising the Royal Navy and designing in 1906 the new *Dreadnought* battleship, which made every other ship afloat obsolete. This, however, only made it easier for the Germans to catch up as it inevitably reduced Britain's overwhelming lead. Thus, when in 1908 the Germans announced a supplementary programme consisting of four capital ships per year for the next four years, often hysterical demands in the British popular press and skilfully orchestrated campaigns by the Navy League pressure group pushed the British government into agreeing to build eight new battleships in 1909 and a further ten over the next two years.

In 1909–10 and then again in 1912 attempts were made to find a formula which could defuse the dangerous tensions generated by the naval race, but each time there were insuperable objections to a settlement. Britain wanted to safeguard its naval supremacy by negotiating a **fixed ratio** for capital ships, while the Germans wanted a cast-iron assurance that Britain would remain neutral if Germany had to fight France and Russia. Britain could not afford to stand aside and see another defeat of France by Germany, which would lead to the German domination of the European continent.

The making of the Anglo-French *Entente*

After their humiliation at Fashoda, the French were determined to occupy Morocco (see page 32). Once it was clear that the Germans would not help them, **Delcassé**, the French foreign minister, began to look to London. Britain had initially been hostile to the prospect of a French **protectorate** in Morocco, as it might threaten the great British naval base in Gibraltar, but by 1902 Morocco was on the verge of civil war and the restoration of order by the French seemed the better option. The looming war in the Far East between Japan and Russia

KEY FIGURES

Alfred von Tirpitz (1849–1930)

German naval minister. His intention was to create a powerful German fleet which would be able to force the British to make major colonial concessions.

Theophile Delcassé (1852–1923)

French foreign minister 1898–1905. He was forced to resign by the Germans in 1905, but during 1911–13 he was naval minister and 1914–15 again foreign minister.

KEY TERMS

Fixed ratio A scheme whereby Germany would agree not to increase the number of ships beyond a certain percentage of the British fleet.

Protectorate A territory that is controlled and protected by another state.

also played an important part in pushing the states into agreement as both feared what the historian John Lowe has called the 'nightmare scenario of Britain and France having to fight each other as the "seconds" of their allies' (see page 34).

Ultimately, of course, the French hoped to associate Britain with the Franco-Russian Dual Alliance, while the British government hoped that an **Anglo-French colonial *entente*** would lead to a similar agreement with Russia. The agreement was signed on 8 April 1904 and settled Anglo-French colonial problems in three main areas:

- The French exchanged their fishing rights around Newfoundland for territorial compensation in west Africa.
- Siam (present-day Thailand) was divided into two zones of influence and a **condominium** was set up in the New Hebrides.
- France agreed not to block British plans for financial reform in Egypt, provided Britain recognised France's right to maintain law and order in Morocco. Secret clauses then made provision for the establishment of a protectorate at some future date by France over Morocco and by Britain over Egypt.

While it improved Anglo-French relations, it is important to grasp that this agreement was not an alliance since neither country was committed to come to the help of the other in the event of war. Arguably, together with the Japanese Alliance, it made Britain even more independent of Continental entanglements and it was only Germany's violent reaction to its provisions for the French control of Morocco that turned the agreement into a virtual Franco-British Alliance against Germany.

The German reaction: the first Moroccan crisis 1905–6

The German chancellor, Count Bernhard von Bülow (1849–1929), decided to challenge the right to control Morocco which had been given to France by the Anglo-French Agreement. Optimistically, he believed that he could destroy both the Dual Alliance and the *Entente cordiale*, and that a new Russo-German Alliance would emerge, which would effectively isolate France.

In early 1905 the French government, ignoring all warnings from Berlin, began to reform the Moroccan administration. The Kaiser interrupted his Mediterranean cruise to land at Tangier and greeted the Sultan of Morocco as an independent ruler. The Germans then demanded a conference on the future of Morocco and the resignation of Delcassé. At first it seemed that Berlin really would win a significant success. The French cabinet agreed to a conference and forced Delcassé to resign. Then, in July, the Kaiser and Nicholas II of Russia met at Björkö and signed a defensive alliance to co-operate against any hostile power in Europe.

Yet all these successes were purely temporary and by April 1906 Germany had suffered a crushing defeat. The Russian government never ratified the Björkö

KEY TERMS

Anglo-French colonial *entente* An understanding reached by Britain and France on colonial issues, sometimes called the *Entente cordiale* because it led to the restoration of good Anglo-French relations.

Condominium Joint control of a territory by two states.

Agreement and let it lapse, and France was significantly strengthened when the British government came down firmly on the side of the French over Morocco.

When the conference opened at Algeçiras in January 1906, Germany secured the backing of only Austria and Morocco. The other nine states agreed that France had a special interest in Morocco. Together with the Spanish, the French were therefore entrusted with the supervision of the Moroccan police, while France was also given control of the state bank. However, the Germans did win the concession that all the powers should enjoy equal economic rights within Morocco.

The Moroccan incident was, as the historian A.J.P. Taylor has stressed, 'a true crisis, a turning point in European history'. For the first time since 1870 a Franco-German war seemed a real possibility. There were no armies or fleets mobilised, but the senior official in the German foreign ministry, Friedrich von Holstein, and the German military high command were certainly ready to risk war, as Russia was weak and the French army was inadequately equipped. In December 1905 the **Schlieffen Plan** was perfected for a **two-front war**, while the British and French military staffs also began seriously to discuss what action should be taken if Germany invaded France.

SOURCE D

From David Lloyd George, *War Memoirs*, Odhams, 1938, p. 1.

In the year 1904 on the day when the Anglo-French entente was announced, I arrived at Dalmeny [in Scotland] on a couple of days' visit to the late Lord Roseberry. His first greeting to me was: 'Well, I suppose you are just as pleased as the rest of them with this French agreement?' I assured him that I was delighted that our snarling and scratching relations with France had come to an end at last. He replied: 'You are all wrong. It means war with Germany in the end!'

… Had anyone then told me that before I ceased to hold office in the British Cabinet I should … have witnessed a war between Britain and Germany … I should have treated such a forecast as [a] … wild prediction … .

The Anglo-Russian *Entente* 1907

The Anglo-Russian *Entente* of 1907, like the Anglo-French Agreement, was not initially aimed at Germany. The British had long wished to negotiate a compromise with Russia that would take the pressure off Afghanistan and northern India. On the Russian side, the Anglo-French *Entente* and Japan's victory in the Far East made an agreement with Britain increasingly necessary. It had little option but to improve its relations with London if it was to maintain its alliance with France.

The Anglo-Russian Agreement was signed in August 1907. Like the Anglo-French Agreement it was concerned only with colonial matters:

Schlieffen Plan Planned a two-front war against France and Russia. France was to be defeated within a month by a flanking movement through Belgium, the Netherlands and Luxembourg and then the mass of the German army would move eastwards to deal with Russia. The plan was later revised to omit the Netherlands.

Two-front war A war in which fighting takes place on two geographically separate fronts.

Study Source D. Why did Lloyd George welcome the Anglo-French *Entente* in 1904, while Lord Roseberry was fiercely critical of it?

- The Russians gave up all claims to Afghanistan and recognised British interests in Tibet.
- Persia (present-day Iran) was divided into zones of influence: the north went to Russia, the south to Britain, with a neutral zone in between.
- Both empires recognised Chinese sovereignty over Tibet.

Germany on the defensive

The **Triple *Entente*** was not a formal alliance system, but it did mark a shift in the balance of power in Europe. No longer could the Germans assume that an Anglo-Russian war would break out that would enable them to force Britain – or Russia – into becoming a subordinate ally. The *ententes* did not, however, completely remove all friction between their members. Anglo-Russian friction continued, for instance, in Persia. Nor did they necessarily mean that Germany would be isolated and encircled. There were influential voices in France arguing for a settlement with Germany. In 1909 the French and Germans even signed an agreement for economic co-operation in Morocco.

Yet by the end of 1910 Franco-German relations were again rapidly worsening, as local French officials in Morocco were breaking the Algeçiras Agreement by steadily increasing their power in administrative, economic and financial affairs. In Germany, the new foreign secretary, von Kiderlen-Wächter, was also determined to pursue a more decisive and aggressive foreign policy.

 **KEY TERM**

Triple *Entente* The name often applied to the co-operation of Britain, France and Russia in 1907–17.

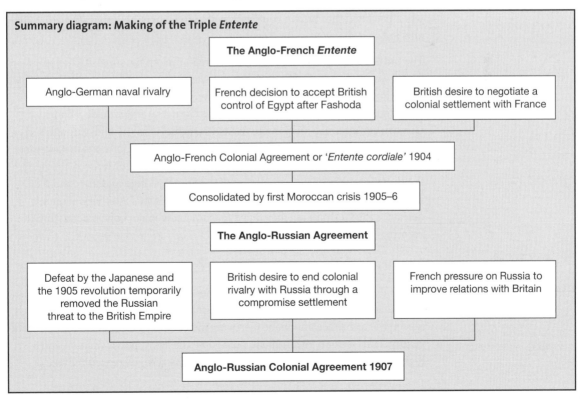

Summary diagram: Making of the Triple *Entente*

The Anglo-French *Entente*

| Anglo-German naval rivalry | French decision to accept British control of Egypt after Fashoda | British desire to negotiate a colonial settlement with France |

Anglo-French Colonial Agreement or '*Entente cordiale*' 1904

Consolidated by first Moroccan crisis 1905–6

The Anglo-Russian Agreement

| Defeat by the Japanese and the 1905 revolution temporarily removed the Russian threat to the British Empire | British desire to end colonial rivalry with Russia through a compromise settlement | French pressure on Russia to improve relations with Britain |

Anglo-Russian Colonial Agreement 1907

The second Moroccan crisis 1911 and its consequences

► *What were the causes and consequences of the second Moroccan crisis?*

Kiderlen-Wächter's opportunity to reassert Germany's rights in Morocco came when in May 1911 French troops intervened in Fez after riots against the Sultan of Morocco had broken out. It soon became clear that France, contrary to the agreement of 1906, was going to occupy the whole country. The German government immediately insisted on territorial compensation from territory in the French Congo, and on 1 July sent the *Panther*, a gunboat, to the south Moroccan port of Agadir. The hope was, as Kiderlen-Wächter expressed it, that 'By seizing a [territorial] pawn, the Imperial government will be placed in a position to give the Moroccan affair a turn which should cause the earlier setbacks of 1905 to pass into oblivion.'

Initially, the French government was ready to negotiate with the Germans as the Russians, still resenting the lack of French help during the Bosnian crisis (see page 46), made it clear that they could offer the French no military assistance at all. But then on 21 July Britain intervened decisively. The chancellor of the exchequer, David Lloyd George (see page 89), voiced his government's policy when he stated that Britain could not 'be treated where her interests were vitally affected as if she were of no account'.

The British were anxious to prevent a German diplomatic success which they feared would destroy the *Entente*, but they were also signalling to the French that Britain must not be ignored in any new Moroccan agreement. In fact, the warning was seen as an ultimatum against Germany and it made a Franco-German compromise much more difficult to achieve. In the end, through secret negotiations, the French reached an agreement with the Germans in November 1911, which allowed France to establish a protectorate over Morocco, provided that Germany was given a small part of the French Congo and its economic interests in Morocco were respected. Essentially this was another diplomatic defeat for the Germans as they failed to extract any major concessions from the French.

The acceleration of the arms race

The second Moroccan crisis had very serious consequences for the peace of Europe. It heightened tension between Germany and Britain and France, which fuelled the arms race and made Germany increasingly desperate for a diplomatic victory. The German government, pushed by the army, public opinion and a highly effective pressure group called the **Wehrverein**, increased the size of the army by about 29,000 men in 1912 and then a year later a further increase of 117,000 men and 119 officers and non-commissioned officers was approved. In Britain, the Navy League (see page 38) and the **National Service League** subjected their own government to similar pressures.

The French meanwhile compensated for their smaller population by extending the period of conscription from two to three years and by modernising their artillery and equipment. Russia had to rebuild its armed forces after the disaster of the Russo-Japanese War. By the financial year 1913–14 Russia was spending over 800 million roubles on rearmament. By June 1914 the peacetime strength of the Russian army was on target to reach almost 2 million men, which was three times as large as Germany's.

The strengthening of the Triple *Entente*

When **Poincaré** became French prime minister in 1912 he was determined as a consequence of the second Moroccan crisis to strengthen the Triple *Entente*:

- A Franco-Russian naval convention was signed in July 1912 in which both navies agreed to work out joint tactics in the event of war.
- The French and Russian military chiefs of staff also met and decided that should war break out with Germany both armies would immediately attack.
- At the same time, talks between the British and French naval staff also took place about the part each navy would play in the event of war with Germany in the Mediterranean and the English Channel.

In November the French and British governments exchanged letters defining the *Entente*. In essence they stated that the naval and military agreements between the two countries did not constitute a proper alliance, but if either state were attacked by a third power, they would immediately meet to discuss whether they would take any joint measures. This was as far as the British cabinet was willing to go.

By the end of 1912 both the Dual Alliance and the Anglo-French *Entente* had been greatly strengthened. Germany, facing isolation, was consequently all the more determined to cling to its alliance with Austria. It was this that was to make the Balkan crises of 1908–14 so dangerous.

KEY TERM

National Service League
A British pressure group founded in February 1902 to alert the country to the inability of the army to fight a major war and to propose the solution of national service.

KEY FIGURE

Raymond Poincaré (1860–1934)
A popular right-wing patriot, as prime minister and then president he did all he could to strengthen France's relations with Russia and Britain.

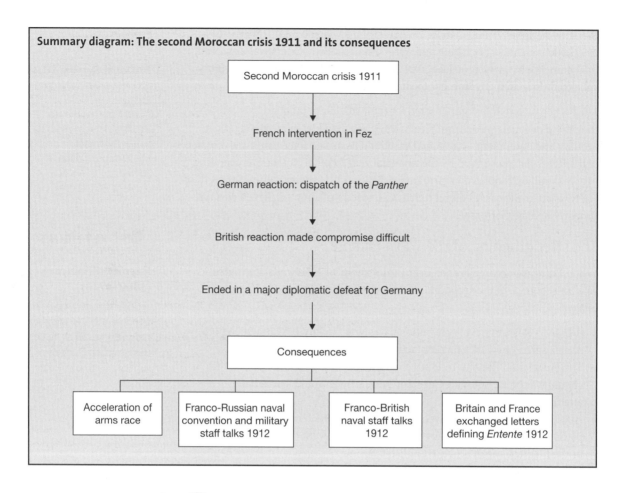

Summary diagram: The second Moroccan crisis 1911 and its consequences

5 The Balkans and the Great Powers 1906–14

▶ *Why were the Balkans a major crisis point during the years 1906–14?*

Between 1890 and 1905 the Balkans remained relatively quiet. Britain was no longer concerned by the Russian threat to the straits of the Bosphorus and the Dardanelles as it could now protect its interests in the eastern Mediterranean from bases in Egypt. As Russia wished to concentrate on the Far East, in May 1897 it signed with Austria an agreement whereby both states would do as little as possible to disturb the existing situation in the Balkans and Near East. In 1905, weakened by defeat in the Far East and the subsequent turmoil at home, the Russian government hoped to maintain this agreement, but Russia's very weakness upset the balance of power in the Balkans and tempted Austria to take advantage of it to defend its interests against an increasingly aggressive Serbia.

In 1903 the pro-Austrian Serbian king, Alexander Obrenovich (1876–1903), had been assassinated by Serbian nationalists and replaced by Peter (1844–1921), of the rival Karageorgevich dynasty. Peter followed a fiercely anti-Austrian and strongly nationalist policy, which he hoped would attract Russian support. Ultimately, his aim was to free the South Slavs, who increasingly resented being part of the Austro-Hungarian Empire. Austria's main aim in the Balkans was now at all costs to weaken Serbia.

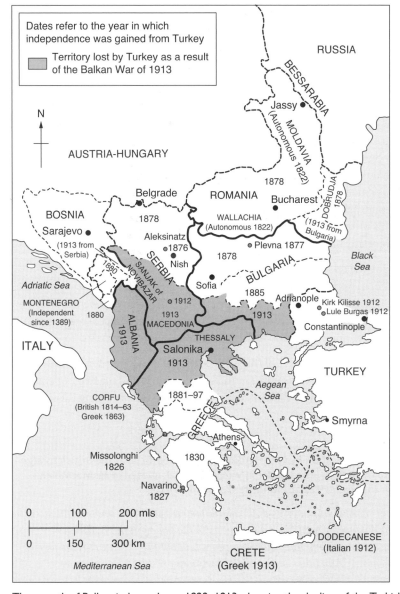

How far does this map explain the growing threat to Austria caused by the decline of the Turkish Empire in Europe?

The growth of Balkan independence 1822–1913, showing the decline of the Turkish Empire within Europe.

The Bosnian crisis 1908–09

In 1908 a group of army officers seized power in Turkey. This temporarily revived Austro-Russian co-operation as both powers feared that this would lead to the strengthening of the Turkish Empire. In September 1908 the Russian and Austrian foreign ministers approved an agreement whereby Russian warships would be able to pass through the Straits, while this right would still be denied to the other powers. In exchange, Austria would be able formally to annex Bosnia and Herzegovina, which it had in fact administered since 1878 (see page 17). The Russian foreign minister claimed that any Austrian move would have to be confirmed later by a European conference, but this was never put down on paper, a fact that explains much of what was to follow.

The Austrians went ahead and annexed Bosnia and Herzegovina in October, while the Russians found little international support for their plans at the Straits. The annexation, however, met with a storm of complaint throughout Europe. In Russia and Serbia, which eventually hoped to make these provinces part of a greater Serb state, there were demonstrations calling for war against Austria. Facing strong criticism in the Russian press, Isvolsky, the Russian foreign minister, demanded the calling of the European conference, to which he insisted the Austrians had in principle agreed. The Austrian government immediately vetoed this proposal as it feared a repetition of what had happened at Algeçiras, where Germany and Austria had been heavily outvoted (see page 40).

What made the crisis so dangerous was that Austria, which had the unconditional backing of Germany, was ready to fight Serbia even if supported by Russia. However, the Russians received no backing from the French, who were busy negotiating an economic agreement covering Morocco (see page 41) with Germany, and were ready to accept the annexation.

The dangerous consequences of this crisis were that it did long-term and serious damage to Russia's relations with Germany and Austria and made co-operation in the Balkans much more difficult, while at the same time bringing Russia and Serbia together.

SOURCE E

From a communication by Lord Hardinge, the head official at the British foreign office, to the British ambassador in Vienna in 1909, quoted in M. MacMillan, *The War that Ended Peace*, Profile Books, 2014, p. 410.

I entirely share your views as to the absolute necessity of an understanding of some kind between Austria and Russia as to the policy in the Balkans, otherwise it is unlikely that unbroken peace will obtain in those regions for many years ... Any other policy would inevitably result in European war.

Study Source E. Why, in the aftermath of the Bosnian crisis, did Hardinge believe that an Austro-Russian understanding was so vital?

The First Balkan War 1912

In 1912 the Italians invaded Libya, which was legally still part of the Turkish Empire. This prompted the Balkan states to overcome their internal rivalries, and declare war against Turkey. Within three weeks the Turkish Empire in Europe had collapsed, and Bulgarian troops were advancing on Constantinople. The sheer speed and scale of the victory created an acute crisis for the Great Powers. What made the situation so tense was the following:

- Austria faced a strengthened Serbia, which had occupied part of Albania. Austria, however, was determined to make Albania an independent state so as to deny Serbia access to the Adriatic. At first, Russia supported Serbian claims. Austria began to concentrate troops near the Russian frontier.
- Russia was equally determined to stop Constantinople falling to Bulgaria, as the Straits were becoming increasingly vital for its economic development. Between 1903 and 1912 a growing percentage of Russian exports, particularly of grain, which was the main export, were passing through them.
- The crisis also threatened to activate 'the alliance system'. Behind Austria stood Germany; behind Russia stood France. Although neither wanted war, both powers made clear that they would stand by their ally.
- The German declaration on 2 December 1912, promising help to Austria if attacked by a 'third party', was answered by a statement from London stressing that Britain would not remain neutral in a major conflict.
- Partly in response to this, on 8 December the Kaiser called a conference of his service chiefs. Von Moltke, Chief of the General Staff, argued for 'War – the sooner, the better', but Tirpitz insisted on waiting until the Kiel Canal had been widened to take modern battleships.

The immediate danger to Russia passed when Bulgaria failed to take Constantinople and the Balkan states signed an armistice with Turkey on 3 December. The Great Powers then agreed to call a peace conference in London to settle the territorial problem in the Balkans. By the Treaty of London of 30 May 1913 the Turks gave up all their territory in the Balkans except for a small zone around the Dardanelles and Bosphorus, which satisfied Russia, while Austria's demand that an independent Albania be set up was also agreed.

The Second Balkan War

At the end of June 1913 the Second Balkan War broke out when Bulgaria, which felt cheated of its just share of territory, attacked Serbia. The Greeks, the Romanians and the Turks all supported Serbia and within a month Bulgaria was defeated. The subsequent Treaty of Bucharest increased the territories of Serbia, Greece and Romania, while Turkey, through the Treaty of Constantinople, regained some of the territory it had lost to Bulgaria.

The clear loser in the Second Balkan War was Austria, even though it was not a belligerent, because Serbia had now emerged stronger, and was in a position to resist pressure from Vienna.

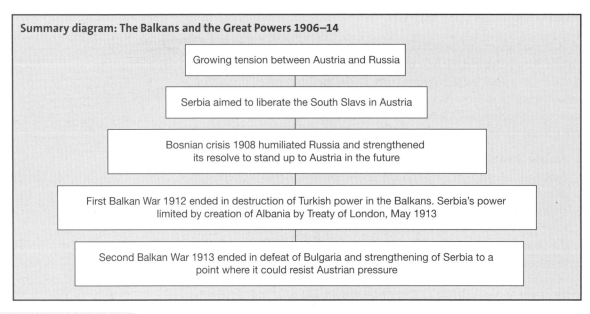

Summary diagram: The Balkans and the Great Powers 1906–14

Growing tension between Austria and Russia

Serbia aimed to liberate the South Slavs in Austria

Bosnian crisis 1908 humiliated Russia and strengthened its resolve to stand up to Austria in the future

First Balkan War 1912 ended in destruction of Turkish power in the Balkans. Serbia's power limited by creation of Albania by Treaty of London, May 1913

Second Balkan War 1913 ended in defeat of Bulgaria and strengthening of Serbia to a point where it could resist Austrian pressure

 **KEY TERMS**

Black Hand This secret terrorist organisation was founded in May 1911 and by 1914 probably had about 2500 members. They included a considerable number of the army officers who had taken part in the Serbian revolution of 1903. Its aim was to work for the union of the Serbs living in the Austrian and Turkish Empires with Serbia.

Blank cheque A free hand, unconditional support.

 KEY FIGURE

Theobold von Bethmann Hollweg (1856–1921)

A Prussian civil servant before becoming *Reich* minister of the interior in 1907. He was appointed *Reich* chancellor in 1909 and forced to resign by the army in 1917.

 Outbreak of the First World War 1914

▶ *Why did Germany give Austria a 'blank cheque'?*

The assassination of Franz Ferdinand

On 28 June 1914, Archduke Franz Ferdinand, the heir to the Austrian throne, and his wife were assassinated in Sarajevo by Gavrilo Princip, who had been recruited by the Serb terrorist group, the **Black Hand**. The assassination at last provided Austria with an excuse to eliminate the Serb threat to Bosnia and its South Slav territories. To succeed, however, Vienna needed to gain German backing in case of Russian intervention and also to move quickly while the horror of the assassination was still fresh in the minds of the European governments. The German government agreed with the Austrian analysis of the Serb threat, and on 5 July the Kaiser and his chancellor, **Bethmann Hollweg**, gave the Austrians their unconditional support: the so-called **blank cheque**, as it was later called.

What did they hope this would achieve? Neither was intending to unleash a major European war, but Bethmann Hollweg believed that a brief punitive war against Serbia could be kept localised. He gambled that Russia would not in the end intervene both because it was financially not ready for war and because it would see the war as justified retribution for the assassination of the heir to the Austrian throne. Bethmann Hollweg hoped that the rapid defeat of Serbia would

SOURCE F

Franz Ferdinand, and his wife Sophie, one hour before their assassination in Sarajevo on 28 June 1914 by the Serb terrorist group the Black Hand.

restore the prestige of the Dual Alliance, weaken Pan Slavism and Russia, and subsequently enable Germany to exploit Austria's success to improve relations with the *Entente* powers from a position of strength.

Study Source F. What was the significance of Franz Ferdinand's murder?

The Austrian ultimatum

Possibly, if Austria had moved quickly, the plan might have worked. On 7 July the Austro-Hungarian ministerial council met to consider what action to take. The chancellor, Count Leopold von Berchtold (1863–1942), was ready to launch a surprise attack on Serbia but on the advice of the Hungarian prime minister, Count Stephen Tisza (1861–1918), he agreed first of all to present Serbia with an ultimatum, and then only declare war if this was rejected.

The crucial part of the ultimatum insisted that Serbia should carry out, under the supervision of Austrian officials, a whole series of anti-terrorist measures. The Austrians calculated that Belgrade would reject this demand, as acceptance would give Vienna effective control of Serbia's security forces, and enable it to intervene in Serbia's internal affairs. It was sent to Belgrade on 23 July.

The Serbs reject the ultimatum

The Serb reply to the ultimatum was skilfully drafted. It rejected, as Vienna expected, and indeed hoped, the crucial demand that Austrian officials should supervise the anti-terrorist measures, yet its tone was so conciliatory that it cunningly appeared to offer Austria most of what it wanted. The Austrians were not fooled by this 'masterpiece of public relations'. They broke off diplomatic relations and then on 28 July declared war on Serbia.

The reaction of the Great Powers

Russia

The Russians accepted the Austrians' right to demand an inquiry into the assassination at Sarajevo, but they were not ready to tolerate the destruction of Serbia and Austro-Hungarian domination of the Balkans. On 28 July, the day Austria declared war on Serbia, the Russian government ordered the **mobilisation** of the military districts of Odessa, Kiev, Kazan and Moscow. Two days later this was changed to full mobilisation despite the initial reservations of the tsar and a personal appeal from the Kaiser. This move certainly heightened the tension, although it would take at least six weeks before the Russian army would be ready for war.

Germany

Russian mobilisation made German mobilisation inevitable given the Schlieffen Plan (see page 40) which depended on defeating the French *before* the Russian army was fully ready. By 28 July the German **general staff** was already urging its government to prepare for war. Germany, therefore, had little option but to act quickly. On 31 July it dispatched an ultimatum to Russia warning its government that unless it stopped mobilisation within twelve hours, Germany would fully mobilise its armed forces. When the ultimatum expired, Germany declared war on Russia. Politically, the fact that the Russians started to set their army on a war footing before the Germans enabled Bethmann Hollweg to claim

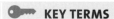

KEY TERMS

Mobilisation Preparing the armed forces for war.

General staff A group of officers which plans operations and administrates an army.

According to Riezler in Source G, why does the murder of Franz Ferdinand confront Bethmann Hollweg with 'difficult decisions'?

SOURCE G

From the diary of Kurt Riezler, the secretary of Bethmann Hollweg, the German chancellor, 7 July 1914, quoted in I. Porter and I. Armour, *Imperial Germany*, Longman, 1991, pp. 99–100.

The Chancellor talks of difficult decisions. Murder of Francis Ferdinand. Official Serbia involved. Austria wants to bestir herself … If we encourage them, they will say we pushed them into it; if we try to dissuade them, then we are supposed to have left them in the lurch. Then they turn to the western powers whose arms are open and we lose our last halfway reliable ally. This time it's worse than 1912; for this time Austria is on the defensive against the subversive activities of Serbia and Russia. A move against Serbia can lead to world war.

that Germany was only acting defensively against the Russian threat. This was to prove an important factor in gaining the support of the German working classes for the war.

France

French reactions to the crisis were confused by the fact that both the French president and prime minister were at sea returning from a visit to St Petersburg and did not reach Paris until 29 July. However, the war minister had taken the precaution of discreetly recalling soldiers from leave and moving some key units back from Morocco.

On 31 July the French cabinet ordered mobilisation to start on the following day. The German ambassador was instructed from Berlin to ask what France's attitude would be to a Russo-German war. If France chose to remain neutral, it would have to surrender the two fortresses of Toul and Verdun to Germany as a pledge of good faith. The prime minister merely commented that 'France will act in accordance with her interests.' In reality, France had little choice. The Dual Alliance bound France to come to the help of Russia. The French could not stand back and allow the defeat of Russia, which would immeasurably increase German power. The Germans, however, could not afford to wait for France to declare war. They had to implement the Schlieffen Plan, part of which involved a flanking attack against France through Belgium as soon as possible. On 2 August they sent an ultimatum to Belgium demanding a free passage for their troops. When this was rejected the following day, orders were given to the German army to advance into Belgium and war was declared on France.

Great Britain

As the seriousness of the crisis in the Balkans became clear, the British foreign minister, **Sir Edward Grey**, on 27 July suggested a conference in London to discuss the crisis. The Italians and the French backed it, but the Germans argued that only direct Austro-Russian negotiations could solve the problem. That same day the cabinet decided that the British fleet, which had just finished manoeuvres, should not be dispersed to its peacetime bases. Ominously, Grey also raised with the cabinet the possibility that Britain might declare war on Germany, should France be attacked.

With the announcement of Russian mobilisation and the German declaration of war on Russia, pressure from both France and Russia on Britain to enter the war increased, while Germany attempted to persuade Britain to remain neutral. The French argued that Britain was morally committed to back them. However, on the vital issue of peace or war the cabinet was divided. On 29 July it could only agree that 'at this stage' it was 'unable to pledge ourselves in advance either under all circumstances to stand aside or on any condition to go in'.

It was finally the German violation of Belgium on 4 August that enabled Grey and the '**war party**' to win over the majority of those in the cabinet, who still

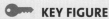

KEY FIGURE

Edward Grey (1872–1933)

British foreign minister, 1905–16, and Liberal MP. He became a great champion of the League of Nations.

KEY TERM

War party A group of ministers supporting Britain's entry into the war.

clung to the hope that Britain could keep out of the war. An ultimatum was sent to Berlin at 2p.m. that afternoon and when it expired at midnight (German time) Britain was at war with Germany.

Italy

Throughout the critical days in late July, Italy, despite being a member of the Triple Alliance, refused to align itself with Germany and Austria-Hungary.

? What does this map tell you about Germany's position in Europe?

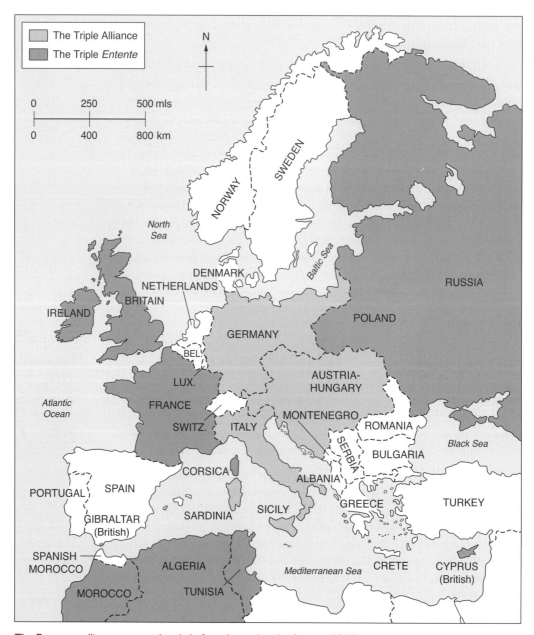

The European alliance system shortly before the outbreak of war in 1914.

There was little public support for Austria, who was still viewed as the 'traditional enemy' (see page 19), and also an awareness of how vulnerable Italy's coastline would be to British and French naval attacks. After the war in Libya (see page 46) the army, too, needed to be re-equipped and rested. However, the Italian prime minister did not rule out eventual entry on either side if promised sufficient territorial reward.

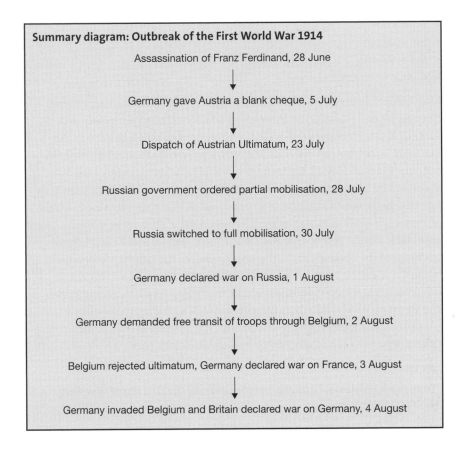

Summary diagram: Outbreak of the First World War 1914

Assassination of Franz Ferdinand, 28 June

↓

Germany gave Austria a blank cheque, 5 July

↓

Dispatch of Austrian Ultimatum, 23 July

↓

Russian government ordered partial mobilisation, 28 July

↓

Russia switched to full mobilisation, 30 July

↓

Germany declared war on Russia, 1 August

↓

Germany demanded free transit of troops through Belgium, 2 August

↓

Belgium rejected ultimatum, Germany declared war on France, 3 August

↓

Germany invaded Belgium and Britain declared war on Germany, 4 August

 # The key debate

▶ *Can it be argued that no one power alone bears the chief responsibility for the causes of the First World War?*

The causes of the First World War are one of the most controversial debates in modern history. At the Paris Peace Conference in 1919 (see Chapter 5) the Allied powers had little doubt that 'this responsibility rests first on Germany and Austria', but in the 1920s and 1930s this view was rejected by historians not only in Germany but in the USA, Britain and even France.

The 'European system' 1871–1914

Revisionist critics after 1919 insisted that the real causes of the war were far more complex and were a result of the 'European system' that came into existence in 1871. In their opinion the key causes were:

- the alliance system
- nationalism
- militarism
- imperialism
- the arms race
- economic rivalry.

Most modern historians accept that nationalism, militarism and imperialism certainly helped to create the atmosphere which made war acceptable and exciting. These ideologies radicalised large sections of public opinion in the European states, but, as Margaret MacMillan argues, by themselves they did not *cause* the war. Indeed, the historians Niall Ferguson and Mark Hewitson stress that by 1914 militarism and imperialism were in decline. For instance, in July 1914 Bethmann Hollweg was worried that the German Socialist Party, the SPD, would not support war unless it was seen to be a defensive struggle against **autocratic** Russia. Neither did economic rivalry, despite Marx's and Lenin's teachings to the contrary, make the war inevitable. The German 'economic miracle' during the period 1890–1914 challenged Britain's former economic supremacy, but the two countries became major trading partners, and British and German banks worked closely together. While strident nationalists in Germany demanded ever more armaments, the majority of the German people saw no need for war and were proud of Germany's progress.

KEY TERM

Autocratic Absolute government by one person.

EXTRACT I

From Mark Hewitson, *Germany and the Causes of the First World War*, Berg, 2004, pp. 224–5.

This study has argued … that the largest parties and most popular newspapers [in Germany] harbor reservations about 'offensive' wars, especially those waged against increasingly familiar and allegedly weaker west European states such as France or even Britain. The … public … were by and large impressed by the scale of Germany's economic progress and proud of the international position and military power of the new German state. Noisy debates about 'world empires' and rapid armament, as well as 'war scares' and international crises appeared to have created anxieties amongst many Wilhelmine observers. Few on the left and in the center were so moved by such fears to contemplate war as a remedy. On the contrary, most seemed to assume – in conjunction with the Reich's industrialists and financiers – that a military conflict would bring instability and potential disaster.

The arms race and the alliance system both contributed towards the outbreak of war. The arms race fuelled political tension and insecurity, as we can see with the Anglo-German naval race, for example. In Germany the generals, faced by the growing strength of the Russian and French armies, positively welcomed the chance to go war in 1914 before the strength of their potential enemies became overwhelming.

The alliance system with its **secret diplomacy** and treaties was much criticised after 1919. The fact that the web of treaties which covered Europe in 1914 contained, or – equally as important – was thought to contain, secret clauses, contributed to the atmosphere of suspicion between the Triple Alliance and the Triple *Entente*. The alliance system also divided Europe up into potential friends and enemies and influenced military and strategic planning. The danger of this was that the admirals and generals had to take planning decisions which in a time of acute crisis could deprive their governments of both time and the freedom of action. The existence of the Schlieffen Plan (see page 40), for instance, made it much more difficult for Bethmann Hollweg to avoid war in July 1914. On the other hand, two American historians, Marc Trachtenberg and Denis Showalter, point out that the option of attacking Russia first was kept open until 1913, and so presumably could still have been put into operation only a year later, and just might have bought valuable time as far as France was concerned.

KEY TERM

Secret diplomacy
Diplomatic contacts, meetings and decisions which are not made public.

Germany's role

From the 1920s to the 1960s it was generally agreed that all the Great Powers were responsible for the war, but then this consensus was challenged by a new generation of German historians led by Fritz Fischer, who argued in two key books that the German leadership by 1912 was more than ready to risk war both to make Germany into a world power and to consolidate its position at home.

EXTRACT 2

From Fritz Fischer, *Germany's War Aims*, Chatto & Windus, 1967, p. 88.

Given the tenseness of the world situation in 1914 – a condition for which Germany's world policy, which had already led to three dangerous crises (those of 1905, 1908, and 1911) was in no small measure responsible – any limited or local war in Europe directly involving one great power must inevitably carry with it the imminent danger of a general war. As Germany willed and coveted the Austro-Serbian war and, in her confidence in her military superiority, deliberately faced the risk of a conflict with Russia and France, her leaders must bear a substantial share of the historical responsibility for the outbreak of the general war in 1914.

Fischer focused the spotlight back on Germany's role in the causes of the war and triggered a bitter debate within Germany. His critics, such as the historians Gerhardt Ritter and Golo Mann, accused him of resurrecting the war guilt accusations of 1919. While his arguments have been modified, few historians would go back to the pre-1960 consensus among the majority of German historians and argue that Germany was a victim of aggression in 1914.

The responsibility of the other powers

Nevertheless, the Fischer controversy inspired historians to look more closely at the record of the other belligerent powers. Samuel Williamson, for instance, stresses the responsibility of Austria-Hungary.

EXTRACT 3

From Samuel Williamson, *Austria-Hungary and the Origins of the First World War*, Palgrave Macmillan, 1999, p. 215.

In Vienna in July 1914 a set of leaders experienced in statecraft, power and crisis management consciously risked a general war to fight a local war. Battered during the Balkan wars by Serbian expansion, Russian activism and now by the loss of Franz Ferdinand, the Habsburg leaders desperately tried to shape their future, rather than let events destroy them. The fear of domestic disintegration made war an acceptable option.

Serbia's willingness to risk a war with Austria even if that should trigger a European war is explored by Mark Cornwall and Joachim Remark, and Edward McCullough argues strongly that Germany and Austria 'fought to maintain the *status quo*, while France and Russia fought to change it'. Britain too is heavily criticised by Niall Ferguson for the ambiguity of its foreign policy and secret military staff talks with the French about which parliament knew nothing.

EXTRACT 4

From Niall Ferguson, *The Pity of War*, Penguin, 1999, p. 443.

Britain's decision to intervene was the result of secret planning by generals and diplomats, which dated back to late 1905. Formally Britain had no 'universal commitment' to France; this was repeatedly stated by Grey and other ministers in parliament and the press between 1907 and 1914 … The key was the conviction of a minority of generals, diplomats and politicians that, in the event of continental war, Britain must send an army to France.

? How far do the views of the historians on the causes of the First World War quoted in Extracts 1, 2, 3 and 4 complement or contradict each other?

Why did war break out in 1914?

Why did war break out in 1914 when previous crises in the Balkans and Morocco had not led to conflict between the Dual Alliance and the Triple *Entente*? Arguably, each crisis increased the likelihood of war. The two Moroccan crises did much to bring together Britain and France, while France's failure to back Russia in the Bosnian crisis of 1908, and Russia's subsequent humiliation at the hands of Austria and Germany, strengthened both Poincaré's resolve to support Russia next time and Russia's determination to stop the destruction of Serbia in July 1914.

The Great Powers did co-operate in containing the fallout from the two Balkan wars, but nevertheless the emergence of a greatly strengthened Serbia in 1913 with its claims on Bosnia and Herzegovina was a deadly threat to the Habsburg Empire, and the following year Austria went to war to crush it.

The constant international tension had created a mood throughout Europe that war was sooner or later inevitable, and that the main thing was to choose the right moment for the struggle to start. For differing reasons and at different stages that moment seemed to have been reached in July 1914. The Sarajevo assassinations brought together all the explosive tensions in Europe. Germany could not allow its only reliable ally to be humiliated by Serbia and Russia. Once Germany declared war on Russia, France could not stand back and see Russia defeated, while Britain, despite initial hesitations, could not afford to run the risk of a German victory. The decisions of the statesmen were backed for the most part by their people, who saw the war as a struggle and a matter of honour and principle to preserve their nation's independence, greatness and future development.

Chapter summary

In 1890, after Bismarck's resignation, Germany did not renew the Reinsurance Treaty but instead hoped to negotiate an alliance with Britain. Not only did this fail but it opened the door to the Franco-Russian Dual Alliance of 1894. For the next decade the focus of European rivalries shifted from Europe and the Balkans to Africa and China, where the Great Powers, joined by Japan, scrambled for territory and influence. The Germans believed that Britain, whose large and vulnerable empire was coming under increasing pressure, would in the end seek to join the Triple Alliance, but the Anglo-Japanese Alliance, the defeat of Russia in Manchuria and the *Entente* with France eased the pressure on Britain. The years 1904–14 saw growing Anglo-German tension largely as a result of naval rivalry and also the re-emergence of Austro-Russian rivalry in the Balkans, made more dangerous by Germany's support for Austria in the Bosnian crisis of 1908–9. By early 1914, with the collapse of the Turkish Empire within Europe, Serbia emerged as a major threat to Austria. The assassination of Franz Ferdinand gave Austria the chance to counter this threat but at the cost of causing a European war triggered by the alliance system.

Refresher questions

Use these questions to remind yourself of the key material covered in this chapter.

1 What was the impact of the Franco-Russian Alliance on the European balance of power?

2 Why did imperial rivalries in Africa and China not lead to a major war?

3 How serious was the Fashoda crisis?

4 Why did the Jameson raid damage Anglo-German relations?

5 How great a role did economic rivalry play in the deterioration in Anglo-German relations?

6 What role did Anglo-German naval rivalry play in the causes of the First World War?

7 What did the Germans hope to achieve by triggering the first Moroccan crisis?

8 Why did Britain and Russia sign the colonial agreement of 1907?

9 What impact did the second Moroccan crisis have on the arms race?

10 To what extent did Poincaré strengthen the Triple *Entente*?

11 Why did the First Balkan War threaten the peace of Europe?

12 Why was Austria the 'clear loser' in the Second Balkan War?

13 Did Russian mobilisation make the First World War inevitable?

14 Why did Germany declare war on Russia on 1 August 1914?

15 Why did Britain not declare war on Germany until 4 August 1914?

 Question practice

ESSAY QUESTIONS

1 'Troubles in the Balkans were the most important factor in causing the outbreak of the First World War?' How far do you agree?

2 'It was Germany that caused the First World War.' Assess the validity of this view.

3 To what extent was the Triple *Entente* a cause of the First World War?

4 'The termination of the Reinsurance Treaty in 1890 by Germany was a major mistake that ultimately made the First World War more likely.' Explain why you agree or disagree with this view.

INTERPRETATION QUESTIONS

1 Read the interpretation and then answer the question that follows: 'The alliances and alignments guaranteed that the [Balkan] crisis [of 1914] would be Europe wide. In this situation the decisions of Austria-Hungary and Germany on the one hand, and of Russia on the other, involved fateful consequences.' (From D.E. Lee, *The Outbreak of the First World War*, D.C. Heath, 1975, p. x.) Evaluate the strengths of this interpretation, making reference to other interpretations that you have studied.

2 Read the interpretation and then answer the question that follows: '[Germany's] leaders must bear a substantial share of the historical responsibility for the outbreak of the general war in 1914.' (From Fritz Fischer, *Germany's War Aims*, W.W. Norton, 1967, p. 88.) Evaluate the strengths and weaknesses of this interpretation, making reference to other interpretations that you have studied.

SOURCE ANALYSIS QUESTIONS

1 With reference to Sources 1 and 2, and your understanding of the historical context, which of these two sources is more valuable in explaining why the state of Austro-Russian relations was a threat to the peace of Europe?

2 With reference to Sources 2, 3 and 4, and your understanding of the historical context, assess the value of these sources to a historian studying the causes of the First World War.

SOURCE I

From a dispatch to the Austrian foreign minister by the German chancellor Bethmann Hollweg, 10 February 1913, quoted in M. Hewitson, *Germany and the Causes of the First World War*, Berg, 2004, p. 204.

As far as I can judge the situation in Russia, on the basis of information which I have cause to believe is reliable, we can reckon with certainty that the forces which stand behind the Pan-Slavist agitation will win the upper hand if Austria should get involved in a conflict with Serbia. One must arrive at the conclusion, after objective enquiry that it is almost impossible for Russia without an enormous loss of prestige, given its traditional relations with the Balkan states to look on without acting during a military advance against Serbia by Austria-Hungary. The consequences of Russian involvement, however, are plain for all to see. It would turn into an armed conflict of the Triple Alliance – predictably not supported by Italy with great enthusiasm – against the powers of the Triple Entente in which Germany would have to bear the entire heavy burden of a French and English attack.

SOURCE 2

From a report to the British foreign secretary from Sir Fairfax Cartwright, British ambassador to Vienna, January 1913, quoted in Joachim Remak, 'Third Balkan War' in D.E. Lee, editor, *The Outbreak of the First World War*, D.C. Heath, 1975, p. 146.

[Serbia] will some day set Europe by the ears and bring a universal war on the Continent … I cannot tell you how exasperated people are getting here at the continual worry which that little country causes to Austria under encouragement from Russia. It may be compared to a certain extent to the trouble we had to suffer through the hostile attitude formerly assumed against us by the Transvaal Republic under the guiding hand of Germany. It will be lucky if Europe succeeds in avoiding war as a result of the present crisis. The next time a [Serbian] crisis arises … I feel sure that Austria-Hungary will refuse to admit of any Russian interference in the dispute and that she will proceed to settle her differences with her little neighbour by herself. …

SOURCE 3

From the Franco-Russian Treaty 1892, quoted in Yale Law School, The Avalon Project, Documents in Law, History and Diplomacy, http://avalon.law.yale.edu/19th_century/frrumil.asp

1. *If France is attacked by Germany, or by Italy supported by Germany, Russia shall employ all her available forces to attack Germany. If Russia is attacked by Germany, or by Austria supported by Germany, France shall employ all her available forces to attack Germany.*

2. *In case the forces of the Triple Alliance, or of any one of the Powers belonging to it, should be mobilized, France and Russia, at the first news of this event and without previous agreement being necessary, shall mobilize immediately and simultaneously the whole of their forces, and shall transport them as far as possible to their frontiers.*

3. *The available forces to be employed against Germany shall be, on the part of France, 1,300,000 men, on the part of Russia, 700,000 or 800,000 men.*

SOURCE 4

From David Lloyd George, *War Memoirs*, Odhams, 1938, p. 1.

In the year 1904 on the day when the Anglo-French entente was announced, I arrived at Dalmeny [in Scotland] on a couple of days' visit to the late Lord Roseberry. His first greeting to me was: 'Well, I suppose you are just as pleased as the rest of them with this French agreement?' I assured him that I was delighted that our snarling and scratching relations with France had come to an end at last. He replied: 'You are all wrong. It means war with Germany in the end!'

... Had anyone then told me that before I ceased to hold office in the British Cabinet I should ... have witnessed a war between Britain and Germany ... I should have treated such a forecast as [a] ... wild prediction ... .

CHAPTER 4

The First World War 1914–18

Once war had broken out the key decisions about the future of Europe were made on the battlefield. It was not the diplomats, but the generals and admirals who now called the tune. To understand why the war lasted so long and ended in the defeat of the Central Powers, it is necessary to examine how events on the battlefields unfolded, as well as the aims and strategies of the belligerents. This chapter therefore examines the history of the war under the following headings:

★ The military and strategic background of the war 1914–15

★ 1916: The deadlock still unbroken

★ 1917: 'No peace without victory'

★ 1918: The final year of the war

★ The armistices of October and November 1918

Key dates

1914	Aug.	Germany invaded Belgium and France	1916	June	Battle of Jutland
		Battle of Tannenberg		July–Nov.	Battle of the Somme
	Aug. 23	Japan declared war on Germany	1917	Jan.	Unrestricted submarine warfare began
	Oct. 28	Turkey joined the Central Powers		Feb.	First Russian Revolution
1915	April 26	Treaty of London signed by Italy, France, Britain and Russia		April 6	USA declared war on Germany
				Oct.	Second Russian or Bolshevik Revolution
	May 23	Italy declared war on Austria-Hungary	1918	March 3	Treaty of Brest-Litovsk
				March–April	German offensive on the Western Front
1916	Feb.–Nov.	Battle of Verdun		Nov. 11	German armistice

The military and strategic background of the war 1914–15

 Why during 1914–15 did the war of movement turn into static trench warfare?

Initial war plans and strategy, August–December 1914

The initial **strategy** of the German invasion of France was determined by the Schlieffen Plan (see the map on page 63). It was imperative for the Germans to defeat the French army, which was the most effective in the Triple *Entente*, in a lightning campaign before Russia had completed mobilisation, and then turn east to deal with Russia.

At first, the German advance under the command of **General von Moltke** made good progress. The Germans swung through Belgium and Luxembourg and on into north-eastern France. The French meanwhile, in accordance with **Plan 17**, attempted to retake Alsace-Lorraine, but were repulsed with huge casualties. Soon, however, the German strategy began to go very wrong. Contrary to expectations, the Russians advanced into east Prussia. This necessitated the dispatch of two army corps from France to Prussia, although by the time they had arrived, the Russians had already been defeated at Tannenberg by **Hindenburg**.

The German's absence on the Western Front had fatal consequences. By the end of August the French had slowed down the German advance and prevented the encirclement of Paris. Then, together with the small British Expeditionary Force of 120,000 men, they counterattacked across the river Marne on 6 September and forced the Germans to retreat behind the river Aisne, where they dug in and repulsed the Allied attack.

By the autumn of 1914 the war was beginning to settle into the pattern it retained until 1918. In the west, German attempts to outflank the Allies in northern France and Belgium failed after they were halted in the first Battle of Ypres in November. The war of movement was turning into static trench warfare, and a line of makeshift trenches now ran from the North Sea to the Swiss border.

On the Eastern Front, East Prussia was cleared of Russian troops but the Russians were still able to invade Austria and threaten Silesia. Clearly, Russia was far from being knocked out of the war; a new Austro-German campaign would have to be mounted in 1915.

How the Schlieffen Plan was supposed to work in the west. The Schlieffen Plan was drawn up in December 1905.

What does this map and key tell you about the aims of the Schlieffen Plan in the west? **?**

The widening war 1914–15

Japan declares war on Germany

Japan quickly seized the chance to declare war on Germany on 23 August 1914 to capture German territory in the Chinese province of Shantung as well as the German Pacific islands. Japan refused to send any troops to the Western Front but its navy helped Britain to ensure the security of the Pacific Ocean. Japan's primary interest was to strengthen its hold on China.

Turkey joins the Central Powers

Both the Germans and the Allies also attempted to secure Turkish support, at least by rival offers of concessions. In the end, the Germans were able to outbid their enemies by promising their support for the Turkish annexation of Russian border territory and possibly the restoration of the Aegean islands, which had been ceded to Greece. Britain also seriously damaged its bargaining position by refusing to hand over two Turkish warships which had just been constructed in British dockyards. Turkey declared war on the *Entente* powers on 28 October 1914.

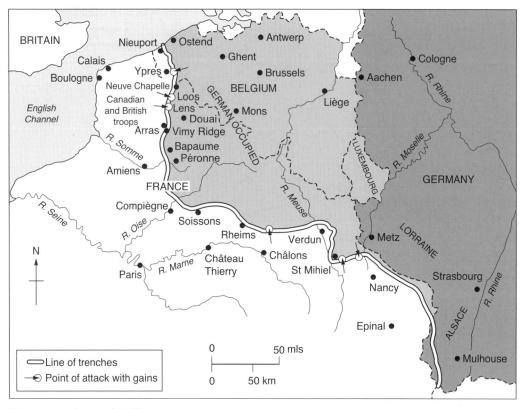

The Western Front, 1915. This map shows the line of trenches stretching from the North Sea to the Swiss border.

What does this map tell you about the nature of the war on the Western Front in 1915?

KEY TERMS

Anzac Australian and New Zealand Army Corps.

Mesopotamia An ancient Greek term literally meaning 'the land between two rivers': the Tigris and Euphrates. Today this area consists of Iraq, as well as some parts of north-eastern Syria, south-eastern Turkey and south-western Iran.

Turkey's entry into the war was a direct threat to Britain's position in Egypt and led to the dispatch of the **Anzac** Corps to defend the Suez Canal. In November, an Anglo-Indian force captured Basra to secure Britain's oil supplies from the Persian Gulf. From there, over the next three years British forces advanced ever deeper in **Mesopotamia**. Despite defeat at Kut in April 1916, Baghdad was finally occupied nearly a year later.

Italy abandons neutrality

Throughout the winter of 1914–15 the Italian government negotiated with both the Central Powers and the Allies to gain the maximum concessions for abandoning neutrality. In the end, Italy entered the war on the Allied side in May 1915, and by the Treaty of London was promised not only the Austrian territories of South Tyrol, Istria and nearly half the Dalmatian coastline (see the map on page 97), but also territory in Africa and the Middle East.

SOURCE A

From Bernhard Fürst von Bülow, *Denkwürdigkeiten*, volume 3, Ullstein, 1931, p. 220 (translated by the author). Von Bülow, who was sent on a special mission to Rome in December 1914 to negotiate a German–Italian alliance, later recorded in his memoirs that the Italian foreign minister, Sonino.

... did not hesitate to make clear his views of the position ... As war objectives the Allies had promised Italy all Austrian territories populated by Italian subjects. If Austria wishes to avoid war with Italy ... she must offer definite binding concessions. Such concessions must then be made in a generous and correct manner. They must not be grudgingly granted to Italy rather as if one was throwing a burdensome beggar some money. They must be the expression of the genuine wish between the old enemies of Austria and Italy to create a lasting, strong and friendly relationship.

The minimum was ... the immediate and unconditional handing over of the purely Italian parts of the Tyrol, the Trentino, autonomy for Trieste within the Austrian Empire as well as better treatment of Italians in Istria and in Dalmatia.

> **?** Study Source A. What light does this source shed on Italy's attitude to the war in December 1914?

The war in Africa

With Germany unable to send reinforcements as a result of British naval power, German colonies in west Africa (Togoland and the Cameroons) were quickly seized by Allied forces. In July 1915 German South West Africa surrendered to British South African forces. It was only in German East Africa (present-day Tanzania) that the Germans, under the leadership of General von Lettow-Vorbeck, managed to win a successful **guerrilla war** against the British right up to November 1918.

> 🔑 **KEY TERM**
>
> **Guerrilla war** An irregular war fought by small groups of troops acting independently.

Military stalemate in the west: the development of trench warfare

By 1915 the key element of the defensive war on the Western Front was the trench. Only through the construction of trenches could troops gain protection from enemy firepower. The trenches were protected with massive barbed-wire entanglements and machine guns. Over the course of the next three years the trench system on both sides of the Western Front became far more elaborate. Trenches were shored up with timber and sandbags, and deep concrete dugouts were built.

In 1915 both Allied and German attacks followed a depressingly similar pattern. Air reconnaissance first located the enemy machine-gun nests and trench system, which were then pounded with heavy artillery shells. The infantry then went 'over the top' in waves about 100 metres (100 yards) apart with men only six to eight metres (6–8 yards) distant from each other. The attackers often took the first line of trenches but were then repulsed by a counterattack. In 1915 no British or French attack managed to gain more than five kilometres of land.

New science and technology

To break the trench warfare deadlock both sides attempted to develop new techniques and new weapons.

Artillery

From the early days of the war it had been clear that only artillery could effectively destroy trench defences and give a frontal attack some chance of success. Throughout 1915, both sides sought to improve their deficiencies in heavy guns and devise new techniques for their use, such as the **creeping barrage**. By 1916 the Germans had developed enormous **howitzers** – 'Big Berthas' as they were called – which could fire a shell weighing nearly a ton.

SOURCE B

British troops in sandbagged trenches in France in 1917. Trenches were sandbagged to prevent them from collapsing as a result of enemy artillery fire.

Gas

As early as October 1914 the German Second Army was considering employing gas as a means to achieve a breakthrough, but it was not until April 1915 that it was first used at Ypres. It failed, largely because the Germans did not exploit the initial surprise and panic. Later, with the development of gas masks, the impact of gas was minimised, but it marked another stage in the development of modern scientific warfare.

? What does Source B reveal about the nature of trench warfare?

SOURCE C

What does Source C indicate about the role of artillery on the Western Front?

In this photograph, taken during the First World War, a British soldier stands among a massive pile of artillery shell cases, the remains of what had been fired into German lines.

Tanks

Essentially, at this stage of the war, military technology favoured defence rather than attack. However, in March 1915 an eventual technical solution to the problem of barbed wire, trenches and machine guns was foreshadowed by the invention of the tank. It linked two ideas: the use of armour plating to protect soldiers while advancing, and caterpillar tracks to help them cross trenches and surmount barbed wire. Trials were first held in February 1916, but it was not until the battle of Cambrai in November 1917 that tanks first effectively displayed their potential (see page 75).

The use of sea power 1914–15: the Gallipoli landing

By January 1915 the Royal Navy unquestionably controlled the seas. The flow of British and Empire troops to France and the Middle East was unimpeded. The German **China Squadron** under Graf von Spee, after some brilliant successes against the British, had been destroyed and Germany itself was blockaded.

Given the stalemate on the Western Front, British politicians increasingly wondered whether sea power could somehow break the military deadlock and lead to a speedy end to the war. Inspired by Winston Churchill, the decision was taken to force the Dardanelles. The plan, according to the British **official historian**, was 'one of the few great strategical conceptions of world war'. It would have knocked Turkey out of the war, opened up Russia to military supplies from western Europe and the USA, and in turn enabled it to export

KEY TERMS

China Squadron Units of the German navy used for protecting their possessions in the Far East.

Official historian A historian appointed by the government to write the history of the war.

Winston Churchill

1874	Born into an aristocratic family
1900	Entered parliament as a Conservative
1904	Joined the Liberal Party
1910	Home secretary
1911–15	First Lord of the Admiralty
1917	Minister of munitions
1918–21	Secretary for war and air
1924	Rejoined the Conservative Party
1924–9	Chancellor of the exchequer
1940–5	Appointed wartime prime minister
1951–5	Elected as prime minister
1965	Died and given a state funeral

Churchill was one of the most original and gifted politicians of the twentieth century. He had great energy and powers of leadership, but at the same time these gifts could lead him into making disastrous errors of judgement. During the 1930s he was excluded from government because he opposed concessions to Indian nationalists and irritated the government with his repeated warnings about the dangers of German rearmament.

In May 1940, Churchill was appointed prime minister and proved to be a charismatic wartime leader, leading Britain to victory in 1945.

wheat supplies to Britain. It could well have altered the course of the war and perhaps even have prevented the Russian Revolution. British and Anzac troops landed on 25 April on Gallipoli but an earlier naval bombardment had deprived them of the element of surprise. The campaign rapidly degenerated into trench warfare and the troops were withdrawn in December.

In October 1915 further Allied troops were landed in Salonika to help Serbia, but they had little success until September 1918 (see page 79). The failure of the Gallipoli campaign and the absence of any early success in Salonika showed that there was no 'easy fix' and that only on the Western Front could a decision be obtained.

The Germans attempt to achieve a decision in the east

In France the Germans remained on the defensive throughout 1915. Eight German divisions were removed from the Western to the Eastern Front and formed the basis of a new German army there. The intention was that they, together with Austrian troops, would deliver a knockout blow against Russia. A brilliantly successful attack was launched against the Russians in southern Poland in early May. The Central Powers broke through the Russian lines between Gorlice and Tarnow and advanced 150 km within two weeks. In August, Warsaw was taken and by September the Central Powers' troops had advanced 200 km to the east of Warsaw. Again, as in the autumn of 1914, spectacular results were achieved. The Russians suffered nearly 2 million casualties.

One consequence of this success was that Bulgaria joined the Central Powers in September. However, great as this success was, Russia had not been defeated. By the autumn the Russians had consolidated their positions. The Central Powers were still locked in a two-front war with no decisive victory in sight.

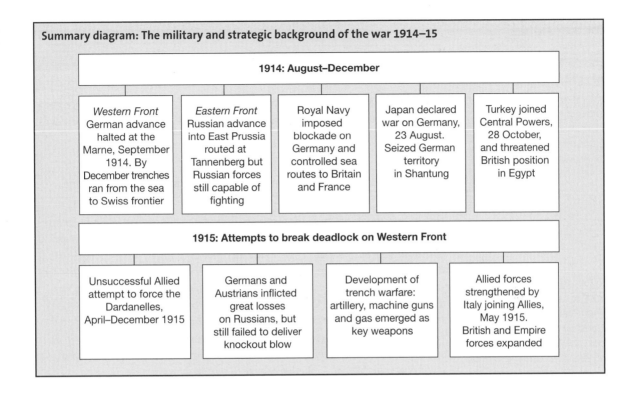

Summary diagram: The military and strategic background of the war 1914–15

1914: August–December

Western Front German advance halted at the Marne, September 1914. By December trenches ran from the sea to Swiss frontier	*Eastern Front* Russian advance into East Prussia routed at Tannenberg but Russian forces still capable of fighting	Royal Navy imposed blockade on Germany and controlled sea routes to Britain and France	Japan declared war on Germany, 23 August. Seized German territory in Shantung	Turkey joined Central Powers, 28 October, and threatened British position in Egypt

1915: Attempts to break deadlock on Western Front

Unsuccessful Allied attempt to force the Dardanelles, April–December 1915	Germans and Austrians inflicted great losses on Russians, but still failed to deliver knockout blow	Development of trench warfare: artillery, machine guns and gas emerged as key weapons	Allied forces strengthened by Italy joining Allies, May 1915. British and Empire forces expanded

 # 1916: The deadlock still unbroken

▶ *Why was neither side able to achieve a decisive victory in 1916?*

Allied plans

What options had the Allied and Central Powers in January 1916? Both had failed to achieve a decisive breakthrough in 1915. The Allies needed to bring to bear on Germany their huge reserves of strength. France had been weakened but its army was still the most effective on the Allied side. The British Empire was mobilising its resources effectively and the British now had over a million men in France. Italy too was an ally, while Russia had unlimited reserves of manpower if only they could be exploited.

The answer, of course, was to plan a co-ordinated attack on the Central Powers by all four Allied nations, which was agreed on in principle at the Inter-Allied Military Conference at Chantilly in December 1915.

German plans

The situation was more difficult for the Germans and Austrians. They had limited manpower resources and needed to force one of their enemies out of the war. Should they renew the offensive against Russia; concentrate on weakening France, as the major military power on the Western Front, to the point where it could no longer take the strain of fighting; or eliminate the British army by driving its troops into the sea?

General von Falkenhayn, the German chief of staff, argued that if France could be defeated, Britain would be fatally weakened by the loss of its ally. To achieve this he came to the conclusion given in Source D.

SOURCE D

General von Falkenhayn, the German chief of staff, quoted in John Terraine, *The First World War, 1914–1918*, Papermac, 1984, p. 97.

As I have already insisted, the strain on France has almost reached a breaking point – though it is borne with the most remarkable devotion. If we succeeded in opening the eyes of her people to the fact that in a military sense, they have nothing more to hope for, that breaking point will be reached and England's best sword knocked out of her hand. We can probably do enough for our purposes with limited resources. Within our reach behind the French sector of the Western Front there are objectives for the retention of which the French General Staff would be compelled to throw in every man they have. If they do so, the forces of France will bleed to death – as there can be no question of a voluntary withdrawal – whether we reach our goal or not.

Why, according to Source D, was it so important to defeat France and how did Falkenhayn intend to achieve this?

Verdun

The place Falkenhayn chose for his decisive attack was the historic fortress of Verdun. He calculated correctly that, while it had only limited military value, its defence would become a priority because its fall would be perceived by the French as a major defeat and so weaken the fighting morale of the nation. Falkenhayn's plan was simple: the Germans would mount a series of limited attacks. These, preceded by brief, intense artillery bombardments, would allow the Germans to make short advances and then consolidate their positions before the French counterattacked. Falkenhayn calculated that the French would be destroyed by the 'mincing machine' of the German artillery.

The attack began on 21 February. The French did indeed suffer terribly, but as the siege wore on until it ended in a German withdrawal in November, it became clear that the Germans too had been sucked into a 'mincing machine'. The Germans sustained 336,831 casualties and the French some 362,000.

France's allies attack

To relieve the pressure on Verdun, the Italians, the Russians and the British all launched offensives in the summer of 1916. The Italians attacked on the Trentino front in May. The Russian attack under General Brussilov (1856–1926) was launched in June and on 1 July the British army advanced on the German positions north of the Somme.

The Italians were quickly halted by 10 June. The Russians initially achieved a brilliant success against the Austrians on the Carpathian front, taking some quarter of a million prisoners, which persuaded Romania to join the war on the side of the Allies and forced Falkenhayn to transfer reserves from the Western Front. However, Brussilov's success was not exploited by any of the other Russian army corps and ground to a halt in the autumn.

The British attack on the Somme in July was successful in taking some of the pressure off the French. It was, too, the first battle in which a small number of tanks were used, but when the advance halted in November it had cost about 415,000 British casualties (killed and injured) for the gain of a strip of land of some 50 km with a maximum depth of 11 km.

The Battle of Jutland

There was also a possibility that the Germans could achieve a major naval success by severely damaging the British fleet, even if in the process the German navy was itself defeated. This would, as the Germans put it in 1898, 'so substantially weaken the enemy that, in spite of a victory he might have obtained, his own position in the world would no longer be secured by an adequate fleet'. In other words, Britain would find it much more difficult to find sufficient ships to escort troops and supplies to France and the Middle East. Admiral Jellicoe, the commander-in-chief of the British Grand Fleet, was aware

> What does Source E indicate about the weather and conditions during the Battle of Jutland? **?**

SOURCE E

The German fleet is deflected from bombarding the British coast by Admiral Beatty's battle cruiser squadron, which forms a protective screen during the Battle of Jutland in June 1916.

of this risk and appreciated that if he led the fleet into defeat he could 'lose the war in a single afternoon'!

On 31 May, Rear-Admiral von Scheer succeeded in tempting the British fleet out of its bases. Although in the subsequent Battle of Jutland, he inflicted more damage on the British than his own fleet sustained, aided by bad weather and poor visibility he rapidly withdrew back to the German North Sea bases. He may have given the Royal Navy a bloody nose but strategically the situation was not changed. The German fleet was not destroyed but it was confined to its bases in northern Germany. The British fleet retained its overwhelming numerical superiority, and the blockade was still in place. As one US newspaper observed: 'The German fleet has assaulted its jailor, but it is still in jail.'

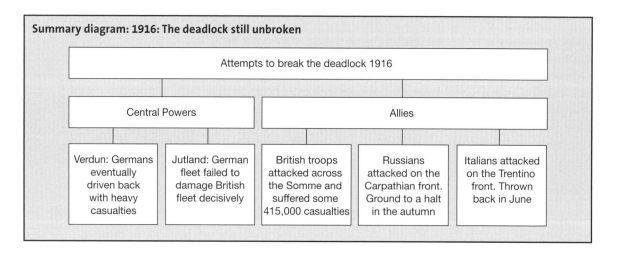

Summary diagram: 1916: The deadlock still unbroken

Attempts to break the deadlock 1916

Central Powers

Verdun: Germans eventually driven back with heavy casualties	Jutland: German fleet failed to damage British fleet decisively

Allies

British troops attacked across the Somme and suffered some 415,000 casualties	Russians attacked on the Carpathian front. Ground to a halt in the autumn	Italians attacked on the Trentino front. Thrown back in June

③ 1917: 'No peace without victory'

▶ *What were the consequences of the German decision to declare unrestricted submarine warfare against the Allies?*

▶ *Why was no compromise peace negotiated between the Central Powers and the Entente in 1917?*

The declaration of unrestricted submarine warfare, January 1917

Bethmann Hollweg was reluctant to risk a rupture with the USA. Yet in January 1917, against his better judgement, he was pushed by the German high command into sanctioning **unrestricted submarine warfare** against all shipping trading with the Allies, on the optimistic assumption that this would rapidly defeat Britain. Inevitably, this ran the risk of drawing the USA into the war on the Allied side, because since 1914 the US economy had become increasingly dependent on exporting to the Allies munitions, food and a wide range of industrial products.

Predictably, US shipping and commerce suffered severely from the U-boat attacks. On 6 April **President Wilson** declared war on the Central Powers as an '**associated power**' rather than an ally of Britain and France. Potentially, this was a development of immense importance because the manpower reserves and economic strength of the USA would now be available to the Allies. On the other hand, it would take the USA at least a year to train and equip an army that could fight in France.

The development of the convoy system

Initially, Germany's gamble that unrestricted submarine warfare would drive Britain out of the war appeared to be paying off. By April a million tons of Allied shipping had been lost, and Admiral Jellicoe told his US counterpart that 'it is impossible for us to go on with the war if losses like this continue'.

In May the **convoy system** was introduced, however, and by the autumn, with the help of the US navy, Allied shipping was escorted in both directions across the Atlantic and the Mediterranean. This, combined with the introduction of rationing in Britain, prevented starvation and thwarted German hopes that they could knock Britain out of the war.

The Hindenburg line

At the end of 1916 General Ludendorff (see page 76) told Bethmann Hollweg that if the war were prolonged without the collapse of one of the Allies, Germany would inevitably be defeated. He feared above all that a renewed offensive on the scale of the Somme would break clean through the German lines. As a result of this advice, the Germans constructed a strongly fortified line in north-eastern France, called the Hindenburg line, to which they retreated in March 1917. The line would also save the Germans manpower because they would require thirteen fewer divisions to defend it.

The Nivelle offensive and the exhaustion of the French army

The strength of the Hindenburg line forced the Allies to abandon plans for a fresh attack across the Somme. Instead, they were persuaded by the new commander-in-chief of the French armies, General Nivelle, that a massive attack, just south of the Hindenburg line, composed of over 50 French divisions, would drive right through the German lines and roll them up in a mere 48 hours.

KEY FIGURE

Woodrow Wilson (1856–1924)
President of the USA 1912–21. In April 1917 he was compelled to declare war on Germany by the resumption of Germany's unrestricted submarine warfare. On 8 January 1918 he issued his Fourteen Points as the basis for a negotiated peace.

KEY TERMS

Associated power The USA was not bound by any treaties with Britain and France in 1917–19, and was free, if necessary, to pursue its own policies.

Convoy system Group of ships travelling together under escort.

? What does Source F reveal about German tactics during the offensive of March–July 1918 (see page 78)?

The attack opened on 16 April. Once again, to quote the military historian John Terraine, 'the machine guns … survived the bombardment – machine guns in undreamt-of-numbers, spaced in depth to trap and decimate the French infantry'. Such was the slaughter that by the middle of May the French army was paralysed by a series of mutinies. By the beginning of June there were only two reliable divisions on the French central front covering Paris.

A French collapse was prevented by Nivelle's replacement, **General Pétain**, who managed by a well-judged combination of firmness and improvement in the living conditions of the French soldier to restore morale and discipline. Miraculously, the extent of the mutinies was concealed from both the Germans and France's allies.

On the Western Front, the main burden of the war now fell on the British, who launched a major offensive at Ypres in July, but by early November, when it ended, only a few miles had been gained. The Germans had suffered heavy losses of over 200,000 men, and Ludendorff was concerned about 'the demoralising effect of the battle' on his troops, but the British losses of 245,000 were even higher.

SOURCE F

Past a twisted iron bed frame, a relic of the civilian world that once existed here, and the body of a French soldier fallen on the edge of a shell hole, German troops advance through smoke and fire. This head-on combat photograph, including the action of a man about to hurl a grenade, was taken as Hindenburg's army overran Allied lines near the Somme in March 1918.

The Battle of Cambrai

Briefly, in November 1917, the future was glimpsed in the battle of Cambrai: 381 British tanks attacked the Hindenburg line at Cambrai. The tank force was divided up into groups of twelve machines each supported by infantry. The tanks carried great bundles of brushwood. These were dropped in the enemy trenches and served as bridges for the tanks to pass over. The Germans were caught completely by surprise and their front lines, which had been considered impregnable, were overrun. The barbed wire was crushed flat and the tanks rolled forward to a depth of six to ten kilometres (four to six miles) on a ten-kilometre (six-mile) front. However, owing to a lack of tank and infantry reserves, the attack ran out of steam and over the next week the Germans won back nearly all the land they had lost.

The Russian Revolutions, February–October 1917

In Russia the February Revolution had swept away the tsarist regime. The new **Provisional Government** initially promised to fight a '**people's war**' against the Germans. It hoped that carrying on the war under a new democratic regime would ignite a great burst of popular enthusiasm, but the Russian army was in no state to fight. Its morale was low and discipline was undermined by the Bolsheviks. In July a badly planned attack against the Austrians in Galicia ended in a rout. In October the Bolsheviks seized power and were determined to pull Russia out of the war.

Why no negotiated peace?

In 1917 there seemed to be a brief window of opportunity for peace negotiations. Karl, the new Austrian emperor, desperate to save his empire from disintegration, had already put out peace-feelers to the Allies in the autumn of 1916. The Pope also appealed to the warring powers in August 1917, as did the International Socialist Conference, which met in Stockholm in June. In Germany the **Reichstag** in July 1917 actually passed a resolution 'for a peace of understanding'.

Both sides were suffering from the war of attrition. Why then did the war not end in 1917? In the past such a situation of mutual exhaustion would have led to a compromise peace, but the First World War was not a war waged by professional armies and diplomats. On the contrary, it was a people's war where whole nations were mobilised against each other. To persuade them to work, fight and ultimately to die for their country, the popular nationalism, militarism and imperialism of the pre-war period (see pages 1–4) had to be appealed to and exploited. The enemy had to be demonised, and the population inspired with the prospect of an absolute victory that would make worthwhile their present suffering. If that failed, then the population might indeed turn against the war and the regime which had led them into war.

 **KEY TERMS**

Provisional Government
A government in power until the holding of elections.

People's war Popular war fought by the mass of the people.

Reichstag German parliament.

In Russia, war weariness did produce revolution, but in 1917 the key belligerents, Britain, France and Germany, were not yet ready to make peace. The entry of the USA into the war gave Britain and France the hope of ultimate victory. In December 1916 Lloyd George (see page 89) came to power to head a political coalition with a mandate to fight on for victory. In France, too, eleven months later Georges Clemenceau (see page 88) was appointed prime minister, and was committed to waging total war against the Central Powers.

In Germany the collapse of Russia also held out the prospect of eventual victory, which would make the struggle worthwhile after all. Generals Hindenburg and Ludendorff, backed by a mass nationalist party, the **Fatherland's Party**, reacted to the *Reichstag*'s peace resolution by insisting on the dismissal of Bethmann Hollweg in July 1917 and his replacement by a chancellor who was essentially a puppet of the high command.

KEY TERM

Fatherland's Party The party was founded close to the end of 1917 and represented political circles supporting the war. By the summer of 1918 it had around 1,250,000 members.

Study Source G. To what extent do the terms of the Peace Resolution explain why it was rejected by the German army under the leadership of Generals Hindenburg and Ludendorff?

SOURCE G

From the Peace Resolution passed by the German *Reichstag* on 19 July 1917, quoted in D.G. Williamson, *Germany Since 1815*, Palgrave, 2005, p. 406.

As on 4 August 1914, the German people, on the threshold of the fourth year of the war, stand behind the words of the speech from the throne: 'we are not driven by a desire for conquest!' Germany took up arms only for the defence of its freedom and independence and for the preservation of its territorial integrity.

The Reichstag strives for a peace of understanding and lasting reconciliation of nations. Such a peace is not in keeping with forcible annexations of territory or forcible measures of political, economic or financial character.

The Reichstag also rejects all plans which would result in economic isolation and hostility among nations after the war. The freedom of the seas must be made secure. Only economic peace will prepare the ground for the friendly living together of the nations.

The Reichstag will actively support the creation of international judicial organizations.

So long as the enemy governments will not agree to such a peace … the German people will stand together as one.

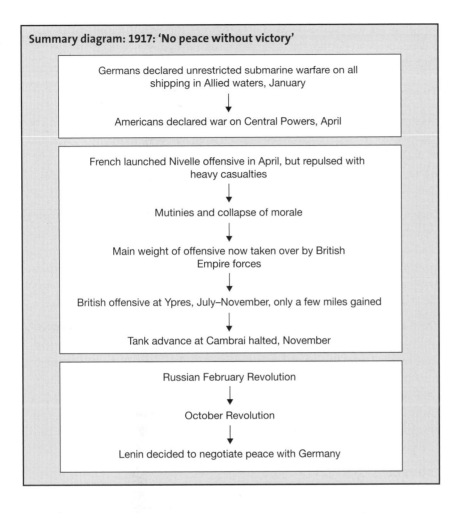

Summary diagram: 1917: 'No peace without victory'

Germans declared unrestricted submarine warfare on all shipping in Allied waters, January

↓

Americans declared war on Central Powers, April

French launched Nivelle offensive in April, but repulsed with heavy casualties

↓

Mutinies and collapse of morale

↓

Main weight of offensive now taken over by British Empire forces

↓

British offensive at Ypres, July–November, only a few miles gained

↓

Tank advance at Cambrai halted, November

Russian February Revolution

↓

October Revolution

↓

Lenin decided to negotiate peace with Germany

4 1918: The final year of the war

▶ *How did the Germans benefit from the Bolshevik Revolution?*

The impact of the Bolshevik Revolution

In Russia, the Bolsheviks overthrew the Provisional Government in October 1917. This not only led to a two-year civil war, but also gave the Germans their best chance of victory since August 1914. **Lenin**, the Bolshevik leader, although hoping that the revolution in Russia would trigger similar revolts throughout Europe, realised that if his regime was to survive he needed to make immediate peace with Germany.

On 22 December Lenin began negotiations with the Germans at Brest-Litovsk after announcing to the world that he supported a peace without annexations or reparations. As the Allies ignored his calls for a general peace, Lenin had

 KEY FIGURE

Vladimir Ilych Lenin (1870–1924)

Leader of the Bolshevik Party from 1903. In 1917 the Bolsheviks seized power but were then faced with a bitter civil war, which they won under Lenin's leadership. In 1922–3 he suffered a series of strokes and power passed to Stalin, Zinoviev and Kamenev.

no option but to sign the Treaty of Brest-Litovsk. Russia was forced to give independence to Poland, the Baltic provinces, the Ukraine, Finland and the Caucasus.

The final German offensive, March–July 1918

In January 1918 on the Western Front, the initiative now lay with Germany. The majority of German troops on the Russian front had been moved to France, and by early March there were 193 German divisions as against 173 Allied. Despite warnings of an imminent offensive, the Allies were slow to withdraw troops from other fronts to make up this deficiency.

Ludendorff's intention was to split the Allied armies and push the British back to the coast. The Germans attacked at the juncture between the British and French fronts where they had a local superiority of 69 divisions to 33. Specially trained groups of storm-troopers armed with light machine guns, light trench mortars and flame throwers infiltrated the enemy trenches and managed to penetrate to the artillery. By the end of March the Germans had advanced nearly 65 km.

The Allies responded by setting up a joint command under **General Foch**, which was able to co-ordinate military operations against the Germans. Troops were recalled from the other theatres and for the first time US divisions were committed to battle. By mid-July the Allies were in a position to counterattack. On 8 August a Franco-British force attacked east of Amiens using over 400 tanks and overwhelmed the forward German divisions. Ludendorff was later to describe this as 'the blackest day of the German army in the history of the war … it put the decline of our fighting power beyond all doubt'.

SOURCE H

The Allied generals photographed in Alsace-Lorraine in 1918. From left to right: Joffre (France), Foch, the Supreme Commander on the Western Front (France), Haig (UK), Pershing (USA), Gillain (Belgium), Albricci (Italy) and Haller (Poland). The generals are attending a ceremony marking the French reconquest of Alsace-Lorraine, which had been taken by Germany in 1870 (see page 14).

KEY FIGURE

Ferdinand Foch (1851–1929)

Commanded a French army group on the Somme, 1916, then in 1917 chief-of-staff to Pétain, and in April 1918 appointed commander-in-chief of the Allied armies on the Western Front. He played a prominent part in the Paris Peace Conference and retired in 1920.

Study Source H. To what extent does this photograph indicate that France was the major military power among the Allied and associated powers?

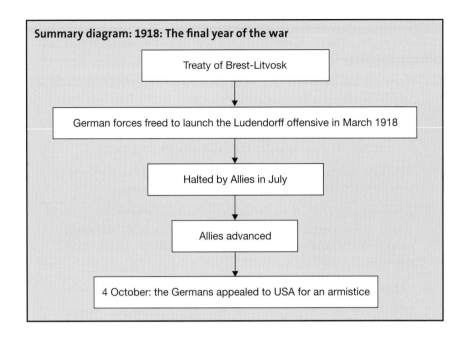

Summary diagram: 1918: The final year of the war

Treaty of Brest-Litvosk

German forces freed to launch the Ludendorff offensive in March 1918

Halted by Allies in July

Allies advanced

4 October: the Germans appealed to USA for an armistice

 5 # The armistices of October and November 1918

▶ *Why were the terms of the armistice agreement with Germany so severe?*

▶ *To what extent did the armistice terms contain the key war aims of the Allies and associated powers?*

By September the Germans were in full retreat on the Western Front. The Austrians were coming under ever greater pressure from Italian forces and the Bulgarians were decisively defeated in Macedonia by an allied army advancing from Salonika in Greece (see page 68 and the map on page 97). On 28 September, Ludendorff and Hindenburg had little option but to concede defeat and advised the Kaiser to form a new **parliamentary government**, which would impress President Wilson with its democratic credentials and facilitate the negotiation of an armistice on the basis of the Fourteen Points. Summing these points up in February 1918, Wilson had proclaimed that the USA wanted a peace of 'no annexations, no contributions, no punitive damages'.

On 4 October the new German government asked Wilson for 'an immediate armistice' on the basis of the Fourteen Points. Similar requests then came from Bulgaria, Austria-Hungary and the Ottoman Empire, all of which faced imminent defeat by Allied forces.

 KEY TERM

Parliamentary government A government that is responsible to a parliament elected by the people.

SOURCE I

Study Source I. To what extent do the Fourteen Points explain why the Germans hoped to negotiate an armistice with Wilson rather than with the Allies?

From the Fourteen Points speech delivered by President Woodrow Wilson to a joint session of the US Congress on 8 January 1918.

1. Open covenants [agreements], openly arrived at … diplomacy shall always proceed frankly and in the public view.

2. Absolute freedom of navigation upon the seas, outside territorial waters …

3. The removal, so far as possible, of all economic barriers …

4. Adequate guarantees given and taken that national armaments will be reduced to the lowest point consistent with domestic safety.

5. A free, open-minded, and absolutely impartial adjustment of all colonial claims … the interests of the populations concerned must have equal weight with the equitable claims of the government whose title is to be determined.

6. The evacuation of all Russian territory …

7. Belgium, the whole world will agree, must be evacuated and restored, without any attempt to limit the sovereignty, which she enjoys in common with all other free nations.

8. All French territory should be freed and the invaded portions restored, and the wrong done to France by Prussia in 1871 in the matter of Alsace-Lorraine … should be righted …

9. A readjustment of the frontiers of Italy should be effected along clearly recognizable lines of nationality.

10. The peoples of Austria-Hungary, whose place among the nations we wish to see safeguarded and assured, should be accorded the freest opportunity of autonomous development.

11. Romania, Serbia and Montenegro should be evacuated … Serbia afforded free and secure access to the sea; and the relations of the several Balkan states to one another determined by friendly counsel along historically established lines of allegiance and nationality …

12. The Turkish portions of the present Ottoman Empire should be assured a secure sovereignty, but the other nationalities … should be assured an absolutely unmolested opportunity of autonomous development, and the Dardanelles should be permanently open as a free passage to the ships and commerce of all nations …

13. An independent Poland should be erected which should include the territories inhabited by indisputably Polish populations, which should be assured a free and secure access to the sea …

14. A general association of nations must be formed under specific covenants for the purpose of political independence and territorial integrity to great and small states alike.

The armistice agreement with Germany

Germany's hopes of dividing its enemies were dashed when Wilson asked the Allies to draft the details of the armistice agreements. They produced tough terms, which anticipated their key aims at the coming Peace Conference:

- In the west, the Germans were to evacuate all occupied territory, including Alsace-Lorraine, and to withdraw beyond a ten-kilometre (six-mile)-wide **neutral zone** to the east of the Rhine.
- Allied troops would move in and occupy the west bank of the Rhine.
- In eastern Europe all German troops were similarly to be withdrawn from the occupied territories.
- The German navy was also to be interned in either a neutral or a British port.

Events in Germany, October–November 1918

Once news of the armistice negotiations became public, the demand for peace by the German people after the years of deprivation caused by the Allied blockade and false hopes of victory became unstoppable.

Rashly, on 28 October, the German Admiralty ordered the fleet out on a suicide mission against the British. In protest, the sailors at the Wilhelmshaven base mutinied. When the ringleaders were arrested, their colleagues organised mass protest meetings and formed **soviets**, which by the evening controlled all the naval bases and prevented the fleet from setting sail. Over the next few days unrest spread, and soviets also sprang up in the cities. On 9 September the Kaiser was forced to abdicate and the German government had little option but to accept the armistice on 11 November.

The armistice agreement with Austria-Hungary

In the summer of 1918, under US pressure, the Allies decided to abandon their former policy of dealing with Austria-Hungary as a sovereign state. Instead, they recognised the right of its subject peoples, especially the Czechs and the **Yugoslavs**, to independence. In Paris, the exiled leaders of the Austrian Yugoslavs had already agreed to form a South Slav state (later to be called Yugoslavia), together with the Serbs, Croats and Slovenes. In October, Wilson brushed aside attempts by Vienna to negotiate on behalf of its empire, and the Czechs and Yugoslavs seized the chance to declare their independence. On 1 November the Austro-Hungarian Empire was dissolved, and two days later the former imperial high command negotiated an armistice with the Italians.

The Turkish armistice

In the meantime the Turkish armistice was signed at Mudros on 30 October. The Turks surrendered their remaining garrisons outside **Anatolia**, and gave the Allies the right to occupy forts controlling the straits of both the Dardanelles and

KEY TERMS

Neutral zone A belt of territory which would be occupied by neither German nor Allied troops.

Soviets Elected councils.

Yugoslavs A term for the South Slav inhabitants of Austro-Hungary.

Anatolia The core territory of the Turkish Empire, covering most of the modern Turkish republic.

the Bosphorus. The Ottoman army was demobilised, and ports, railways and other strategic points were made available for use by the Allies. In the Caucasus, Turkey had to withdraw its troops back to its pre-war borders.

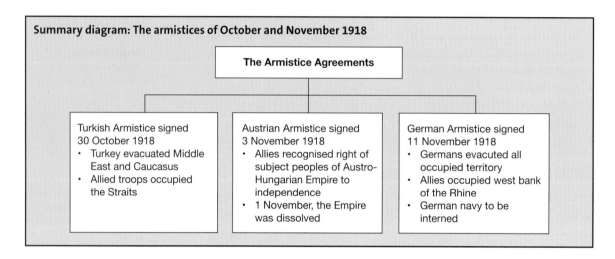

Summary diagram: The armistices of October and November 1918

The Armistice Agreements

Turkish Armistice signed 30 October 1918
- Turkey evacuated Middle East and Caucasus
- Allied troops occupied the Straits

Austrian Armistice signed 3 November 1918
- Allies recognised right of subject peoples of Austro-Hungarian Empire to independence
- 1 November, the Empire was dissolved

German Armistice signed 11 November 1918
- Germans evacuated all occupied territory
- Allies occupied west bank of the Rhine
- German navy to be interned

Chapter summary

The Germans in 1914 attempted to defeat France first before moving eastwards to Russia. However, the Russian advance into East Prussia necessitated the transfer of two German army corps to the east, which enabled the French to counterattack. By the autumn the war settled into a deadlock on the Western Front. Over the next year the war spread: Turkey joined Germany in October 1914, while Japan allied with Britain and France in August 1914 and Italy also became an ally of the *Entente* in May 1915.

Both sides attempted to break the deadlock on the Western Front, but failed. The British plan to knock Turkey out of the war was unsuccessful, as was the German attempt to defeat France at Verdun and sink the British fleet at Jutland. In 1917 two momentous events occurred: the German submarine campaign against Britain brought the USA into the war, while in eastern Europe Russia was paralysed by the revolutions of February and October. In March 1918 Russia made peace with Germany, which then concentrated forces on the Western Front. By July 1918 this attack had been halted, and in October Germany and its allies had little option but to accept stringent armistice terms from the Allied and associated powers.

Refresher questions

Use these questions to remind yourself of the key material covered in this chapter.

1 Why did Turkey join the Central Powers?

2 Why did Italy enter the war on the Allied side?

3 What were the main features of trench warfare?

4 What advantages would the defeat of Russia bring to the Central Powers?

5 What were the German plans for 1916?

6 What did the Germans achieve at Verdun?

7 How did France's allies try to relieve the pressure on the French at Verdun?

8 Why did the Germans declare unrestricted submarine warfare against the Allies?

9 Why did the USA enter the war in April 1917?

10 Why did the German submarine campaign fail?

11 How did the Russian Revolutions weaken the Allied war effort?

12 Why did the German offensive of March–July 1918 fail?

13 Why were the terms of the armistice agreement with Germany so severe?

14 Why was the Austrian Empire dissolved on 1 November 1918?

15 What were the terms of the armistice negotiated with Turkey?

 Question practice

ESSAY QUESTIONS

1 Assess the reasons why the fighting in the First World War only came to an end in November 1918.

2 'Germany's greatest mistake in the First World War was to declare unrestricted U-boat warfare in January 1917 against all neutral shipping trading with the Allies.' How far do you agree?

3 'In 1918 Germany won the war in eastern Europe, but lost in the west.' Explain why you agree or disagree with this view.

4 To what extent was the First World War essentially a European conflict rather than a global conflict?

INTERPRETATION QUESTION

1 Read the interpretation and then answer the question that follows. 'German mobilization sustained a remarkable military feat, a comprehensive national exertion that for more than four years defied material odds to hold at bay a far superior coalition of enemies' (from R. Chickering, *Imperial Germany and the Great War, 1914–1918*, 1998, p. 200). Evaluate the strengths and limitations of this interpretation, making reference to other interpretations you have studied.

SOURCE ANALYSIS QUESTIONS

1 With reference to Sources 1 and 2 (page 84) and your understanding of the historical context, which of these two sources is more valuable in explaining why Germany's fortunes declined so dramatically in 1918?

2 With reference to Sources A (page 65), D (page 70) and G (page 76), and your understanding of the historical context, assess the value of these sources to a historian studying the First World War.

SOURCE 1

On 2 May 1918 F.S. Oliver, a British political commentator and businessman, made the following observation, quoted in J. Terraine, *The First World War, 1914–1918*, Papermac, 1985, p. 156.

… it would appear certain that a crushing victory cannot be hoped for against an admirably trained, disciplined and equipped army of warlike people, unless we have a great preponderance of numbers. There is no chance of this until the Americans come in, and when it is reasonable to think that the Americans will be able to put in that immense army of three million, fully equipped, each man with a hair mattress, a hot water bottle, a gramophone and a medicine chest, which they tell us will get to Berlin and cook the goose of the Kaiser … When? If it comes next year it might produce the desired military results. But is there the slightest reason to imagine that it will come next year, or the year after, or even the year after that? … from a purely military point of view, I don't see victory approaching.

SOURCE 2

On 3 October 1918 Hindenburg wrote the following to the German chancellor, quoted in A. Rosenberg, *Imperial Germany: The Birth of the German Republic*, Oxford University Press, 1970, p. 245.

The Supreme Command continues to hold to its demand expressed on September 29 of this year that a request for an armistice should be sent to our enemies immediately. As a result of the collapse of the Macedonian Front, the consequent weakening of the reserves on our western front, and the impossibility of making good the very severe losses which we have suffered in the last few days, there is, as far as it is humanly possible to judge, no further chance of forcing a peace on the enemy. Our adversaries are continually bringing up fresh reserves. The German army still stands firm and is successfully resisting all attacks. Nevertheless the situation becomes daily more critical; and the Supreme Command may be forced to take very grave decisions. The circumstances call for a cessation of hostilities in order to spare the German nation and its allies needless sacrifices. Each day that is lost costs the lives of thousands of brave soldiers.

CHAPTER 5

Peace settlements 1919–23

This chapter looks at the peace settlements of 1919–23 and the aims and motives of the participants. It also assesses how fair and effective these complex settlements were and what their immediate impact on Europe and the Middle East was. It analyses these problems by examining the following topics:

★ Problems faced by the peacemakers

★ Aims and principles of the victorious Great Powers

★ Organisation of the Paris Peace Conference

★ Settlement with Germany

★ Settlements with Austria, Hungary and Bulgaria

★ Settlement with Turkey 1919–23

★ Enforcing the Treaty of Versailles 1920–3

The key debate on *page 111* of this chapter asks the question: How unjust were the peace treaties of 1919–20?

Key dates

1919	Jan. 18	Peace Conference opened at Paris
	June 28	Treaty of Versailles signed with Germany
	Sept. 10	Treaty of St Germain signed with Austria
	Nov. 27	Treaty of Neuilly signed with Bulgaria
1920	Jan. 10	Treaty of Versailles and League of Nations came into force
	June 4	Treaty of Trianon signed with Hungary

1920	Aug. 10	Treaty of Sèvres signed with Turkey
1921	March	Plebiscite in Upper Silesia
	April	German reparations fixed at 132 billion gold marks
1922	April	Geneva Conference and Rapallo Treaty between Germany and USSR
1923	Jan. 11	French and Belgian troops occupied the Ruhr
	July 23	Treaty of Lausanne

1 Problems faced by the peacemakers

▶ *Why did the economic, political and social conditions of the time make it so much more difficult to negotiate a just and balanced peace settlement?*

In January 1919, the statesmen of the victorious powers were confronted with a Europe in turmoil. The sudden and complete defeat of the Central Powers had made Europe vulnerable to the spread of Communism from Russia. Germany for much of the winter of 1918–19 seemed poised on the brink of revolution. With the disintegration of the Austrian, Turkish and Russian Empires there was no stable government anywhere east of the Rhine. In March, when the communists temporarily seized power in Hungary, it seemed to the Allied leaders that the door to the heart of Europe was now open to communism.

The fear of revolution was intensified by the influenza **pandemic** which by the spring of 1919 had caused the deaths of millions of people, and by the near famine conditions in central and eastern Europe. The problems facing the statesmen in Paris were thus not only the negotiation of peace and the drawing up of new frontiers, but also the pressing need to avert economic chaos and famine. As one Allied official observed, 'There was a veritable race between peace and anarchy.'

The task of rebuilding a peaceful and prosperous Europe was made more difficult by the continued strength of nationalist feeling among the populations of the victorious powers. Public opinion in Britain, the USA, France and Italy viewed the Peace Conference as the final phase of the war in which their leaders must ruthlessly consolidate the gains made on the battlefields and smash the enemy forever.

The greatest blow to the prospects for real peace in Europe was delivered when the **Congressional elections** in the USA in November 1918 gave the Republicans, who opposed the Democratic President Woodrow Wilson, a majority. The Republicans were determined to campaign for a hard peace with Germany and simultaneously insist that the USA should become involved neither in guaranteeing it nor in financing any expensive schemes for European reconstruction.

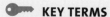

KEY TERMS

Pandemic An epidemic on a global scale.

Congressional elections The elections to the US Senate and House of Representatives took place on 5 November 1918. The Republicans secured an overall majority of two seats in the Senate and 50 in the House.

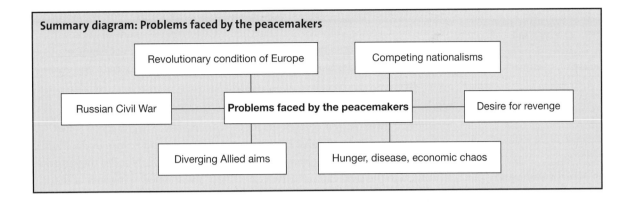

Summary diagram: Problems faced by the peacemakers

2 Aims and principles of the victorious Great Powers

▶ *What did the individual Allied and associated powers hope to achieve from the peace treaties?*

The peace negotiations in Paris are often interpreted as a struggle between the proponents of reconciliation, led by Wilson and Lloyd George, and the ruthless advocates of a peace of revenge, represented by Clemenceau, the French prime minister. The reality, however, was much more complicated.

The USA: Wilson's efforts to implement the Fourteen Points

Although President Wilson strongly believed that Germany needed to be punished for its part in starting the war and that it should be put on 'probation' before joining the League of Nations, he was determined to ensure that the Fourteen Points (see page 80) served as a basis for the coming peace negotiations and to anchor the **Covenant** of the League of Nations in the text of the peace treaties. He was convinced that this was the key to creating a just and lasting peace. This was, however, an optimistic assessment. There was general agreement among the victors to set up independent **nation-states** in eastern Europe and the Balkans and confine Turkey to its ethnic frontiers, all of which was anticipated by points 10–13. Points 7 and 8, covering the liberation of Belgium and the return of Alsace-Lorraine to France, had already been fulfilled the start of the armistice.

On other issues, Wilson was ready to compromise. Britain, for instance, was assured that point 2, which demanded the 'freedom of the seas', did not mean the immediate lifting of the blockade against Germany. The French and Belgians were promised US support for German reparations, despite the absence of any such clause in the Fourteen Points, and Italy was promised the award of former Austrian territory up to the Brenner frontier, even though this would include

 **KEY TERMS**

Covenant Rules and constitution of the League of Nations.

Nation-state A state consisting of an ethnically and culturally united population.

over 200,000 Germans. Wilson was also ready to compromise with Britain over the former German colonies and the Middle Eastern possessions of Turkey. These territories would be the ultimate responsibility of the new League of Nations but would be handed over as '**mandates**' to the appropriate powers to administer.

These concessions did not go far enough to turn the Fourteen Points into a practicable **inter-Allied consensus** for the coming peace negotiations. They failed to overcome imperialist rivalries between Britain and France in the Middle East or between the USA, Japan and Britain in the Far East. Nor did they provide a solution to the rival claims in 1919–20 of Italy and the new 'kingdom of the Serbs, Croats and Slovenes' (which later became Yugoslavia) to Dalmatia (see page 103).

France's priorities

More importantly, the Fourteen Points failed to impress the French premier, **Clemenceau**, who was convinced that only an effective balance of power in Europe could contain Germany. He was painfully aware that France, with its reduced birth rate and a total number of casualties of 1.3 million dead and another 2.8 million wounded, faced a Germany which, as a consequence of the collapse of Austria-Hungary and tsarist Russia, was potentially stronger than in 1914.

Clemenceau was anxious to enforce maximum disarmament and reparation payments on the Germans, and to set up strong independent Polish, Czechoslovak and Yugoslav states, and in addition an independent Rhineland state. He also wanted an alliance with Britain and the USA and to continue inter-Allied financial and economic co-operation into the post-war years. He was ready to make considerable concessions to achieve his aims. For instance, in the Middle East, he offered to cede Palestine and the Mosul oilfields to the British in the hope of gaining their support in Europe.

SOURCE A

From a speech to the French parliament on 29 December 1918 by Clemenceau, quoted in W.A. Jordan, *Great Britain, France and the German Problem, 1918–1939*, Frank Cass, 1971, p. 37.

There was a system, which seems condemned today and to which I do not hesitate to say that I remain to some extent faithful: nations tried to organise their defence. It was very prosaic. They tried to have strong frontiers … this system seems condemned today by the very high authorities. Yet I believe that if this balance, which had been spontaneously produced during the war, had existed earlier: if, for example, England, America and Italy had agreed in saying that whoever attacked one of them had attacked the whole world, this war would have never taken place.

KEY TERMS

Mandates Ex-German or Turkish territories entrusted by the League of Nations to one of the Allied powers to govern in accordance with the interests of the local population.

Inter-Allied consensus Agreement between the Allies.

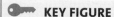

KEY FIGURE

Georges Clemenceau (1841–1929)

A French politician whose outspokenness won him the title of 'the tiger'. As prime minister, he was a charismatic war leader, 1917–18, and presided over the Paris Peace Conference of 1919, but lost power in 1920. He foresaw the re-emergence of Germany as a great power and even predicted war in 1940.

? According to Clemenceau in Source A, what was the most effective way for France to organise its defence against any future German threats?

Great Britain: a satisfied power?

In contrast to France, Britain, even before the Great Powers met in Paris, had already achieved many of its aims: the German fleet had surrendered, German trade rivalry was no longer a threat and Germany's colonial empire was liquidated, while the German army in western Europe had been driven back into the *Reich*. Britain's territorial ambitions lay in the Middle East, not Europe.

Lloyd George realised that a peaceful, united Germany would act as a barrier against the spread of Bolshevism from Russia. Above all, he wanted to avoid long-term British commitments on the continent of Europe and prevent the annexation of German minorities by the Poles or the French creating fresh areas of bitterness, which would sow the seeds of a new war. Inevitably, then, these objectives were fundamentally opposed to the French policy of securing definite guarantees against a German military revival either by negotiating a long-term Anglo-American military alliance or by a partial dismemberment of Germany.

The logic of British policy pointed in the direction of a peace of reconciliation rather than revenge, but in two key areas, **reparations** and the question of German **war guilt**, Britain adopted a much harder line. Lloyd George and Clemenceau agreed in December 1918 that the Kaiser should be tried by an international tribunal for war crimes. Under pressure from the **Dominions**, who also wanted a share of reparations, the British delegation at Paris was authorised 'to secure from Germany the greatest possible indemnity she can pay consistently with the well-being of the British Empire and the peace of the world without involving an army of occupation in Germany for its collection'.

Italy and Japan

Italy

The Italian prime minister, **Orlando**, was anxious to convince the voters that Italy had done well out of the war, and concentrated initially on attempting to hold the *Entente* to their promises made in the Treaty of London (see page 64), as well as demanding the port of Fiume in the Adriatic.

Japan

Japan wanted recognition of the territorial gains made in the war (see page 63). The Japanese also pushed hard, but ultimately unsuccessfully, to have a racial equality clause included in the Covenant of the League of Nations. Japan hoped that this would protect Japanese immigrants in the USA.

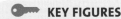

KEY FIGURES

David Lloyd George (1863–1945)

A Liberal politician, he was a highly effective minister of munitions, and then in 1916–18 an inspirational war leader, who remained in power until 1922.

Vittorio Orlando (1860–1952)

Professor of law and Italian prime minister 1917–19. He withdrew from politics when Mussolini came to power in 1922.

KEY TERMS

Reparations Compensation paid by a defeated power to make good the damage it caused in a war.

War guilt Carrying the blame for starting the war.

Dominions The British Dominions of Australia, Canada, New Zealand and South Africa were self-governing, but part of the British Empire and the Commonwealth, of which to this day they are still members.

Summary diagram: Aims and principles of the victorious Great Powers

The aims of the Allied and associated powers at the Peace Conference 1919

Great Britain	*France*	*Italy*	*USA*	*Japan*
• Destruction of German navy and colonial empire • Extension of influence in the Middle East • Preservation of a united Germany as a barrier against Bolshevism • Acceptance of the Covenant of the League of Nations • Independent Poland • Determination to prove German war guilt • Reparations	• Recovery of Alsace-Lorraine • Independent Rhineland • Strengthen influence in Middle East • Strong independent Poland • Reparations • Disarmed Germany • Alliance with Britain and USA • Acceptance of Covenant of the League of Nations • Determination to prove German war guilt	• Implementation of Treaty of London • Annexation of Trentino and S. Tyrol and much of Istria • Colonial gains in Africa and Middle East • Acceptance of Covenant of League of Nations	• Implementation of the 14 Points: (a) Independence for subject nations (b) International rule of law through the League of Nations (c) Disarmament (d) Creation of League of Nations	• Recognition of territorial gains made in the war • Inclusion of a racial equality clause in Covenant of the League of Nations

---

(3) Organisation of the Paris Peace Conference

▶ *How effective was the organisation of the Peace Conference?*

▶ *Why did the organisation of the Paris Peace Conference have to be streamlined?*

Compared to the Vienna Congress of 1814–15, the Paris Conference was a showpiece of sophisticated organisation. The British delegation, for instance, which was composed of 207 officials, compared with a mere seventeen in 1814, had its own printing press, telephone lines to London and the capitals of the British Empire, and a direct daily air link to Croydon airfield.

Yet despite this impressive evidence of outward efficiency, the conference got off to a slow start and for the first two months little progress was made towards a German settlement. The reasons for this were partly organisational and partly that the Allied statesmen formed what Lloyd George called a 'Cabinet of Nations', which could not ignore the pressing problems of immediate post-war Europe. They had to consider the emergency consignments of food to central and eastern Europe, set up the **Supreme Economic Council** to

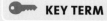
KEY TERM

Supreme Economic Council Allied body with the power to deal with economic issues.

deal with the financial and economic problems affecting both occupied and unoccupied Germany, and negotiate the easing of the food blockade of Germany in exchange for the surrender of the German merchant fleet. Above all, they ceaselessly monitored the progress of the civil war in Russia and weighed up the pros and cons of Allied military intervention.

The Council of Ten

When the Peace Conference opened on 18 January 1919 the delegates of 27 states attended, but in reality power lay with the 'big five': Britain, France, Italy, Japan and the USA. Each, with the exception of Japan, which to a great extent relied on its professional diplomats, was at first represented by its wartime leaders in the Council of Ten (two representatives per country). Neither Russia nor the defeated enemy powers attended. Russia was torn by a civil war between the Bolsheviks and the **White Russians**. At first, the Allies attempted to secure Russian representation at Paris, but their efforts to negotiate a truce between the factions in the civil war failed.

Right up to April, the Allies were not sure whether to follow the pattern of previous peace conferences and plan for a preliminary peace with Germany and the other Central Powers that would only contain the disarmament terms and the outlines of the territorial settlement. Then, at a later date, when passions had cooled, an international congress would be called to which the ex-enemy states would be invited. Thus, unsure in their own minds whether they were working on a preliminary or final treaty, the members of the Council of Ten grappled with the intricate problems of peace-making. Fifty-eight committees were set up to draft the clauses of not only the German treaty but also the treaties with Austria, Bulgaria, Hungary and Turkey. Their work was handicapped by the absence of any central co-ordinating body, and consequently the different committees worked in isolation from each other, sometimes coming up with contradictory solutions.

The emergence of the Council of Four

It was not until 24 March that the organisation of the conference was streamlined as a result of Lloyd George's controversial Fontainebleau memorandum. Inspired by the fear that the Allies might drive Germany into the arms of the Bolsheviks, this urged major concessions to Berlin, and so raised important issues which could only be resolved by secret discussions among Clemenceau, Lloyd George, Orlando and Wilson. This 'Council of Four' proved so effective that it became the key decision-making committee of the conference. It briefly became the Council of Three when Orlando left it in protest against its refusal to agree to Italian claims in Fiume and Dalmatia (see page 103).

As most of the territorial committees had finished their reports by March, it was also decided to drop the idea of a preliminary peace with Germany, which would be followed by a congress attended by all the former belligerent nations, and to

KEY TERM

White Russians The name given to members and supporters of the counter-revolutionary 'White' armies, which fought against the Bolshevik Red Army in the Russian Civil War (1918–21).

proceed quickly to a final settlement with Germany. Inevitably, this decision had serious repercussions on the drafting of the treaty and possibly for the future peace of Europe, as the Germans were not admitted to the peace conference as equals and had little chance to negotiate the terms of the treaty.

SOURCE B

? What is the importance of Source B for understanding the terms of the Treaty of Versailles?

From Harold Nicolson, *Peacekeeping 1919*, Methuen, 1964, p. 100. This book was first published in 1933. Nicolson was a member of the British delegation in Paris.

Many paragraphs of the treaty, and especially in the economic section, were in fact inserted as 'maximum statements' such as would provide some area of concession to Germany at the eventual congress. This congress never materialised: the last weeks flew past us in a hysterical nightmare; and these 'maximum statements' remained unmodified and were eventually imposed by ultimatum. Had it been known from the outset that no negotiations would ever take place with the enemy, it is certain that many of the less reasonable clauses of the Treaty would never have been inserted.

On the other hand, it is arguable that such were the problems the Allied statesmen faced in 1919 that, as the historian Max Beloff has observed, it is surprising 'not that the treaties were imperfect but that they were concluded at all'.

Summary diagram: Organisation of the Paris Peace Conference, 1919

Representatives of 27 states attended

↓

Power lay with the Council of Ten, attended by two representatives each from Britain, France, Italy, Japan and the USA

↓

58 Committees set up to draft clauses of the treaties of peace

↓

March, Council of Ten became Council of Four to streamline decisions. Attended by Clemenceau, Lloyd George, Orlando and Wilson

↓

Decision taken to drop idea of signing a preliminary peace with the Central Powers, and instead proceed quickly to a final settlement

---

Settlement with Germany

▶ *To what extent was the Treaty of Versailles a harsh treaty?*

▶ *How justified was German criticism of the Treaty of Versailles?*

All the peace settlements were to a greater or lesser extent the result of compromises between the Allied powers. Versailles was no exception. Its key clauses were the result of fiercely negotiated agreements, which were often only reached when the conference appeared to be on the brink of collapse. The first 26 articles (which appeared in all the other treaties as well) contained the Covenant of the League of Nations (see page 128) and were agreed unanimously.

German war guilt

Despite some US and Italian reservations, which were eventually overcome by Lloyd George and Clemenceau, about the legality of demanding the surrender of the Kaiser and other German leaders for trial for committing acts against 'international morality', there was universal agreement among the victorious powers that Germany was guilty of having started the war. It was this principle of war guilt which was to provide the moral justification for the reparation clauses of the treaty, as was stressed in Article 231.

SOURCE C

From the Treaty of Versailles, Part VIII, Section 1 [I], Article 231, 1919.

The Allied and associated governments affirm and Germany accepts the responsibility of Germany and her allies for causing all the loss and damage to which the Allied and associated governments and their nationals have been subjected as a consequence of the war imposed up them by the aggression of Germany and her allies.

> What, according to Source C, is Germany guilty of?

Reparations

Although there was general agreement that Germany should pay compensation to the victors, there was considerable debate about the amount to be paid, the nature of the damage deserving compensation and how Germany could raise such large sums of money without rebuilding an export trade which might then harm the Allied industries. Essentially, the major issue behind the Allied demands was the compelling need to cover the costs of financing the war. Britain had covered one-third of its war expenditure through taxation; France just one-sixth. At a time of severe social unrest, no Allied country could easily face the prospect of financing debt repayments by huge tax increases and savage cuts in expenditure. Initially, it was hoped that the USA could be persuaded to continue wartime inter-Allied economic co-operation and, above all, cancel the repayment of Allied war debts, but by the end of 1918 it was obvious that this was not going to happen, as Wilson dissolved all the agencies for inter-Allied co-operation in Washington. Without US participation the British Treasury was reluctant to continue its wartime co-operation with the French finance ministry, and in March 1919 all further financial assistance from Britain to France was stopped. France had no option therefore but to seek financial reparation from Germany.

French demands for reparations

The French finance minister, **Klotz**, backed by the press and the Chamber of Deputies, urged a policy of maximum claims, and coined the slogan that 'Germany will pay' (for everything). Behind the scenes, however, **Loucheur**, the minister for reconstruction, pursued a more subtle policy and informed the Germans that such was the need of the French economy for an immediate injection of cash, that his government would settle for a more moderate sum which the Germans would be able to raise quickly through the sale of bonds on the world's financial markets. The German government, however, suspected that these overtures were merely a means of dividing Germany from the USA, which was seen in Berlin as the country potentially most sympathetic to the German cause. The USA's reparation policy was certainly more moderate than either Britain's or France's as it recommended that a modest fixed sum should be written into the treaty.

British reparation demands

The British delegation consistently maximised their country's reparation claims on Germany. Some historians explain this in terms of the pressure exerted on the government by the electorate. On the other hand, Lloyd George himself claimed that 'the imposition of a high indemnity … would prevent the Germans spending money on an army'. It was arguable that a high indemnity would also ensure that there would be money left over for Britain and the Dominions after France and Belgium had claimed their share. To safeguard Britain's percentage of reparations, the **Imperial War Cabinet** urged that the cost of war pensions should be included in the reparation bill. By threatening to walk out of the conference, Lloyd George then forced the Council of Four to support his arguments.

Setting up the Reparation Commission

The British pension claims made it even more difficult for the Allied financial experts to agree on an overall figure for reparations. Consequently, at the end of April, it was agreed that the Reparation Commission should be set up to assess in detail by 1 May 1921 what the German economy could afford. In the meantime, the Germans would make an interim payment of 20 **milliard** gold marks and raise a further 60 milliard through the sale of bonds. It was not until December 1919 that Britain and France agreed on the ratio 25:55 as the percentage of the total reparations which each of the two powers should

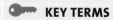

eventually receive. Belgium was the only power to be awarded full compensation for its losses and priority in payment of the first sums due from Germany, largely because it too had threatened to withdraw from the conference in May, at a time when Italy had already walked out and the Japanese were also threatening to do so (see page 98).

German disarmament

As with reparations, the Allied and associated nations agreed on the necessity for German disarmament, but there were differences in emphasis. The British and Americans wished to destroy Germany's tradition of conscription, which they regarded as 'the taproot of militarism'. Instead, they wanted a small professional army created along the lines of the British or US peacetime armies. General Foch, more wisely as it turned out, feared that a professional German army would merely become a tightly organised nucleus of trained men which would be capable of quick expansion when the opportunity arose.

Foch was overruled and the Council of Ten accepted in March proposals for the creation of **inter-Allied commissions** to monitor the pace of German disarmament, the abolition of the general staff, the creation of a regular army with a maximum strength of 100,000 men, the dissolution of the air force and the reduction of the navy to a handful of ships.

The territorial settlement

It was accepted, even by many Germans, that the predominantly Danish northern Schleswig, annexed by Bismarck in 1866, should be returned to Denmark. There was therefore general agreement that a **plebiscite** should be held to determine the size of the area to be handed back. The former German territories of Eupen and Malmedy, together with Moresnet, which before 1914 had been administered jointly by Germany and Belgium, were ceded to Belgium, and the neutrality of the Grand Duchy of Luxembourg was confirmed.

The Saarland

The French proposals for the future of the Saarland proved more controversial. Clemenceau insisted on the restoration to France of that part of the Saar which had been given to Prussia in 1814. He also aimed to detach the mineral and industrial basin to the north, which had never been French, and place it under an independent non-German administration. Finally, he demanded full French ownership of the Saar coalmines to compensate for the destruction of the pits in northern France by the Germans.

Wilson immediately perceived that here was a clash between the national interests of France and the principle of self-determination as enshrined in the Fourteen Points. While he was ready to agree to French access to the coalmines until the production of their own mines had been restored, he vetoed outright other demands. To save the conference from breaking down, Lloyd George

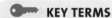

KEY TERMS

Inter-Allied commissions Allied committees set up to deal with particular tasks.

Plebiscite A referendum, or vote, by the electorate on a single issue.

persuaded Wilson and Clemenceau to accept a compromise whereby the mines would become French for fifteen years, while the actual government of the Saar would be entrusted to the League. After fifteen years the people would have the right to decide in a plebiscite whether they wished to return to German rule. (In 1935 the plebiscite was duly held and the territory reverted to German control.)

The Rhineland

Over the future of the Rhineland there was an equally bitter clash between Britain and France. The British had no ambitions on the Rhine, but to the French, the occupation of the Rhine was a unique opportunity to weaken Germany permanently by making the whole region independent of Berlin. This would deprive Germany of the natural defensive line of the Rhine. The British feared that this would not only create a new area of tension between France and Germany but also tilt the balance of power in Europe decisively towards France.

Only after heated and often bitter arguments was a compromise at last reached. Clemenceau agreed to limit the Allied occupation of the Rhineland to a fifteen-year period in return for an Anglo-American treaty guaranteeing France against a new German attack. The Rhineland would be divided into three zones, which would be evacuated after five, ten and fifteen years. Thereafter, the Rhineland would be permanently **demilitarised**. Lloyd George was unwilling to accept even this length of occupation, and right up to the signature of the treaty he sought to evade the commitment.

Germany's eastern frontiers

Anglo-French disagreements again dominated negotiations on Germany's eastern frontiers. The Commission on Polish Affairs recommended on 12 March that Danzig, Marienwerder and Upper Silesia should all be included in the new Polish state, so as to give it access to the sea and make it economically viable. Only the future of Allenstein would be decided by plebiscite. Lloyd George vigorously opposed the inclusion of Danzig and Marienwerder as he feared the long-term resentment of the local, and predominantly German-speaking, population and dreaded that an embittered Berlin might turn to Bolshevik Russia for help. By threatening to withdraw from the Anglo-American guarantee pact, he forced Clemenceau to agree to the holding of a plebiscite in Marienwerder and the establishment of a free and autonomous city of Danzig. The city was to be presided over by a High Commissioner appointed by the League of Nations and to form a **customs union** with Poland. It was also to be linked with Poland through a narrow corridor of territory – the Danzig, or Polish, Corridor.

Germany's colonies

President Wilson insisted that the League should also have ultimate control over the former German colonies. This was accepted only reluctantly by the British Dominions of New Zealand, Australia and South Africa, each arguing that

KEY TERMS

Demilitarised Having all military defences removed.

Customs union An economic bloc, the members of which trade freely with each other.

In comparison with 1914 (see page 52), what changes were made to the map of central Europe in 1919–20?

Central Europe after the peace settlements 1919–23.

the outright annexation by themselves of the South Pacific islands, Samoa and South West Africa, respectively, was vital for their security. In May, agreement was reached on the division of the German colonies. Britain, France and South Africa were allocated most of the former German colonial empire in Africa, while Australia, New Zealand and Japan secured the mandates for the scattered German possessions in the Pacific. Italy was awarded control of the Juba valley in east Africa, and a few minor territorial adjustments were made to its Libyan frontier with Algeria. Essentially Britain, the Dominions and France had secured what they wanted, despite paying lip service to the League by agreeing to mandated status for the former German colonies.

Kiaochow In 1897 the Germans seized Kiachow in revenge for the murder of two missionaries. They also secured mining rights in the neighbouring province of Shantung.

SPD Social Democratic Party of Germany. Its leaders were hostile to Bolshevism and believed in parliamentary government.

Japan and former German territory in Shantung

A more serious clash arose between Japan and the USA. The Japanese were determined to hold on to the ex-German leasehold territory of **Kiaochow** in Shantung in China. The Chinese government, however, on the strength of its declaration of war against Germany in 1917, argued that all former German rights should automatically revert to the Chinese state, despite the fact that in 1915 it had agreed to recognise Japanese rights in Shantung. Wilson was anxious to block the growth of Japanese influence in the Pacific and supported China, but Lloyd George and Clemenceau, wanting to protect their own rights in China, backed Japan. Wilson, already locked in conflict with the Italians over their claims to Fiume (see page 103) and facing Japanese threats to boycott the conference and sign a separate peace with Germany, had no option but to concede. It is arguable that this humiliating defeat did much to turn the US Senate against the Treaty of Versailles.

The German reaction

While the Allies were working on the treaty, the German government could only prepare for the time when it would be summoned to Paris to receive the draft terms. Optimistically, in what one German intellectual, Ernst Troeltsch, called 'the dreamland of the armistice period', Berlin hoped that it would be able to protect Germany from excessive reparation claims and so keep the way open for a rapid economic recovery. Germany had become a republic in November 1918 and in elections held in January voted for a democratic coalition government in which the moderate socialist **SPD** was the largest party.

On 7 May the draft peace terms were at last presented to the Germans, who were given a mere fifteen days to draw up their reply. The German government bitterly criticised the treaty on the basis that it did not conform to the Fourteen Points and demanded significant concessions:

- immediate membership of the League of Nations
- a guarantee that Austria and the ethnic Germans in the Sudetenland, which was a part of the new Czechoslovak state, should have the chance to decide whether they wished to join Germany (see the map on page 97)
- the setting up of a neutral commission to examine the war guilt question.

Allied and US concessions to the Germans

These demands, which if met, would have strengthened Germany's position in central Europe, were rejected outright by the Allied and associated powers, but nevertheless some ground was conceded. Lloyd George, fearful that the Germans might reject the treaty, persuaded the French to agree to a plebiscite in Upper Silesia. He failed to limit the Rhineland occupation to five years, but did manage to secure the vague assurance, which later became Article 431 of the treaty, 'that once Germany had given concrete evidence of her willingness to fulfil her obligations', the Allied and associated powers would consider 'an earlier termination of the period of occupation'.

The signature of the Treaty of Versailles

On 16 June the Germans were handed the final version of the treaty incorporating these concessions. Not surprisingly, given the depth of opposition to it among the German people, it triggered a political crisis splitting the cabinet and leading to the resignation of the chancellor. Yet in view of its own military weakness and the continuing Allied blockade, the Berlin government had little option but to accept the treaty, although it made very clear that it was acting under duress.

SOURCE D

Gustav Bauer, the German Chancellor, announcing Germany's reluctant acceptance of the Treaty of Versailles, quoted in G. Schutz, *Revolutions and Peace Treaties, 1917–1921*, Methuen, 1972, p. 189.

Surrendering to superior force but without retracting its opinion regarding the unheard of injustice of the peace conditions, the government of the German Republic therefore declares its readiness to accept and sign the peace conditions imposed by the Allied and associated governments.

According to Source D, why did the Germans sign the Treaty of Versailles? **?**

On 28 June 1919 the treaty was signed in the Hall of Mirrors at Versailles, where in 1871 the German Empire had been proclaimed (see page 14).

SOURCE E

Why did the French choose the Hall of Mirrors, shown in Source E, as the venue for the peace signature? **?**

In the Hall of Mirrors in Versailles, French Prime Minister Georges Clemenceau adds his signature to the Treaty of Versailles on 28 June 1919. As president of the Paris Peace Conference and prime minister of France, he was the senior statesman among the Allied and associated powers.

Ratified Having received formal approval from parliament.

Isolationists US politicians who were opposed to any US commitments or entanglements in Europe or elsewhere.

KEY FIGURE

Henry Cabot Lodge (1850–1924)

A US statesman, a Republican politician and a historian. He was chairman of the Senate Foreign Relations Committee.

The American refusal to ratify the treaty

By January 1920 the treaty had been **ratified** by all the signatory powers with the important exception of the USA. In Washington, crucial amendments had been put forward by a coalition of **isolationists**, led by **Senator Lodge**, rejecting the Shantung settlement and seriously modifying the covenant of the League. In essence, the isolationists feared that if the USA joined the League, it would be committed to defend the independence of other League members from aggression, even if this meant going to war. They therefore proposed that Congress should be empowered to veto US participation in any League initiative that clashed with the USA's traditional policy of isolationism and independence. Wilson felt that these amendments would paralyse the League and so refused to accept them. He failed twice to secure the necessary two-thirds majority in the Senate.

This was a major defeat for Wilson, and the consequences for Europe were serious. Without US ratification, the Anglo-American military guarantee of France lapsed and the burden of carrying out the Treaty of Versailles fell on Britain and France.

Summary diagram: Settlement with Germany

The settlement with Germany			
Territorial changes	*Reparations*	*Disarmament*	*League of Nations*
Independent Poland	Reparation Commission fixed amount of 132 billion gold marks in May 1921	Abolition of conscription	Collective security
Plebiscites in Upper Silesia, Schleswig and West Prussia		Regular German army of 100,000	New principle of mandates
Alsace-Lorraine to France	Prolonged struggle to force Germany to pay 1921–3	Very small fleet	Weakened by absence of USA
Saar administered by League of Nations	France occupied Ruhr in January 1923	Allied control of commissions in Germany until 1927	Germany and defeated powers initially excluded
Germany lost colonies and foreign investments	Dawes Commission, January 1924	Rhineland occupied for 15 years	

Settlements with Austria, Hungary and Bulgaria

▶ *To what extent were the treaties with Austria, Hungary and Bulgaria unworkable and full of contradictions?*

After the ceremony at Versailles, the Allied leaders returned home, leaving their officials to draft the treaties with Germany's former allies. The outlines of a settlement in eastern Europe and the Balkans were already clear: Austria-Hungary and the tsarist Russian empire had collapsed, the Poles and Czechs had declared their independence and the South Slavs had decided to federate with Serbia to form what was later to be called Yugoslavia. The bewildering diversity of races in the Balkans, who were in no way concentrated in easily definable areas, would ensure that however the Great Powers drew the frontiers, the final settlement would be full of contradictions. The three defeated powers, Austria and Hungary (both treated as the heirs to the former Austro-Hungarian Empire) and Bulgaria, all had to pay reparations, disarm and submit to the humiliation of a war guilt clause. The basis of the settlement in south-central Europe and the Balkans was the creation of the new Czecho-Slovak state, or Czechoslovakia, and the Serbo-Croat-Slovene state, or Yugoslavia.

The Treaty of St Germain, 10 September 1919

The Treaty of St Germain split up the diverse territories which before the war had been part of the Austrian Empire. Austria itself was now reduced to a small German-speaking state of some 6 million people:

- Italy was awarded South Tyrol, despite the existence there of some 230,000 ethnic Germans.
- Bohemia and Moravia were ceded to Czechoslovakia. Any second thoughts the British or Americans had about handing over to the Czechs the 3 million Germans who made up nearly one-third of the population of these provinces were quickly stifled by French opposition. The French wanted a potential ally against Germany to be strengthened by a defensible frontier and the possession of the Škoda munitions works in Pilsen, both of which entailed the forcible integration of large German minorities into Czechoslovakia.
- Slovenia, Bosnia-Herzegovina and Dalmatia were handed over to Yugoslavia.
- Galicia and Bukovina were ceded to Poland and Romania, respectively.
- Only in Carinthia, where the population consisted of German-speaking Slovenes who did not want to join Yugoslavia, did the Great Powers consent to a plebiscite. This resulted in 1920 in the area remaining Austrian.

- To avoid the dangers of an **Anschluss** with Germany, Article 88 (which was identical to Article 80 in the Treaty of Versailles) stated that only the Council of the League of Nations was empowered to sanction a change in Austria's status as an independent state. Effectively this meant that France, as a permanent member of the Council, could veto any proposed change.

The Treaty of Trianon, 4 June 1920

Of all the defeated powers in 1919 it is arguable that Hungary suffered the most severely. By the Treaty of Trianon, Hungary lost over two-thirds of its territory and 41.6 per cent of its population. It was particularly vulnerable to partition, as essentially only the heartlands of Hungary, the great Central Plain, were **Magyar**. Its fate was sealed when, in November 1918, Serb, Czech and Romanian troops all occupied the regions they claimed. The completion of the treaty was delayed by the communist coup in March 1919 (see page 86), but negotiations resumed after its defeat. The Treaty of Trianon was signed in June 1920:

- Most of the German-speaking area in the west of the former Hungarian state was ceded to Austria.
- The Slovakian and Ruthenian regions in the north went to Czechoslovakia.
- The east went to Romania.
- The south went to Yugoslavia (see the map on page 97).

The Treaty of Trianon was justified by the Allies according to the principle of national self-determination, but in the context of Hungary this was a principle almost impossible to realise.

SOURCE F

From C.A. Macartney, *Hungary and Her Successors: The Treaty of Trianon and its Consequences*, Oxford University Press, 1937, p. 3. Macartney was a British historian and an expert on Hungary and the successor states.

… the ethical line was practically nowhere clear cut … long centuries of interpenetration, assimilation, migration and internal colonization had left in many places a belt of mixed and often indeterminate population where each national group merged into the next, while there were innumerable islands of one nationality set in seas of another, ranging in size from the half-million of Magyar-speaking Szekely in Transylvania through many inter-determinate groups of fifty or a hundred thousand down to communities of a single village or less … No frontier could be drawn which did not leave national minorities on at least one side of it.

? What, according to Source F, were the main problems involved in redrawing the boundaries of Hungary?

Wherever there was a clash of interests between Hungary and the **successor states** or Romania, the Allies ensured that the decision went against Hungary.

The Treaty of Neuilly, 27 November 1919

The same principle operated in the negotiations leading up to the Treaty of Neuilly with Bulgaria, which was signed on November 1919. Essentially, Britain and France regarded Bulgaria as the '**Balkan Prussia**' which needed to be restrained. They were determined, despite reservations from Italy and the USA, to reward their allies, Romania, Greece and Serbia (now part of Yugoslavia), at its expense. Thus, southern Dobruja, with a mere 7000 Romanians out of a total population of 250,000, was ceded to Romania and western Thrace was given to Greece (see the map on page 97).

Fiume, Istria and Dalmatia

These post-war settlements were accompanied by bitter quarrels between the Allied and associated powers. The most serious clash of opinions took place between Italy and the USA over Italian claims to Fiume, Istria and Dalmatia (see the map on page 97). Orlando was desperate to prove to the Italian electorate that Italy was not a '**proletarian nation**' which could be dictated to by the Great Powers, and insisted on its right to annex the port of Fiume in which, it could be argued, there was a bare majority of ethnic Italians, if the Croat suburb of Susak was conveniently left out of the picture. The Italian annexation of Fiume would have the added bonus of denying Yugoslavia its only effective port in the Adriatic, thereby strengthening Italy's economic grip on the region. Agreement could have been achieved, especially as Orlando was ready in April 1919 to accept Fiume as a compromise for giving up Italian claims on Dalmatia; but Wilson made the major political mistake of vetoing this option publicly in a statement in the French press. After compromising over the Saar and Shantung, Wilson was stubbornly determined to make a stand on the Fourteen Points in the Adriatic. Italy's Prime Minister Orlando and Foreign Secretary Sonnino walked out of the Peace Conference in protest and did not return until 9 May 1919.

Orlando's resignation and his replacement by Nitti in June opened the way up for secret negotiations in Paris, but the lynching of nine French troops in Fiume by an Italian mob in July and then the seizure of the city in September by the Italian nationalist poet **D'Annunzio** merely prolonged the crisis. It was not until November 1920 that Yugoslavia and Italy agreed on a compromise and signed the Treaty of Rapallo. Istria was partitioned between the two powers, Fiume was to become a self-governing free city, while the rest of Dalmatia went to Yugoslavia. In December Italian troops cleared D'Annunzio out of Fiume, although in late 1923 Mussolini ordered its reoccupation.

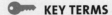

KEY TERMS

'**Balkan Prussia**' Bulgaria was compared to Prussia, which in the eyes of the Allies had an aggressive and militarist reputation.

Proletarian nation
A nation that lacked an empire and raw materials. Like the proletariat (workers) it was poor.

KEY FIGURE

Gabriele D'Annunzio (1863–1938)

Italian nationalist poet, writer and leader of the coup in Fiume.

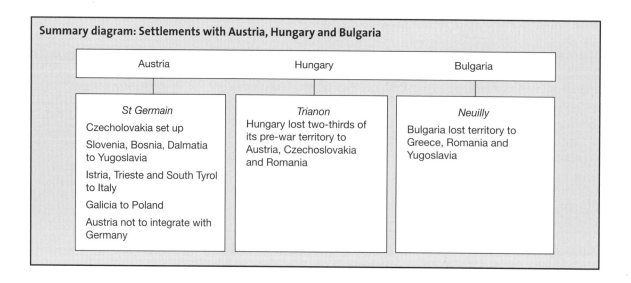

Summary diagram: Settlements with Austria, Hungary and Bulgaria

Austria	Hungary	Bulgaria
St Germain Czecholovakia set up Slovenia, Bosnia, Dalmatia to Yugoslavia Istria, Trieste and South Tyrol to Italy Galicia to Poland Austria not to integrate with Germany	*Trianon* Hungary lost two-thirds of its pre-war territory to Austria, Czechoslovakia and Romania	*Neuilly* Bulgaria lost territory to Greece, Romania and Yugoslavia

6 Settlement with Turkey 1919–23

▶ *To what extent was the Treaty of Sèvres so harsh that it was bound to provoke a backlash?*

The Treaty of Sèvres was another Anglo-French compromise. Lloyd George hoped drastically to weaken Turkey, not only by depriving it of Constantinople and of the control of the Straits, but also by forcing it to surrender all territories where there was no ethnic Turkish majority. He now envisaged Greece, which entered the war on the Allied side in 1917, rather than Italy, as filling the vacuum left by the collapse of Turkish power and, in effect, becoming the agent of the British Empire in the eastern Mediterranean. The French, on the other hand, concerned to protect their pre-war investments in Turkey, wished to preserve a viable Turkish state. Above all, they wanted the Turkish government to remain in Constantinople, where it would be more vulnerable to French pressure.

The end product of this Anglo-French compromise was a harsh and humiliating treaty. Constantinople remained Turkish, but Thrace and most of the European coastline of the Sea of Marmara and the Dardanelles were to go to Greece. In the Smyrna region the Greeks were also given responsibility for internal administration and defence, while an Armenian state was to be set up with access across Turkish territory to the Black Sea. The Straits were to be controlled by an international commission, and an Allied financial committee was to have the right to inspect Turkey's finances. By a separate agreement zones were also awarded to France and Italy in southern Turkey (see the map on page 105).

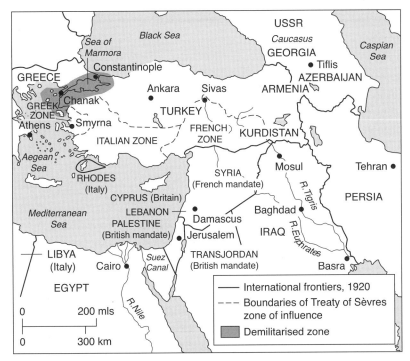

The Near and Middle East after the Treaty of Sèvres.

The division of Turkey's Arabian territories

The Sykes–Picot Agreement

In May 1916 Britain and France signed the Sykes–Picot Agreement. By this they committed themselves to dividing up Mesopotamia, Syria and the Lebanon into Anglo-French spheres of interest once the war against Turkey had been won. Britain, however, was the only power with a large army in the Middle East, and consequently was able to revise the Sykes–Picot Agreement unilaterally. In 1917 Britain insisted on claiming the whole of Palestine, which was quite contrary to the agreement. By announcing support for the **Zionists**' ambition to establish a national home for the Jews in Palestine through the **Balfour Declaration**, Britain cleverly managed to secure the USA's backing for its aims.

The Middle East mandates

In February 1919, in deference to Wilson and the Fourteen Points, Britain and France agreed that they could only exercise power over these territories in the name of the League of Nations. It took several more months of bitter argument before the British agreed to a French mandate in Syria and also French access to the oil wells in Mosul in Iraq. The frontiers between the British mandates of Palestine and Iraq and the French mandate of Syria were then finalised in December (see the map above).

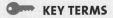 **KEY TERMS**

Zionists Supporters of Zionism, a movement for re-establishing the Jewish state.

Balfour Declaration A communication of November 1917 to the Zionists by A.J. Balfour, British foreign secretary, declaring British support for establishing a national home for the Jews in Palestine.

Mustapha Kemal and the revision of the treaty

Of all the treaties negotiated in 1919–20, Sèvres, signed on 10 August 1920, was the most obvious failure as it was never put into effect by the Turkish government. When the Allies imposed it, they took little account of the profound changes in Turkey brought about by the rise of **Mustapha Kemal**, the leader of the new nationalist movement. Kemal had set up a rebel government which controlled virtually the whole of the Turkish interior, and was determined not to accept the treaty. The long delay until August 1920 ensured that growing Turkish resentment, particularly at the Greek occupation of Smyrna (see page 104), which the Allies had encouraged in May 1919, made its enforcement an impossibility.

By settling the dispute over the Russo-Turkish frontier in the Caucasus, Kemal was able to concentrate his forces against the Greeks without fear of Russian intervention from the north. By August 1922 he was poised to enter Constantinople and the **Straits zone**, which were still occupied by Allied troops. Both the Italians and French rapidly withdrew, leaving the British isolated. Kemal, however, avoided direct confrontation with the British forces and negotiated an armistice, which gave him virtually all he wanted: the Greeks withdrew from eastern Thrace and Adrianople, and the British recognised Turkish control over Constantinople and the Straits.

In 1923 an international conference met at Lausanne to revise the Treaty of Sèvres. Kemal, anxious not to be dependent on Russia, agreed to the creation of small demilitarised zones on both sides of the Straits and the freedom of navigation through them for Britain, France, Italy and Japan. He also insisted on the abolition of foreign control over Turkish finances. This was a serious blow to the French hopes of re-establishing their pre-war influence over Turkish finances, and arguably they, apart from the Greeks, lost more than any other power as a consequence of the new Treaty of Lausanne. Treaty revision did not affect the fate of Turkey's former Arab provinces, which remained under the control of Britain and France.

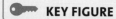

KEY FIGURE

Mustapha Kemal (1880–1938)

Kemal created the Turkish Republic in 1923. He was a great moderniser who emancipated women, introduced the Latin alphabet and encouraged Western-style dress. He started to industrialise Turkey and to free it from traditional Islamic loyalties.

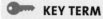

KEY TERM

Straits zone The shores along the Straits of Dardanelles were occupied by Allied troops.

Summary diagram: Settlement with Turkey 1919–23

The peace settlement with Turkey

Treaty of Sèvres, 1919

Turks ceded Middle East empire; Greeks gained Thrace; Straits controlled by Allies

Revised at Lausanne 1923: Greeks expelled, Constantinople back to Turkey

7 Enforcing the Treaty of Versailles 1920–3

▶ *How effectively did the* Entente *Powers enforce the Treaty of Versailles 1920–3?*

▶ *Why and how did Britain's and France's views on how to implement the Treaty of Versailles conflict between 1920 and 1923?*

The organisation for carrying out the treaties

Once the Treaty of Versailles had been ratified the victorious powers set up a series of inter-Allied commissions to organise the plebiscites, monitor German disarmament and examine Germany's financial position with a view to payment of its reparations. These reported to the **Conference of Ambassadors** in Paris, which represented the Allied powers, but the real decisions were taken by the Allied prime ministers, who between January 1920 and January 1924 met 24 times to review progress made in carrying out the Treaty of Versailles.

KEY TERM

Conference of Ambassadors Standing committee set up to supervise the carrying out of the Treaty of Versailles.

Anglo-French differences

Both Britain and France had conflicting ideas of how best to ensure that Germany carried out the Treaty of Versailles. Essentially Britain, as the centre of a worldwide empire, wanted to see a balance of power in Europe that would prevent either French or German domination and leave it free to deal with the growing challenges to its power from nationalist movements in India, Egypt and Ireland. Britain was also convinced that only a prosperous and peaceful Germany could pay reparations and play its part in Europe as one of the main engines of the European economy.

For France, the German problem was an overriding priority. French policy swung uneasily between occasionally exploring the possibilities of economic co-operation with Germany, and more usually of applying forceful measures designed permanently to weaken Germany and to force it to fulfil the treaty.

Drawing up Poland's borders

The eastern frontier with Russia

The Poles exploited the chaos caused by the Russian Civil War to extend their eastern frontier deep in the Ukraine and Belorussia. In December 1919 they rejected the proposed eastern frontier based on recommendations put forward by Lord Curzon, the British foreign secretary, and in early 1920 embarked on a full-scale invasion of Ukraine.

By August, Bolshevik forces had pushed the Poles back to Warsaw. However, with the help of French equipment and military advisers, the Poles rallied and managed to inflict a decisive defeat on the Red Army just outside Warsaw. Soviet troops were pushed back, and in March 1921 Poland's eastern frontiers were at last fixed by the Treaty of Riga. Poland annexed a considerable area of Belorussia and the western Ukraine, all of which lay well to the east of the proposed **Curzon line**.

Upper Silesia

By the end of 1920 the Marienwerder and Allenstein plebiscites had been held, in both of which the population voted to stay in Germany, and Danzig had became a free city under the administration of the League of Nations in November 1920.

Fixing the Upper Silesian frontiers, however, proved to be a much greater problem. Upper Silesia had a population of some 2,280,000 Germans and Poles, who were bitterly divided along ethnic lines, and a concentration of coalmines and industries that were second only in size to the Ruhr.

The plebiscite on 17 March 1921 produced an ambiguous result which did not solve the Anglo-French disagreements over Poland. The British argued that its result justified keeping the key industrial regions of the province German, while the French insisted that they should be awarded to Poland. Fearing that once again British wishes would prevail, the Poles seized control of the industrial area, which was still legally German, and an uprising broke out in May 1921. On French insistence the Germans were forbidden to intervene and order was eventually restored by British and French troops in July 1921 and the whole question was handed over to the League of Nations in August. In 1922 the League, bowing to French pressure, decided to hand over most of the industrial areas to Poland.

SOURCE G

From Prime Minister Lloyd George's speech in the House of Commons, on 13 May 1921, from *House of Commons Debates*, volume 141, fifth session, cols 2382–5.

*Without waiting for discussions between governments, the Polish population under the leadership of Mr. **Korfanty** raised an insurrection … and put us in the difficulty of having to deal with a **fait accompli** … It is a complete defiance of the Treaty …*

… Either the Allies ought to insist upon the treaty being respected, or they ought to allow Germans to do it. Not merely to disarm Germany, but to say that such troops as she has got are not to be permitted to take part in restoring order [in Upper Silesia, which], until the decision comes, is their own province – that is not fair. Fair play is what England stands for, and I hope she will stand for it to the end.

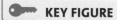

Reparations

By far the most difficult problem facing the British and French governments was the reparation problem. Both the British and French hoped to solve the problem by fixing a global total as soon as possible on the assumption that once Germany knew the full sum of its debts it would be able to raise money in the USA from the sale of government bonds and begin payments.

At the end of April 1921 the Reparation Commission at last fixed a global total for reparations of 132 billion gold marks to be paid over a period of 42 years. When this was rejected by Germany, on the grounds that the sum was too high, an ultimatum was dispatched to Berlin giving the Germans only a week to accept the new payment schedule, after which the Ruhr would be occupied.

To carry out the terms of the London ultimatum, a new government was formed by Joseph Wirth (1879–1956) on 10 May. Assisted by **Walther Rathenau**, his minister for reconstruction, he was determined to pursue a policy of negotiation rather than confrontation. The first instalment was paid, and Rathenau made some progress in persuading the French to accept the payment of a proportion of reparations in the form of the delivery of industrial goods and coal. However, by the end of the year the German government dropped a bombshell by announcing that, as a consequence of escalating inflation, it could not raise sufficient hard currency to meet the next instalment of reparation payments.

The Geneva Conference, April 1922

Germany's default gave Lloyd George the opportunity to launch a major initiative. He was convinced that Germany needed a temporary **moratorium**, to put its economy in order, while in the longer term the key to the payment of reparations and a European economic revival lay in creating a European group of industrial nations, including Germany, to rebuild Russia. He hoped that this would generate an international trade boom, which would also benefit Germany, and enable it to pay reparations without damaging the commerce of the other European nations.

Raymond Poincaré (see page 43), who had just became French prime minister again, grudgingly consented to holding an international conference at Geneva, to which both the Russia and Germany would be invited to discuss these plans, but he vetoed any concession on reparations. The Russians agreed to attend, but were highly suspicious of Lloyd George's plans for opening up their economy to foreign capital.

During the conference, the Russians pulled off a major diplomatic triumph by secretly negotiating the Rapallo Agreement with Germany, whereby both countries agreed to write off any financial claims on each other dating from the war. Germany also pledged to consult with the Russians before participating in any international plans for investing in the Soviet economy.

KEY FIGURE

Walther Rathenau (1867–1922)

The son of the founder of the German electrical company AEG. In 1914–15 he saved Germany from the impact of the British blockade by setting up the German Raw Materials Department. He was murdered by German nationalists in 1922.

KEY TERM

Moratorium Temporary suspension of payments.

Rapallo effectively killed Lloyd George's plan. It is hard not to see Rapallo as a miscalculation by the Germans. While it helped Germany to escape from isolation, it did so at the cost of intensifying French suspicions of its motives. In many ways these were justified, as a **secret annex** signed in July allowed Germany to train its soldiers in Russian territory, thereby violating the terms of the Treaty of Versailles.

The Ruhr occupation

In July 1922 a major confrontation between France and Germany seemed inevitable when the German government requested a three-year moratorium. At the same time Britain announced that, as the USA was demanding the repayment of British wartime debts, it must in turn insist on the repayment of money loaned to former allies, particularly France. To the French, Britain's demand for these repayments contrasted painfully with the concessions Lloyd George was ready to offer the Germans.

On 27 November the Poincaré cabinet decided finally that the occupation of the Ruhr was the only means of forcing Germany to pay reparations, and on 11 January French and Belgian troops moved into the Ruhr. Significantly, Britain did not join in but adopted a policy of '**benevolent neutrality**' towards France.

For nine months the French occupation of the Ruhr was met by **passive resistance** and strikes which were financed by the German government. This increased the cost of the occupation, but it also triggered **hyperinflation** in Germany. In September, Germany was on the brink of collapse and the new chancellor, Gustav Stresemann, called off passive resistance.

France, too, had exhausted itself and seriously weakened its currency, the franc, in the prolonged Ruhr crisis. France's attempts to back **Rhineland separatism** and to create an independent Rhineland currency were unsuccessful. Separatist leaders were assassinated by German nationalist agents from unoccupied Germany or lynched by angry crowds. Poincaré had thus little option but to co-operate with an Anglo-American initiative for setting up a commission chaired by the US financier **Charles G. Dawes**. Its two committee experts, one to study Germany's capacity for payment, and the other to advise on how it could best balance the budget and restore its currency, began work in early 1924.

As one French official accurately observed, the time was now past for dealing with Germany as 'victor to vanquished'. The Ruhr crisis marked the end of the attempts to carry out the Treaty of Versailles by force and the beginning of the gradual revision of the treaty itself.

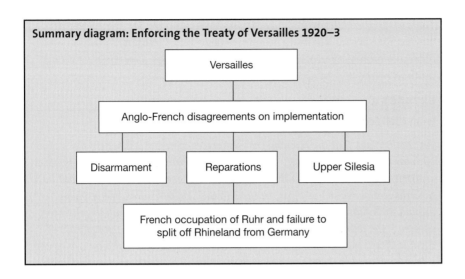

Summary diagram: Enforcing the Treaty of Versailles 1920–3

 # The key debate

▶ *How unjust were the peace treaties of 1919–20?*

The peace treaties of 1919–20 were seen by some contemporaries as a triumph of democracy, the rule of law, self-determination and collective security against militarism, and yet by others as a hypocritical act of vengeance, a profound injustice and a product of economic ignorance, which contributed to the rise of Hitler and the outbreak of the Second World War.

The Treaty of Versailles

EXTRACT I

From J. Hiden, *Republican and Fascist Italy*, Longman, 1996, pp. 11–12.

The peace treaties came to be seen [in the 1940s] as a central cause of the second World war, an idea exemplified by [the historian] E.H. Carr's description [in 1942] of the inter-war period as the 'twenty years crisis'. Carr located unrest in the division caused by the settlement between powers who were 'satisfied' – Great Britain, France, the United States – and those who were 'dissatisfied'. The latter included Germany, the Soviet Russia, Japan and Italy. German resentment against the Versailles terms … was certainly a factor aiding Hitler's power … .

Yet viewed from the perspective of 1945, when Germany was totally defeated, the Treaty of Versailles does not appear as harsh as it did in 1919. Germany was still potentially a Great Power. It had lost part of Upper Silesia, its eastern territories and Danzig, but retained the great industrial centre of the Ruhr.

In fact, given the collapse of the Austrian Empire and the Treaty of Riga, which excluded Russia from Central Europe (see page 108), Germany's position was potentially more powerful in central and eastern Europe after the First World War than before it.

EXTRACT 2

From Niall Ferguson, *The Pity of War*, Penguin, 1999, p. 412.

The reality was that the economic consequences were far less severe for Germany than the Germans … claimed. Apart from the US, all the combatant countries had emerged from the war with heavy losses … The sums owed by the prospective recipients of reparations to the US were already equivalent to around 40 billion gold marks. Similarly it was not just Germany that had lost shipping: the total losses to world shipping during the war (the better part of them inflicted by Germany) had totalled more than 15 million tons … Nor can it be maintained that the reparation total set in 1921 constituted an intolerable burden … the German debt burden in 1921 was actually slightly less than the ratio of the total British national debt to gross national product in the same year.

The Treaties with Austria, Hungary and Bulgaria

The treaties with Austria, Hungary and Bulgaria were an attempt both to give the people of south-eastern Europe a right to self-determination as laid down in the Fourteen Points (see page 80) and to secure territorial and strategic advantages for the allies of France and Britain. The latter aim often overrode the former.

EXTRACT 3

From Margaret MacMillan, *Peacemakers*, John Murray, 2002, p. 259.

Austria's borders had been largely left to specialist committees, which had heard from countries such as Czechoslovakia or Italy about what they wanted, but not of course from Austria itself. Galicia went to Poland and Bohemia to Czechoslovakia. Some three million German speakers went with them. Otto Bauer, Austria's … foreign minister, made an impassioned speech back in Vienna: 'No less than two-fifths of our people are to be subjugated to foreign dominion, without any plebiscite and against their indisputable will, being thus deprived of their right to self-determination.' He had a point but few in Paris were prepared to listen.

Yet given the problems facing the Allied leaders in Paris, it is worth remembering the historian Max Beloff's observation that it is surprising, 'not that the treaties were imperfect but that they were concluded at all'.

EXTRACT 4

From R. Butler, 'The peace settlement of Versailles, 1918–1933', quoted in C.L. Mowat, editor, *The New Cambridge Modern History: The Shifting Balance of World Forces*, Cambridge University Press, 1968, p. 223.

*[It was] the **balkanisation** of Central Europe with which the peacemakers were later reproached, not with full justice. For the settlement did, despite shortcomings, unravel a horrid tangle of conflicting claims and considerations broadly according to fresh concepts of ethnic self-determination. This principle was not, indeed the inevitable **panacea** which people then tended to suppose; much depended, for instance upon the size and choice of the units selected for self-determination.*

 **KEY TERMS**

Balkanisation Breaking up of empires into small and often hostile states, as was done with Austria-Hungary.

Panacea Remedy supposed to cure every problem.

The Treaty of Sèvres

EXTRACT 5

From M.S. Anderson, *The Eastern Question*, Macmillan, 1966, p. 368.

It was already clear that [the enforcement of Sèvres] would be enormously difficult. In April Marshal Foch … reported that an army of 27 divisions would be needed to make Turkey accept such sacrifices and humiliations; and even if Greece were willing to make a large contribution a force of that size simply could not be raised.

Kemal forced the Allies to negotiate a new treaty at Lausanne in 1923. Yet Turkey did not regain the Arab territories, which it lost in the war to the British and French.

> How far do the historians quoted in Extracts 1–5 agree that the peace treaties of 1919–20 were, despite much contemporary criticism, actually realistic attempts to make peace and reconstruct a war-shattered Europe?

Chapter summary

In January 1919 the statesmen of the victorious powers met in Paris to work out their peace aims. Germany was not invited to take part in the negotiations. The Allied demands were therefore presented to Germany in June without any serious negotiation. Germany lost its colonies and some thirteen per cent of its territory. Justified by Article 231 of the Treaty of Versailles, Germany also had to pay reparations, the exact sum of which was to be fixed by the Reparation Commission. Despite vehement protests, Germany signed the treaty on 28 June as it was too weak militarily to defy the Allies.

Over the next years, peace treaties were concluded with Germany's allies. The Allies were committed to creating independent nation states out of the ruins of the former Austro-Hungarian Empire, but in reality the diversity of races in the Balkans, which were often not concentrated in easily definable areas, ensured that large racial minorities were included against their wishes in the new states, a sure recipe for future trouble.

Although Turkey signed the Treaty of Sèvres, Kemal forced the Allies to make major concessions to Turkey in the Treaty of Lausanne. The Germans were less successful in modifying Versailles, even though Britain became increasingly sympathetic to their demands.

Refresher questions

Use these questions to remind yourself of the key material covered in this chapter.

1 What problems faced the peacemakers in early 1919?

2 Why did the Allies disagree about Wilson's Fourteen Points?

3 What were France's aims at the Peace Conference?

4 To what extent had Britain achieved its war aims by December 1919?

5 What did both Italy and Japan hope to gain from the peace treaty?

6 Why did Foch disagree with the British and Americans over the abolition of conscription?

7 What were French aims in the Rhineland?

8 How were Germany's colonies divided up among the victorious powers?

9 What concessions were made to Germany during the negotiation of the Treaty of Versailles?

10 Why did the Americans not ratify the Treaty of Versailles?

11 Why was Kemal able to force the revision of the Treaty of Sèvres?

12 Why did it take so long to regulate Poland's eastern frontier with Russia?

13 Why did the British and French disagree about the Upper Silesian frontier?

14 Why did all efforts to solve the reparation question fail by the end of 1922?

15 Why did the Ruhr crisis mark a turning point in post-war European history?

 Question practice

ESSAY QUESTIONS

1 How important were the consequences of the territorial changes made in the peace treaties of 1919–20 for eastern and south-eastern Europe?

2 Which of the following did more to divide Britain and France during the negotiations leading up to the Treaty of Versailles, 1919–20: i) the reparation question or ii) the territorial settlement? Explain your answer with reference to both i) and ii).

3 'The Versailles treaty was a compromise that satisfied nobody.' Assess the validity of this view.

SOURCE ANALYSIS QUESTION

1 With reference to Sources 1, 2 and 3 below, and your understanding of the historical context, assess the value of these sources to a historian studying the Treaty of Versailles and the efforts made to carry it out 1920–4.

SOURCE 1

From a German government proclamation issued on the date of the coming into force of the Treaty of Versailles on 10 January 1920.

The unfavourable result of the war has surrendered us defenceless to the mercy of our adversaries, and imposes upon us great sacrifices under the name of peace. The hardest, however, which is forced upon us is the surrender of German districts in the east, west and north. Thousands of our fellow Germans must submit to the rule of foreign states without the possibility of asserting their right of self-determination. … Together we keep the language, which our mother taught us, … By all the fibres of our being, by our love and by our whole life we remain united.

Everything that is in our power to preserve your mother tongue, your German individuality, the intimate spiritual connection with your home country will be done. Just as before, whenever we had a possibility to negotiate, we made it our secret task to preserve your vital national rights in spite of your separation.

SOURCE 2

From Prime Minister Lloyd George's speech in the House of Commons, on 13 May 1921, from *House of Commons Debates*, volume 141, fifth session, cols 2382–5.

Without waiting for discussions between governments, the Polish population under the leadership of Mr. Korfanty raised an insurrection … and put us in the difficulty of having to deal with a fait accompli *… It is a complete defiance of the Treaty …*

… Either the Allies ought to insist upon the treaty being respected, or they ought to allow Germans to do it. Not merely to disarm Germany, but to say that such troops as she has got are not to be permitted to take part in restoring order [in Upper Silesia, which] until the decision comes, is their own province – that is not fair. Fair play is what England stands for, and I hope she will stand for it to the end.

SOURCE 3

From President Wilson's address to Congress on the Fourteen Points, 8 January 1918.

We have no jealousy of German greatness and there is nothing in this program that impairs it. We grudge her no achievement or distinction of learning or of pacific enterprise such as have made her record very bright and enviable. We do not wish to injure her or block in any way her legitimate influence and power. We do not wish to fight her either with arms or hostile arrangements of trade if she is willing to associate herself with us and the other peace loving nations of the world in covenants of justice and law and fair dealing. We wish her only to accept a place of equality among the peoples of the world – the new world in which we now live – instead of a place of mastery.

CHAPTER 6

Reconciliation and disarmament 1924–30: the Locarno era

This chapter covers the period after the failure of the Ruhr occupation. Confrontation was now slowly replaced with co-operation between Britain, France and Germany. This chapter looks at the following themes:

★ The impact of the Dawes Plan

★ The Locarno Treaties

★ The 'Locarno spirit' and Germany's re-emergence as a Great Power

★ Russia and eastern Europe during the Locarno era

★ Development of the League of Nations

★ Progress towards disarmament

Key dates

1921	March	Franco-Polish Alliance	1926	Sept.	Germany joined the League of Nations	
1921–2		Washington Conference and Five-Power Naval Convention	1928	Aug. 27	Kellogg–Briand Pact signed by fifteen states	
1925	Oct.	Locarno Conference				
1926	Jan.	Allies evacuated Cologne zone	1929	Aug.	Hague Conference	
	April	German–Soviet Treaty of Friendship		Oct. 29	Wall Street Crash	

1 The impact of the Dawes Plan

▶ *What were the terms of the Dawes Plan, and why did it help to stabilise Europe after the Ruhr crisis?*

The Dawes Plan played a crucial part in ending the bitter conflict over reparations which had nearly escalated into open war during the Ruhr occupation.

The recommendations of the Dawes Plan

The Dawes Plan recommended the following:

- Although the plan did not alter the overall reparation total, which had been fixed in 1921, it did recommend a loan of 800 million gold marks, which was to be raised mainly in the USA, to assist the restoration of the German economy. This was a crucially important component of the plan because it opened the way for US investment in Germany.
- Annual reparation payments were to start gradually and rise at the end of five years to their maximum level. These payments were to be guaranteed by the revenues of the German railways and of several key industries.
- A committee of foreign experts sitting in Berlin under the chairmanship of a US official was to ensure that the actual payments were transferred to Britain, France and Belgium in such a way that the German economy was not damaged. The plan was provisional and was to be renegotiated over the next ten years.

The reaction to the Dawes Plan

The British

The plan was welcomed enthusiastically in April 1924 by the British Treasury as 'the only constructive suggestion for escape from the present position, which if left must inevitably lead to war, open or concealed, between Germany and France'. It also had the advantage of involving the USA in the whole process of extracting reparations from Germany.

The French

There was much that the French disliked about the plan. For instance, it was not clear to them how the Germans could be compelled to pay if they again defaulted and refused to pay, as they had in 1922. However, with the defeat of Poincaré in the elections of June 1924, their willingness to co-operate increased markedly. Essentially, if the French were ever to receive any reparation payments and to avoid isolation, they had little option but to go along with the Dawes Plan.

The Germans

The Germans also disliked the plan as it placed their railways and some of their industry under international control and did nothing about scaling down their reparation debts. **Gustav Stresemann**, who, after the fall of his cabinet in November 1923, was now foreign minister, realised, however, that Germany had no alternative but to accept the plan if the French were to be persuaded to evacuate the Ruhr sooner rather than later.

 **KEY FIGURE**

Gustav Stresemann (1878–1929)

During the war an ardent nationalist but in August 1923, as chancellor, he halted passive resistance in the Ruhr. As foreign minister he negotiated the Locarno Treaties and secured Germany a seat on the council of the League of Nations.

The London Conference

Agreement to implement the Dawes Plan and to withdraw French and Belgian forces from the Ruhr within twelve months was achieved at the London Conference in August 1924. The new balance of power in Europe was clearly revealed when Britain and the USA devised a formula for effectively blocking France's ability to act alone against Germany in the event of another default in reparation payments. If Germany again refused to pay, it was agreed that Britain as a member of the Reparation Commission would have the right to appeal to the **Permanent Court of International Justice** and that a US representative would immediately join the Reparation Commission. Joint Anglo-American pressure would then be more than enough to restrain France from reoccupying the Ruhr. Deprived of much of their influence on the Reparation Commission, the French had undoubtedly suffered a major diplomatic defeat at the London Conference.

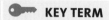

KEY TERM

Permanent Court of International Justice
An institution set up at The Hague, in the Netherlands, by Article 14 of the Covenant of the League of Nations in 1920.

? Study Source A.
According to the British prime minister, why could the London Conference be regarded as the 'first Peace Treaty' between Germany and the former Allies?

SOURCE A

From the concluding speech of the British prime minister, Ramsay MacDonald, at the London Conference, August 1924, quoted in M. Gilbert, *The Roots of Appeasement*, Weidenfeld & Nicolson, 1966, p. 111.

We are now offering Europe the first fully negotiated agreement since the War; every party here represented is morally bound to do its best to carry it out because it is not the result of an ultimatum …

This agreement may be regarded as the first Peace Treaty, because we sign it with a feeling that we have turned our backs on the terrible years of war and war mentality.

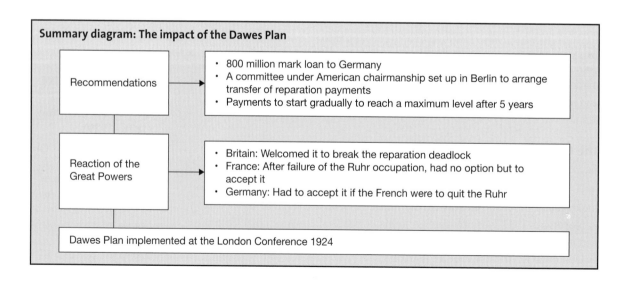

Summary diagram: The impact of the Dawes Plan

Recommendations →
- 800 million mark loan to Germany
- A committee under American chairmanship set up in Berlin to arrange transfer of reparation payments
- Payments to start gradually to reach a maximum level after 5 years

Reaction of the Great Powers →
- Britain: Welcomed it to break the reparation deadlock
- France: After failure of the Ruhr occupation, had no option but to accept it
- Germany: Had to accept it if the French were to quit the Ruhr

Dawes Plan implemented at the London Conference 1924

2 The Locarno Treaties

▶ *How did France seek to gain security from future German aggression?*

▶ *What did Britain, France and Germany gain from the Locarno Agreements?*

France's need for security

The Dawes Plan, by bringing the Ruhr crisis to an end, had, together with the German measures to **stabilise the mark**, made Germany an attractive prospect for US investment. To a certain extent, one of the preconditions for a European economic recovery was now in place, but investment was to come from individuals and banks and was not guaranteed by the US government. Nor was it accompanied by offers of military security to the French. Thus, should a new economic crisis blow up, US money could melt away and France could be left facing a strong and aggressive Germany.

Initially, the French had little option but to continue to insist, in as far as they still could, on the literal implementation of the Treaty of Versailles. They refused, for instance, to agree to the evacuation of the Cologne zone, which was due in January 1925 (see page 96), on the grounds that Germany had not yet carried out the military clauses of the treaty 'either in the spirit or in the letter'.

Negotiating the Locarno Treaties 1925

The urgent need to reassure the French of Germany's peaceful intentions, and so secure the evacuation of Cologne, prompted Gustav Stresemann, on the unofficial advice of the British ambassador in Berlin, to put forward a complex scheme for an international guarantee by the European Great Powers of the Rhineland and of the *status quo* in western Europe.

Austen Chamberlain, the British foreign secretary, at first suspected the proposals of being an attempt to divide France and Britain. Then he rapidly grasped that it was potentially a marvellous opportunity to square the circle by achieving both French security and the evacuation of Cologne without committing Britain to a military pact with France, which the cabinet would never tolerate. **Aristide Briand**, now back in power in France, was aware that only within the framework of an international agreement on the lines put forward by Stresemann could he in any way commit Britain to coming to the assistance of France if it were again attacked by Germany.

In the ensuing negotiations Briand successfully persuaded Chamberlain and Stresemann to widen the international guarantee to cover the Belgian–German frontier. He also attempted to extend it to Germany's eastern frontiers, but this was rejected by both Stresemann and Chamberlain. However, Stresemann

 KEY TERM

Stabilise the mark
In November 1924 the devalued German currency was replaced temporarily by the *Rentenmark* and then, in August 1924, by the new *Reichsmark*, which was put on the gold standard. Theoretically, this meant that banknotes could be converted into agreed, fixed quantities of gold.

 KEY FIGURES

Austen Chamberlain (1863–1937)
Member of Lloyd George's government 1919–22 and then British foreign secretary 1924–9. He was the half-brother of Neville Chamberlain.

Aristide Briand (1862–1932)
Between 1906 and 1929 Briand headed eleven French governments and was also foreign minister from 1925 to 1932. He supported the League of Nations and Franco-German reconciliation. He was awarded the Nobel Peace Prize jointly with Stresemann and Chamberlain.

did undertake to refer disputes with Poland and Czechoslovakia to arbitration, although he refused to recognise their frontiers with Germany as permanent. Chamberlain was quite specific that it was in Britain's interests only to guarantee the *status quo* in western Europe. He told the House of Commons in November 1925, in words that were to return to haunt the British government (see Chapter 8), that extending the guarantee to the Polish Corridor would not be worth 'the bones of a British grenadier'.

The negotiations were completed at the Locarno Conference, 5–16 October 1925, and resulted in a number of treaties that were signed on 1 December. The most important of these were agreements confirming the **inviolability** of the Franco-German and Belgian–German frontiers and the demilitarisation of the Rhineland.

The treaties were underwritten by an Anglo-Italian guarantee to assist the victims of aggression. If a relatively minor incident on one of the frontiers covered by Locarno occurred, the injured party (for example, France) would first appeal to the Council of the League of Nations (see page 128), and if the complaint was upheld, the guarantors would assist the injured state to secure compensation from the aggressor (for example, Germany). In the event of a serious violation of the treaty the guarantors could act immediately, although they would still eventually refer the issue to the council.

KEY TERM

Inviolability Not to be changed or violated.

? How does the message conveyed by Source B of the signature of the Locarno Treaties differ from that of the signing of the Treaty of Versailles on page 99?

SOURCE B

After the signing of the Locarno Treaties in 1925 in London, Briand stands in the middle of the front row; behind him, third from left, Stresemann; third row on left, Chamberlain (with monocle).

Assessing the agreements

Throughout western Europe and the USA, the Locarno Treaties were greeted with enormous enthusiasm. It appeared as if real peace had at last come. Had France now achieved the security it had for so long been seeking? Of all the Great Powers the French gained least from Locarno. It is true that France's eastern frontier was now secure, but under Locarno it could no longer threaten to occupy the Ruhr in order to bring pressure to bear on Berlin in the event of Germany breaking the Treaty of Versailles. The British had managed to give France the illusion of security, but the provision for referring all but major violations of the Locarno Agreements to the League before taking action ensured that the British government would in practice be able to determine, through its own representative on the Council, what action, if any, it should take. For Britain there were two main advantages to Locarno: it tied France down and prevented it from repeating the Ruhr occupation. Also, by improving relations between Germany and the Western powers and by holding out the prospect of German membership of the League, it discouraged any close co-operation between Moscow and Berlin.

Locarno was deeply unpopular with the German nationalists, but for Stresemann it was the key to the gradual process of revising the treaty.

SOURCE C

From Stresemann's letter of 7 September 1925 to the former heir to the German throne, quoted in E. Sutton, editor, *Gustav Stresemann: His Diaries, Letters and Papers*, volume 3, Macmillan, 1937, p. 505.

There are three great tasks that confront German foreign policy in the more immediate future. In the first place the solution of the reparation question in a sense tolerable for Germany, and the assurance of peace, which is essential for the recovery of our strength. Secondly the protection of the Germans abroad, those 10–12 millions of our kindred who now live under a foreign yoke in foreign lands. The third great task is the readjustment of our Eastern frontiers: the recovery of Danzig, the Polish frontier, and a correction of the frontier of Upper Silesia. [He warned against] flirting with Bolshevism … they will be quite content to have Bolshevized Europe as far as the Elbe and they will leave the rest of Germany to be devoured by the French … the most important thing … is the liberation of German territory from foreign occupation. We must first get the strangler from our neck. Therefore German policy must in this respect consist first in showing finesse [skill].

> According to Stresemann in Source C, what are the aims of German foreign policy?

By assuring Germany of peace in the west, and by not placing its eastern frontiers with Poland under international guarantee, Locarno left open the eventual possibility of revision of the German–Polish frontier. Stresemann's aims were therefore diametrically opposed to Briand's, but both desired peace and therein lay the real importance of Locarno. It was a symbol of a new age of reconciliation and co-operation. Locarno, as Ramsay MacDonald (1866–1937), the leader of the British Labour Party, observed, brought about a 'miraculous change' of psychology on the Continent.

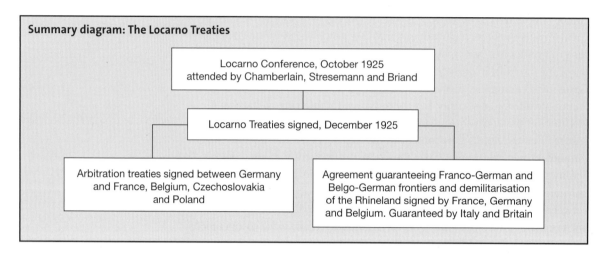

Summary diagram: The Locarno Treaties

Locarno Conference, October 1925 attended by Chamberlain, Stresemann and Briand

Locarno Treaties signed, December 1925

Arbitration treaties signed between Germany and France, Belgium, Czechoslovakia and Poland

Agreement guaranteeing Franco-German and Belgo-German frontiers and demilitarisation of the Rhineland signed by France, Germany and Belgium. Guaranteed by Italy and Britain

3 The 'Locarno spirit' and Germany's re-emergence as a Great Power

▶ *To what extent did the Locarno Treaties lead to a revision of the Treaty of Versailles?*

KEY TERMS

Locarno spirit The optimistic mood of reconciliation and compromise that swept through Europe after the signing of the Locarno Treaties.

Fulfilment A policy by Germany aimed at extracting concessions from Britain and France by at least temporarily accepting the main demands of the Treaty of Versailles.

Détente A process of lessened tension or growing relaxation between two states.

The '**Locarno spirit**' was an elusive concept which was interpreted differently in London, Paris and Berlin. All three powers agreed that it involved goodwill and concessions, yet the scope and timing of these concessions were a matter of constant and often bitter debate. Both Stresemann and Briand had to convince their peoples that the Locarno policy was working. Briand had to show that he was not giving too much away, while Stresemann had to satisfy German public opinion that his policy of '**fulfilment**' was resulting in real concessions from the ex-Allies. It can be argued that the survival not only of Stresemann's policy but possibly of the German Republic itself depended on ever more ambitious diplomatic successes. What would happen once these were unobtainable?

Stresemann's initial successes and failures 1925–7

The atmosphere of *détente* created by Locarno quickly led to the evacuation of the Cologne zone in January 1926, and in September 1926 Germany at last joined the League of Nations and received a permanent seat on the Council.

Stresemann exploited every opportunity both inside and outside the League to accelerate the revision of Versailles. In 1926 he attempted to exploit France's financial weakness by proposing that Germany pay the French nearly 1.5 billion gold marks, most of which Germany would raise in the USA by the sale of bonds. In return, France would evacuate the Rhineland and give back the Saar and its coalmines to Germany. Despite initial interest, the plan was rejected in December. The French government's finances had, contrary to expectation, improved, and it also emerged that the US government was not ready to approve the sale of more German bonds to US investors.

Stresemann did, however, manage to extract further concessions from both Britain and France. In January 1927 the Allied Disarmament Commission was withdrawn from Germany, and in the following August Britain, France and Belgium withdrew a further 10,000 troops from their garrisons in the Rhineland.

The Young Plan and the evacuation of the Rhineland

Two years later Stresemann achieved his greatest success when he managed to negotiate a permanent reduction in reparations with an Anglo-French evacuation of the Rhineland five years before the Treaty of Versailles required it. At The Hague Conference in 1929, under the terms of the **Young** Plan, the overall reparation sum was reduced from 132 billion gold marks to 112 billion, to be paid over the course of 59 years, and Britain and France agreed to evacuate the Rhineland in 1930.

The agreement to end the Rhineland occupation helped to make the Young Plan acceptable in Germany, but even so in December the government faced a referendum forced on them by the Nazi and Nationalist parties declaring that its signature would be an act of high treason on the grounds that Germany was still committed by it to paying reparations. This was easily defeated and the Young Plan was officially implemented on 20 January 1930.

Proposals for a European customs union and a common currency

With the evacuation of the Rhineland, Germany's restoration to the status of a great European power was virtually complete. Briand, like his successors in the 1950s, appears to have come to the conclusion that Germany could only be peacefully contained through some form of European federation. At the tenth assembly of the League of Nations in 1929, he outlined an ambitious, but vague scheme for creating 'some kind of federal link … between the peoples of Europe'.

Stresemann reacted favourably and urged both a European customs union and a common currency. Briand was then entrusted by the 27 European members of the League with the task of formulating his plan more precisely; but when it was circulated to the chancelleries of Europe in May 1930, the whole economic and political climate had dramatically changed. Stresemann had died and the

KEY FIGURE

Owen D. Young (1874–1962)

US industrialist, businessman, lawyer and diplomat. He chaired the committee that proposed what came to be called the Young Plan.

SOURCE D

From Aristide Briand's speech to the Assembly of the League of Nations, Plenary Session, 5 September 1929, pp. 51–2.

I believe there should be some kind of federal link between peoples who are grouped together geographically, like the peoples of Europe. These peoples should be able to come into contact at any time to discuss their common interests, and to make a joint resolution … Obviously the association will function most of all in the economic field … this is the most immediate necessity … I am also sure, however, that from the political or social point of view, the federal link could be beneficial, without interfering with the sovereignty of any of the nations which might form part of an association of this kind.

🔑 KEY FIGURE

Heinrich Brüning (1885–1970)

Leader of the German Centre Party and chancellor of Germany 1930–2.

🔑 KEY TERM

Federation A system of government in which several countries or regions form a unity but still manage to remain self-governing in internal affairs.

political crisis in Germany caused by the onset of the Great Depression (see page 144) brought to power a government under **Heinrich Brüning** that was more interested in a customs union with Austria than in a European **federation**. The German cabinet finally rejected the memorandum on 8 July 1930. A week later it was also rejected by Britain.

It is tempting to argue that Briand's plans for a European federation, which were killed off by the economic crisis that was eventually to bring Hitler to power, were one of the lost opportunities of history. On the other hand, it would be a mistake to view them through the eyes of early twenty-first-century European federalists. Essentially, Stresemann hoped that it would open the door to an accelerated revision of the Treaty of Versailles, while Briand calculated that it would have the opposite effect. Perhaps under favourable circumstances it could at least have provided a framework within which Franco-German differences could have been solved.

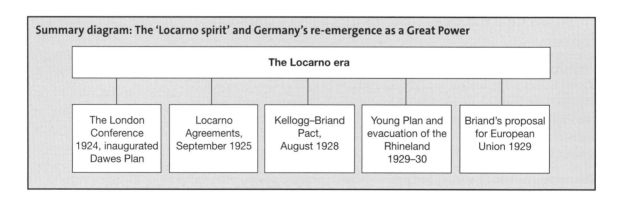

Summary diagram: The 'Locarno spirit' and Germany's re-emergence as a Great Power

The Locarno era				
The London Conference 1924, inaugurated Dawes Plan	Locarno Agreements, September 1925	Kellogg–Briand Pact, August 1928	Young Plan and evacuation of the Rhineland 1929–30	Briand's proposal for European Union 1929

Russia and eastern Europe during the Locarno era

▶ *What were the aims of Russian foreign policy towards Germany 1924–9?*

Russia and Germany

The Soviet government, which after the death of Lenin in January 1924 increasingly fell under the control of Stalin (see page 154), viewed the progress made in stabilising western Europe through the Dawes Plan and the Locarno Agreements with both dismay and hostility, as it feared that this would strengthen the anti-Bolshevik forces in Europe and delay revolution in Germany. The Soviets initially attempted to deflect Stresemann from his Locarno policy, first with the offer of a military alliance against Poland, and then, when that did not work, with the contradictory threat of joining with France to guarantee Poland's western frontiers.

Stresemann, aware of the USSR's attempts to stir up revolution in Germany in 1923, was not ready to abandon the Locarno policy, but he was anxious to keep open his links with Moscow and consolidate the Rapallo Agreement of 1922 (see page 109), if only as a possible insurance against Anglo-French pressure in the west. Thus, the Soviets were able first to negotiate a commercial treaty with Germany in October 1925. Then in April 1926, at a time when the Poles and the French were trying to delay Germany's membership of the League council, they persuaded Stresemann to sign the German–Soviet Treaty of Friendship (the Berlin Treaty). Essentially, this was a neutrality pact in which both powers agreed to remain neutral if either party was attacked by a third power.

Anglo-Russian relations

Relations between Russia and Britain sharply deteriorated when the incoming Conservative government refused in October 1924 to ratify the Anglo-Soviet General Treaty which had been negotiated by the outgoing Labour administration. In 1927, after ordering a raid on the offices of the official Soviet trading company, Arcos, in an attempt to discover evidence of espionage, the British government severed all official relations with Russia. Only in 1929, with the return of Labour, were ambassadors again exchanged. This outbreak of the first 'Anglo-Soviet cold war', as US historian Jon Jacobson has called it, strengthened Stalin's determination to cut Russia off from the West. Increasingly, the main thrust of Soviet foreign policy in the late 1920s was to exploit anti-Western feeling in the Middle East, China and India.

France and eastern Europe

With the victory of the Bolsheviks in the Russian Civil War, the French began to build up a series of alliances in eastern Europe to take the place of their original pre-war alliance with Tsarist Russia (see page 30). In March 1921 they concluded an alliance with Poland which, because it was hated by Russia and Germany and was on bad terms with Czechoslovakia and Lithuania, was the most vulnerable of the east European states. Further French attempts to strengthen it met with little success. Paris failed to persuade Stresemann to agree to a guarantee of Poland's frontiers or to ensure that Poland gained a permanent seat on the League council. In 1925–6 it even looked as if the Polish state would suffer financial collapse, but by 1927 its financial position stabilised and for the time being the USSR and Germany had to tolerate its existence.

The French were less successful in organising the other new states created by Versailles into a defensive alliance against Germany. In August 1920 Czechoslovakia and Yugoslavia signed a pact which became known as the Little *Entente,* and were joined by Romania in 1921. However, it was primarily directed against Hungary and was designed to prevent the return of the Habsburgs and the revision of the Trianon Treaty. Only in 1924 did Paris succeed in concluding a treaty with Czechoslovakia but, again, it was not strictly an anti-German alignment. It would only come into operation in the event of a restoration of the royal families of Austria or Germany or of an Austrian *Anschluss* with Germany. Despite attempts by Italy to challenge French influence in the Balkans, the French government was able to exploit the suspicions caused by the growth of Italian influence in Albania to sign first a treaty with Romania guaranteeing its frontiers (1926) and then a treaty of friendship with Yugoslavia (1927). By the end of the decade French influence was preponderant in the Balkans.

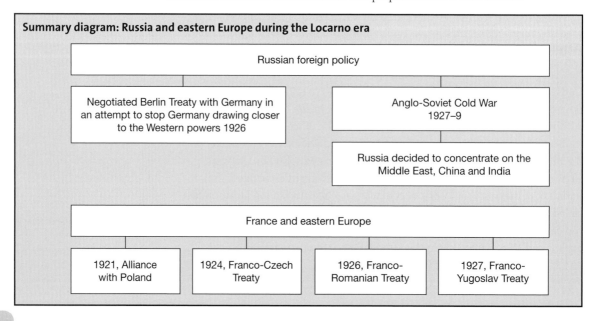

Summary diagram: Russia and eastern Europe during the Locarno era

Russian foreign policy

Negotiated Berlin Treaty with Germany in an attempt to stop Germany drawing closer to the Western powers 1926

Anglo-Soviet Cold War 1927–9

Russia decided to concentrate on the Middle East, China and India

France and eastern Europe

1921, Alliance with Poland

1924, Franco-Czech Treaty

1926, Franco-Romanian Treaty

1927, Franco-Yugoslav Treaty

5 Development of the League of Nations

▶ *How successful was the League of Nations?*

▶ *How did the League of Nations work?*

The League was a part of the international settlements negotiated in 1919–20. Inevitably, the tensions and divisions inherent in these were also present in the League. The absence in 1920 of Germany, Russia and the USA from the League reflected the reality of the international situation where both Germany and the Russia licked their wounds in defensive isolation, while the US government, after having played such a key role in negotiating the new peace settlement, had been forced by Congress to disengage from most of its international responsibilities. The League's ultimate success or failure was dependent on the progress made by the Great Powers in stabilising Europe after the First World War. Not surprisingly, the League's golden age coincided with the new stability created by the Locarno era.

The Covenant of the League of Nations

In retrospect, it is possible to argue that the League's Covenant, or constitution, provided too many loopholes for war, supported the *status quo* which favoured the Great Powers and, in the final analysis, lacked the machinery for collective action against an aggressor. Yet even if it had had a theoretically perfect constitution, would its history have been any different?

SOURCE E

From the official British commentary on the Covenant quoted in F.S. Northedge, *The League of Nations, Its Life and Times, 1920–1946*, Leicester University Press, 1986, p. 54.

[The ultimate and most effective sanction] must be the public opinion of the civilised world. If the nations of the future are in the main selfish, grasping and warlike, no instrument or machinery will restrain them. It is only possible to establish an organisation which may make peaceful co-operation easy and hence customary, and to trust in the influence of custom to mould opinion.

Study Source E. What point is the commentary making?

The organs of the League of Nations

The initial members of the League were the 32 Allied states which had signed the peace treaties and twelve neutral states. By 1926 all the ex-enemy states including Germany had joined, but the USSR did not do so until 1934, and the USA never did. The League at first consisted of three main organs: the Assembly, the Council and the Permanent Secretariat.

KEY TERMS

Deliberative chamber An assembly appointed to debate or discuss issues.

Executive committee A committee which can take key decisions.

The Assembly

The Assembly was essentially a **deliberative chamber** where each state, regardless of its size, was allotted three representatives. It was a jealously guarded principle that even the smallest state had the right to be heard on international issues.

The Council

The Council in 1920 had four permanent members: Britain, France, Italy and Japan. In 1926 this was increased by one when Germany joined. The smaller states were represented by a changing rota of four temporary members, later increased to seven, who were all selected by the Assembly. As the Council met more frequently than the Assembly and was dominated by the Great Powers, it gradually developed as an **executive committee** or 'cabinet' of the Assembly, and worked out the details and implementation of policies which the Assembly had endorsed in principle. Decisions in both bodies were normally taken by unanimous vote. The votes of states involved in a dispute under discussion by the League were discounted when the Assembly and Council voted on recommendations for its settlement. In this way they could be prevented from vetoing an otherwise unanimous decision.

SOURCE F

What information does Source F convey about the League of Nations?

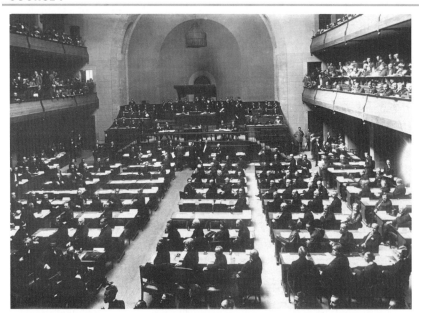

Ambassadors from around the world assemble in the Reformation Hall at Geneva's Palais de Nations, for the first session of the League of Nations, in November 1920. The formation of the League was one of the results of the peace settlements of 1919–20.

Permanent Secretariat

The routine administrative work of the League was carried out by the Permanent Secretariat, which was staffed by a relatively small **international civil service**.

Permanent Court of International Justice

In 1921 a fourth organ was added to the League when the Permanent Court of International Justice was set up at The Hague in the Netherlands with the task of both advising the council on legal matters and judging cases submitted to it by individual states.

What powers did the League of Nations possess to solve international disputes?

The heart of the Covenant, Articles 8–17, was primarily concerned with the overriding question of the prevention of war. The League's long-term strategy for creating a peaceful world was summed up in the first section of Article 8:

> *The members of the League recognise that the maintenance of peace requires the reduction of national armaments to the lowest point consistent with national safety, and the enforcement by common action of international obligations.*

The process for solving disputes between sovereign powers was defined in Articles 12–17. Initially (Article 12), disputes were to be submitted to some form of arbitration or inquiry by the League. While this was happening, there was to be a cooling-off period of three months. By Article 13 members were committed to carrying out the judgements of the Permanent Court of International Justice or the recommendations of the Council. Even if a dispute was not submitted to arbitration, the Council was empowered by Article 15 to set up an inquiry into its origins. The assumption in these articles was that states would be only too willing to eliminate war by making use of the League's arbitration machinery. If, however, a state ignored the League's recommendations, Article 16 would be enforced (see Source G).

In Article 17 the League's powers were significantly extended by its right to intervene in disputes between non-members of the League, while in Article 11 member states were encouraged to refer to the assembly or council any international problem which might threaten the peace.

In theory, the League seemed to have formidable powers, but it was not a world government in the making, with powers to coerce independent nations. Its existence was based, as Article 10 made clear, on the recognition of the political and territorial independence of all member states. Article 15, for instance, recognised that if a dispute arose from an internal issue, the League had no right to intervene. There were, too, several gaps in the League Covenant which allowed a potential aggressor to wage war without sanction. War had to be officially declared before the League could act effectively. It had, for instance,

KEY TERM

International civil service
A permanent administration made up of officials from all the member states.

? What powers, according to Source G, does Article 16 ultimately give the League if its recommendations were ignored by a state?

SOURCE G

From Article 16 of the Constitution of the League of Nations, quoted in F.S. Northedge, *The League of Nations, Its Life and Times, 1920–1946*, Leicester University Press, 1986, p. 323.

I. Should any member of the League resort to war in disregard of its Covenants under Articles 12, 13 and 15, it shall … be deemed to have committed an act of war against all other members of the League, which hereby undertake immediately to subject it to the severance of all trade or financial relations …

II. It shall be the duty of the Council in such case to recommend to the several governments concerned what effective military, naval or air force the members of the League shall severally contribute to the armed forces to be used to protect the covenants of the League.

III. The members of the League agree further that they will mutually support one another in the financial and economic measures which are taken under this Article … and they will mutually support one another in resisting any special measures aimed at one of their number by the Covenant-breaking state and they will take the necessary steps to afford passage through their territory to the forces of any members of the League which are co-operating to protect the Covenants of the League.

no formula for dealing with acts of guerrilla warfare, which the instigating state could disown. Even in the event of a formal declaration of war, if the International Court or the Council could not agree on a verdict, then League members were free to continue with their war.

The League of Nations struggles to find a role

In January 1920 the governments of the Great Powers viewed the League with either cynicism or open hostility. The French doubted its ability to outlaw war, while the Germans saw it as a means for enforcing the hated Versailles Treaty. For a short time after the Republican victory in November 1920, the US government was openly hostile to the League and its officials were instructed to avoid any co-operation with the organisation.

Under the Treaty of Versailles the League was responsible for the administration of the Saar and Danzig (see pages 95–6). This inevitably involved the danger of it becoming too closely associated with the policy of the Allies. Indeed, in the Saar, it made the mistake of appointing a French chairman to the governing commission which then administered the territory in the interests of France. The League was also the guarantor of the agreements, signed by the Allies and the successor states created in 1919, which were aimed at ensuring that the various racial minorities left isolated behind the new frontiers enjoyed full civil rights.

The mandates

Article 22 of the Covenant marked a potentially revolutionary new concept in international affairs: see Source H.

SOURCE H

From Article 22 of the Constitution of the League of Nations, quoted in F.S. Northedge, *The League of Nations, Its Life and Times, 1920–1946*, Leicester University Press, 1986, pp. 324–5.

To those colonies and territories, which as a consequence of the late war, have ceased to be under the sovereignty of the states which have formerly governed them, and which are inhabited by peoples not yet able to stand by themselves under the strenuous conditions of the modern world, there should be applied the principle that the well-being and development of such peoples should form a sacred trust of civilisation, and that securities for the performance of this trust should be embodied in this Covenant.

What is meant in Source H by the phrase 'sacred trust of civilisation'?

When the Allies distributed the former German and Turkish territories among themselves, they were divided into three groups according to how developed they were. The most 'advanced' were in the Middle East, while the most 'backward' were the ex-German islands in the Pacific. The League was determined to avoid becoming a façade for colonialism in a new form. Thus, mandate powers were required to send in annual reports on their territories to the League's Permanent Mandates Commission, which rapidly gained a formidable reputation for its expertise and authority.

The League's attitude towards the mandates was by modern standards paternalistic and condescending, but nevertheless, as Northedge has argued, 'it helped transform the entire climate of colonialism', since the imperialist powers were forced by moral pressure to consider the interests of the native populations and to begin to contemplate the possibility of their eventual independence.

The League's welfare, medical and economic work

Economic and financial work

The League was excluded from dealing with the key financial issues of reparations and war debts, but nevertheless in 1922 its Financial Committee was entrusted by the Allied leaders with the task of rebuilding first Austria's and then Hungary's economy. Its Economic Committee had the far greater task of attempting to persuade the powers to abolish **protection** and create a worldwide **free-trade zone**. It organised two world economic conferences, held in 1927 and 1933, which both the USSR and the USA attended. But not surprisingly, given the strongly protectionist economic climate of the times, it failed to make any progress towards free trade.

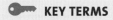 **KEY TERMS**

Protection Stopping foreign goods by levying tariffs or taxes on imports.

Free-trade zone An area where countries can trade freely without restrictions.

The International Labour Organisation

One of the greatest successes of the League was the International Labour Organisation (ILO). This had originally been created as an independent organisation by the Treaty of Versailles, but it was financed by the League. In some ways it was a league in miniature. It had its own permanent labour office at Geneva, staffed by 1000 officials. Its work was discussed annually by a conference of labour delegates. Right up to 1939 the ILO turned out an impressive stream of reports, recommendations and statistics which provided important information for a wide range of industries all over the world.

Health Organisation

The League's Health Organisation provided an invaluable forum for drawing up common policies on such matters as the treatment of diseases, the design of hospitals and health education. The League also set up committees to advise on limiting the production of opium and other addictive drugs, on the outlawing of the sale of women and children for prostitution and on the effective abolition of slavery.

The League as peacemaker and arbitrator 1920–5

Until 1926, when the foreign ministers of Britain, France and Germany began to attend the meetings of the Council and turn it into a body which regularly discussed the main problems of the day, the League of Nation role in the many post-war crises was subordinated to the Allied leaders and the Conference of Ambassadors, which had been set up to supervise the carrying out of the Treaty of Versailles (see page 107). For the most part it therefore dealt with minor crises only.

In 1920 the inability of the League to act effectively without the backing of the Great Powers was clearly demonstrated when it failed to protect Armenia from a joint Russo-Turkish attack, as neither Britain, France nor Italy was ready to protect it with force. One of the French delegates caustically observed in the Assembly that he and his colleagues were 'in the ridiculous position of an Assembly which considers what steps should be taken, though it is perfectly aware that it is impossible for them to be carried out'.

Polish–Lithuanian quarrel over Vilna

In October 1920, in response to appeals from the Polish foreign minister, the League negotiated an armistice between Poland and Lithuania, whose quarrel over border territories was rapidly escalating into war. The ceasefire did not, however, hold, as shortly afterwards **General Żeligowski** with a Polish force, which the Warsaw government diplomatically pretended was acting on its own initiative, occupied the city of Vilna and set up the new puppet government of Central Lithuania under his protection. The League first called for a plebiscite and then, when this was rejected, attempted in vain to negotiate a compromise

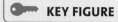

KEY FIGURE

Lucjan Żeligowski (1865–1947)

A Polish general of Lithuanian origin. He fought in both the First World War and the Polish–Soviet War.

settlement. In March 1922 Poland finally annexed Vilna province. A year later, after it was obvious that the League could not impose a solution without the support of the Great Powers, the Conference of Ambassadors took the matter into its own hands and recognised Polish sovereignty over Vilna. Britain, France and Italy, by failing to use the machinery of the League to stop Polish aggression, had again effectively marginalised it.

The Aaland Islands dispute

In less stubborn disputes, however, where the states involved were willing to accept a verdict, the League did have an important role to play as mediator. The League enjoyed a rare success in the dispute between Finland and Sweden over the Aaland Islands. These had belonged to the Grand Duchy of Finland when it had been part of the Russian Empire. Once Finland had broken away from Russia in 1917, the islanders, who were ethnically Swedish, appealed to Stockholm to take over the islands. When Sweden began to threaten to use force, the British referred the matter to the League. In 1921 the League supported the *status quo* by leaving the islands under Finnish sovereignty, but insisted on itself ensuring the civil rights of the Swedish population there. Neither government liked the verdict, but both accepted it and, what is more important, made it work.

Albania, Upper Silesia, Memel and the Ruhr

In the second half of 1921 the League did serve as a useful means of focusing the attention of the Great Powers on the plight of Albania when it urgently appealed for help against Greek and Yugoslav aggression. As the Conference of Ambassadors had not yet finally fixed its frontiers, the Greeks and Yugoslavs were exploiting the ambiguous situation to occupy as much Albanian territory as they could. The Council responded by dispatching a commission of inquiry, but it took a telegram from Lloyd George, the British prime minister, both to galvanise the Conference of Ambassadors into finalising the frontiers and to push the League Council into threatening economic sanctions against Yugoslavia if it did not recognise them. When this was successful, the League was then entrusted with supervising the Yugoslav withdrawal. Thus, in this crisis the League had played a useful but again secondary role to the Allied powers. The fact that the Conference of Ambassadors then made Italy the protector of Albania's independence indicates where the real power lay.

In August 1921 the League played a key role in solving the bitter Anglo-French dispute over the Upper Silesian plebiscite, which was referred to the League Council (see page 108). It again proved useful in the protracted dispute over Memel. When the Lithuanians objected to the decision by the Conference of Ambassadors to internationalise the port of Memel, and seized the port themselves in 1923, the League was the obvious body to sort out the problem. Its decision for Lithuania was accepted by Britain and France.

Attempts by Britain and Sweden to refer the question of the Ruhr occupation of 1923 (see page 110) to the League were blocked by the French, who had no intention of allowing the League to mediate between themselves and the Germans.

The Corfu incident

In the Corfu incident of August–September 1923 the League's efforts to intervene were yet again blocked by a major power. The crisis was triggered by the assassination in Greek territory near the Albanian frontier of three Italians, who were part of an Allied team tracing the Albanian frontiers for the Conference of Ambassadors. Mussolini, the Italian Fascist leader, who had come to power the preceding October (see his profile below), immediately seized the chance to issue a deliberately unacceptable ultimatum to Athens. When the Greeks rejected three of its demands, Italian troops occupied Corfu. The Greeks wanted to refer the incident to the League, while the Italians insisted that the Conference of Ambassadors should deal with it. The Conference, while initially accepting some assistance from the League, nevertheless ultimately settled the case itself and insisted that Greece should pay 50 million lire in compensation to Italy. Once this was agreed, Italian forces were withdrawn from Corfu. The Corfu incident, like the Ruhr crisis, underlined the continuing ability of the major powers to ignore the League and to take unilateral action when it pleased them.

Benito Mussolini

1883	Born in Romagna in Italy
1904–14	Socialist agitator and journalist
1915–18	Supported the war against Germany
1919	Founded the Italian Fascist Party
1922–43	Gained power in Italy and gradually established a Fascist dictatorship
1943–5	After the Allied invasion of Italy he was kept in power in northern Italy by the Nazis
1945	Captured and shot by Italian partisans

Mussolini was the son of a blacksmith and originally a socialist, but was expelled from the party when he supported Italy's entry into the war. He created the Fascist Party in 1919 and successfully exploited the post-war economic crisis, fear of Bolshevism and disappointment with the peace treaties to gain power in 1922. By 1929 he had consolidated his position and established a one-party government. Mussolini was determined to re-establish the Roman Empire and turn the Mediterranean into an 'Italian lake'. In October 1935 Italian forces invaded Abyssinia and in May 1936 Mussolini declared it part of the Italian Empire.

Mussolini's fatal mistake was to enter the Second World War as an ally of Hitler in June 1940 on the assumption that Germany would win. After a series of defeats in Greece and North Africa, the Germans had to send troops to stop Italy from being knocked out of the war. From that point on Italy became a German satellite. In the 1930s Hitler had been a great admirer of Mussolini and in many ways regarded him as a role model.

The League's successes: Mosul and the Greco-Bulgarian dispute

In 1924 the League was confronted with another crisis involving a greater power and a lesser power. On this occasion it was able to mediate successfully. It provided a face-saving means of retreat for Turkey in its dispute with Britain over the future of Mosul, which according to the Treaty of Lausanne (see page 106) was to be decided by direct Anglo-Turkish negotiations. When these talks broke down and the British issued in October 1924 an ultimatum to Turkey to withdraw its forces within 48 hours, the League intervened and recommended a temporary demarcation line, behind which the Turkish forces withdrew. It then sent a commission of inquiry to consult the local Kurdish population, which, as total independence was not an option, preferred British to Turkish rule. The League's recommendation that Mosul should become a mandate of Iraq for 25 years was then accepted. As Iraq was a British mandate, this effectively put it under British control.

In October 1925, the League's handling of the Greco-Bulgarian border conflict, like its solution to the Aaland Islands dispute, was to be a rare example of a complete success. When the Bulgarians appealed to the Council, its request for a ceasefire was heeded immediately by both sides. So too was the verdict of its commission of inquiry, which found in favour of Bulgaria.

Ending the Greco-Bulgarian conflict was an impressive example of what the League could do, and in the autumn of 1925 this success, together with the new 'Locarno spirit', seemed to auger well for the future. Briand was able to claim at the meeting of the Council in October 1925 that 'a nation which appealed to the League when it felt that its existence was threatened, could be sure that the Council would be at its post ready to undertake its work of conciliation'.

The League was not put to the test again until the Manchurian crisis of 1931. Unfortunately, Briand's optimism was then shown to be premature (see Chapter 9). The League could function well only if the Great Powers were in agreement.

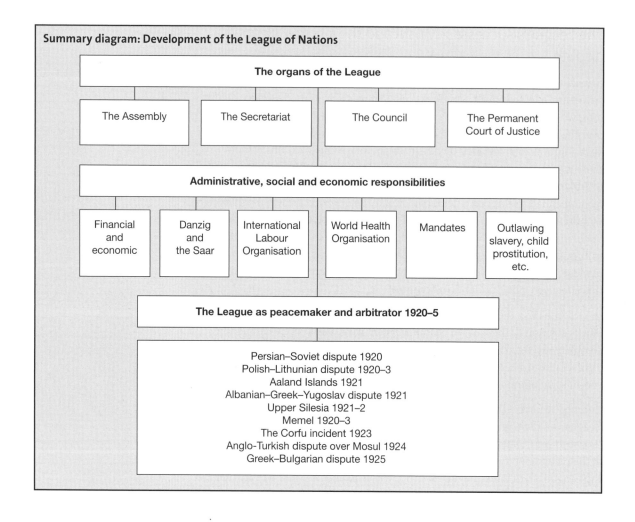

Summary diagram: Development of the League of Nations

The organs of the League

| The Assembly | The Secretariat | The Council | The Permanent Court of Justice |

Administrative, social and economic responsibilities

| Financial and economic | Danzig and the Saar | International Labour Organisation | World Health Organisation | Mandates | Outlawing slavery, child prostitution, etc. |

The League as peacemaker and arbitrator 1920–5

Persian–Soviet dispute 1920
Polish–Lithunian dispute 1920–3
Aaland Islands 1921
Albanian–Greek–Yugoslav dispute 1921
Upper Silesia 1921–2
Memel 1920–3
The Corfu incident 1923
Anglo-Turkish dispute over Mosul 1924
Greek–Bulgarian dispute 1925

 Progress towards disarmament

▶ *Why did Britain reject the Geneva Protocol?*

▶ *What role did the USA play in the disarmament question 1921–33?*

 **KEY TERM**

Collective security
Security gained through joining an alliance or signing an agreement where the security of each state is guaranteed by the others.

The Geneva Protocol

One of the major tasks of the League was to work out an acceptable world disarmament programme. Disarmament, however, could not be divorced from the question of security, for if a state did not feel secure, it would hardly disarm. To solve this problem the League in 1924 drafted an ambitious **collective security** agreement, the Geneva Protocol, but this was rejected by the British, who feared that it would commit them to policing the world.

Washington Conference and Five-Power Naval Treaty

With the USA outside the League, the twin problems of growing Anglo-American naval rivalry and deteriorating US–Japanese relations in the Pacific could only be tackled by negotiations between the powers concerned. By 1919 the USA had become alarmed by the rise of Japanese power in the Pacific. Japan, already possessing the third largest navy in the world, had begun a major naval construction programme. The USA responded by forming a Pacific fleet and embarking on its own formidable building programme, which, when completed, would make the US navy the largest in the world.

This escalation in battleship building pushed Britain in early 1921 into announcing its own naval programme, but privately it told Washington that it desired a negotiated settlement as it could not afford a naval race. **President Harding** was anxious both to reduce armaments and to economise, but he would only negotiate with Britain if it agreed to terminate the twenty-year-old Anglo-Japanese Alliance, which, theoretically at least, could have involved Britain as Japan's ally in a war against the USA (see page 34). As the treaty was due for renewal in July 1921, the British and Japanese agreed under pressure from Washington to replace it by a new four-power treaty, which committed Britain, France, Japan and the USA to respect each other's possessions in the Pacific and to refer any dispute arising out of this agreement to a conference of the four signatory powers.

With the Anglo-Japanese Treaty out of the way, the first Washington Naval Convention was signed in February 1922 for a duration of fourteen years. It halted the building of capital ships for ten years, provided for the scrapping of certain battleships and battle cruisers, and, for those capital ships which were spared the breaker's yard, established a ratio of three for Japan and 1.67 each for Italy and France to every five for Britain and the USA. In 1930 the five powers in the London Naval Treaty agreed to extend the main principle of this agreement to smaller fighting ships.

Kellogg–Briand Pact

From 1922 onwards the USA's attitude towards the League began to alter. The Americans saw the value of participating in some of the League's committees on social, economic and health matters, and President Harding even considered US membership of the Permanent Court of International Justice in 1923, but the Senate again vetoed it. When the League set up a Preparatory Commission in 1926 to prepare for a world disarmament conference, both the USA and the USSR participated.

Peace movements, such as the **Carnegie Endowment for International Peace**, put considerable moral pressure on the US government to play a greater role in the disarmament question. In March 1927, Professor Shotwell, a director of the Carnegie Endowment, on a visit to Paris persuaded Briand to propose a

 KEY FIGURE

Warren Harding (1865–1923)

US President 1921–3. He was a Republican and had been an opponent of President Wilson's internationalism.

 KEY TERM

Carnegie Endowment for International Peace
An organisation founded by industrialist Andrew Carnegie. It describes itself as being dedicated to advancing co-operation between nations.

Frank B. Kellogg (1856–1937)

US lawyer, statesman, senator and secretary of state. He was awarded the Nobel Peace Prize in 1929 for his part in negotiating the Kellogg–Briand Pact.

? What, according to Source I, do the signatory powers of the Kellogg–Briand Pact agree to?

Franco-US pact that would outlaw war. **Frank B. Kellogg**, the US secretary of state, replied cautiously in December and suggested a general pact between as many states as possible, rejecting war 'as an instrument of national policy'. On 27 August 1928 the Kellogg–Briand Peace Pact was signed by fifteen states, and by 1933 a further 50 had joined it.

SOURCE I

From the Kellogg–Briand Pact, quoted in R. Birley, editor, *Speeches and Documents in American History, 1914–1939*, volume IV, Oxford University Press, 1951, pp. 83–4.

1. The high contracting powers solemnly declare in the names of their respective peoples that they condemn recourse to war for the solution of international controversies, and renounce it as an instrument of national policy in their relations with one another.

2. The high contracting parties agree that the settlement or solution of all disputes or conflicts of whatever nature or of whatever origin they may be, which may arise among them, shall never be sought except by pacific means.

3. This treaty … shall remain open … for adherence by all other powers of the world.

Optimists saw the pact as supplementing the Covenant. It outlawed war, while the League had the necessary machinery for setting up commissions of inquiry and implementing cooling-off periods in the event of a dispute. Pessimists, however, pointed to the fact that it was just a general declaration of intention, which did not commit its members. Perhaps, in reality, all that could be said for it was that it would give the US government a moral basis on which it could intervene in world affairs, should it desire to do so.

The World Disarmament Conference 1932–4

In 1930 the Preparatory Commission, after protracted discussions on different models of disarmament, produced its final draft for an international convention. The League's Council called the long-awaited World Disarmament Conference in February 1932 at Geneva. It could not have been convened at a more unfortunate time: the Manchurian crisis (see Chapter 9) had weakened the League, the rise of nationalism in Germany was making France and Poland less likely to compromise over German demands for equality in armaments, while the impact of the Great Depression on the USA was reviving the isolationist tendencies of the early 1920s. Long before the Germans withdrew in November 1933 (see page 147) it was clear that the conference would fail.

Summary diagram: Progress towards disarmament

1922	Washington Naval Convention	Halted building of capital ships for 10 years Established ratio of capital ships comprising three for Japan and 1.67 for Italy and France to every five for Britain and the USA
1924	Geneva Protocol	Attempted to provide worldwide security by obliging members of the League to come to the assistance of any state which was the victim of aggression and was situated in the same continent as themselves – rejected by Britain
1928	Kellogg–Briand Pact	Rejected war as a 'national instrument' – by 1933 65 states had signed it
1932–4	World Disarmament Conference	Failed to achieve any agreement. November 1933, Germany withdrew

Chapter summary

The acceptance of the Dawes Plan and the signature of the Locarno Agreements together marked a fresh start after the bitterness of the immediate post-war years. For the next four years the pace of international co-operation quickened and the League of Nations, despite a hesitant start, grew in authority and influence. After Germany joined the League in 1926 a new framework for Great Power co-operation evolved. The foreign ministers of Britain, France and Germany regularly attended the meetings of the League Council and Assembly and played a key part in drawing up their agenda and influencing their decisions. The partnership of these three statesmen came to symbolise the new era of peace and apparent stabilisation. However, good relations between the Western powers were viewed with suspicion by the USSR, which feared an anti-Bolshevik alliance.

These years also marked the partial end of US isolation. The US played a key role in negotiating the Washington Naval Convention and ending the Franco-German deadlock over reparations through the Dawes Plan. It was also one of the principal architects of the Kellogg–Briand Pact. The Great Depression and rise of nationalism in Germany ensured the failure of the World Disarmament Conference in 1932–4 and effectively the end of the Locarno era.

Refresher questions

Use these questions to remind yourself of the key material covered in this chapter.

1 What were the recommendations of the Dawes Plan?

2 What was the reaction of the British, French and Germans to the Dawes Plan?

3 What steps were taken to ensure that France would not again be able to act alone if Germany defaulted on reparation payments?

4 What were the terms of the Locarno Treaties?

5 What was the 'Locarno spirit' and how justified was it?

6 What did Stresemann achieve at The Hague Conference in 1929?

7 Why did Briand's proposals for a European federation fail?

8 Why were relations so bad between Britain and the USSR 1924–9?

9 To what extent did France consolidate its influence in eastern Europe?

10 How effective were the League's powers for solving international disputes?

11 How effective was the League's welfare, medical and economic work?

12 How effective was the League in solving international disputes 1920–5?

13 Why did the USA want Britain to terminate the Anglo-Japanese Treaty?

14 How important was the Kellogg–Briand Pact?

15 Why did the World Disarmament Conference fail?

 Question practice

ESSAY QUESTIONS

1 To what extent did the Locarno Agreements mark the beginning of a new era of conciliation?

2 'In the long run Stresemann's policy helped pave the way for warlike expansion' (from [the East German historian] W. Ruge, *Stresemann. Ein Lebensbild* [*A Portrait*], VEB Deutscher Verlag der Wissenschaften, 1965, p. 226). Assess the validity of this view.

3 How successful was the impact of the League of Nations on international relations during 1920–9?

4 Which of the following played the major role in creating a new and more peaceful mood in Europe in 1924–9: i) the Dawes Plan or ii) the Locarno Treaties? Explain your answer with reference to both i) and ii).

SOURCE ANALYSIS QUESTIONS

1 With reference to Sources 1, 2 and 3 (opposite), and your understanding of the historical context, assess the value of these sources to an historian studying the Locarno Treaties.

2 With reference to Sources 4, 5 and 6 (page 142), and your understanding of the historical context, assess the value of these sources to a historian studying the apparent peacefulness of the 'Locarno era' 1924–30.

SOURCE 1

From Stresemann's letter of 7 September 1925 to the former heir to the German throne, quoted in E. Sutton, editor, *Gustav Stresemann: His Diaries, Letters and Papers*, volume 3, Macmillan, 1937, p. 505.

There are three great tasks that confront German foreign policy in the more immediate future. In the first place the solution of the reparation question in a sense tolerable for Germany, and the assurance of peace, which is essential for the recovery of our strength. Secondly the protection of the Germans abroad, those 10–12 millions of our kindred who now live under a foreign yoke in foreign lands. The third great task is the readjustment of our Eastern frontiers: the recovery of Danzig, the Polish frontier, and a correction of the frontier of Upper Silesia. [He warned against] flirting with Bolshevism … they will be quite content to have Bolshevized Europe as far as the Elbe and they will leave the rest of Germany to be devoured by the French … the most important thing … is the liberation of German territory from foreign occupation. We must first get the strangler from our neck. Therefore German policy must in this respect consist first in showing finesse [skill].

SOURCE 2

From the speech of Austen Chamberlain, the British foreign minister in the House of Commons, 18 November 1925.

I believe a great work of peace has been done. I believe it above all because of the spirit in which it was done and the spirit which it has engendered. It would not have been done unless all the governments, and I will add all the nations, had felt the need to start a new and better chapter of universal relations, but it would not have been done unless this country was prepared to take her share in guaranteeing the settlements so come to ….

And we ask the House of Commons to approve the ratification of the Treaty of Locarno in the belief that by that treaty, we are averting danger from our own country and from Europe, that we are safeguarding peace, and that we are laying the foundations of reconciliation and friendship with the enemies of a few years ago.

SOURCE 3

From the Locarno Treaties.

Article 2. Germany and Belgium and also Germany and France mutually undertake that they will in no case attack or invade each other or resort to war against each other.

This stipulation shall not, however, apply in case of –

(1) The exercise of the right of legitimate defence, that is to say resistance to a violation of the undertaking contained in the previous paragraph or to a flagrant breach of articles 42 and 43 of the said Treaty of Versailles, if such breach constitutes an unprovoked act of aggression and by reason of the assembly of armed forces in the demilitarized zone immediate action is necessary.

(2) Action in pursuance of article 16 of the Covenant of the League of Nations.

Article 3 … Germany and Belgium and Germany and France undertake to settle by peaceful means … all questions of every kind which may arise between them and which it may not be possible to settle by normal methods of diplomacy.

Any questions … to which the parties are in conflict as to their respective rights shall be submitted to judicial decision … All other questions shall be submitted to a conciliation commission.

SOURCE 4

From a letter from Ramsay MacDonald, the leader of the British Labour Party, 16 June 1925, to Gilbert Murray, Professor of Greek at Oxford University.

We can make pacts and agreements by the thousand on matters which of themselves are of little importance from the point of view of possible causes of war …

The problem of security is mainly psychological, and as a matter of fact, it is met only to a small degree by coming to agreements of a military nature regarding it. It is in fact the dramatic form of a deep seated suspicion that no country is really safe from the [threats] of another

SOURCE 5

From Article 16 of the Constitution of the League of Nations.

I. Should any member of the League resort to war in disregard of its Covenants under Articles 12, 13 and 15, it shall … be deemed to have committed an act of war against all other members of the League, which hereby undertake immediately to subject it to the severance of all trade or financial relations …

II. It shall be the duty of the Council in such case to recommend to the several governments concerned what effective military, naval or air force the members of the League shall severally contribute to the armed forces to be used to protect the covenants of the League.

III. The members of the League agree further that they will mutually support one another in the financial and economic measures which are taken under this Article … and they will mutually support one another in resisting any special measures aimed at one of their number by the Covenant-breaking state and they will take the necessary steps to afford passage through their territory to the forces of any member of the League which are co-operating to protect the Covenants of the League.

SOURCE 6

From the Kellogg–Briand Pact, quoted in R. Birley, editor, *Speeches and Documents in American History, 1914–1939*, Oxford University Press, volume IV, 1951, pp. 83–4.

1. The high contracting powers solemnly declare in the names of their respective peoples that they condemn recourse to war for the solution of international controversies, and renounce it as an instrument of national policy in their relations with one another.

2. The high contracting parties agree that the settlement or solution of all disputes or conflicts of whatever nature or of whatever origin they may be, which may arise among them, shall never be sought except by pacific means.

3. This treaty shall when it has come into effect … remain open … for adherence by all other powers of the world. Every instrument evidencing the adherence of a power shall be deposited at Washington and the treaty shall immediately upon such deposit become effective.

CHAPTER 7

Democracies on the defensive 1930–6

This chapter analyses how the Great Depression unleashed forces that destroyed the peace settlement of 1919. It considers the following interlocking themes:

★ The Great Depression 1929–33

★ Hitler's rise to power

★ Reaction of the Great Powers to Nazi Germany 1933–5

★ The Abyssinian crisis 1935

★ Remilitarisation of the Rhineland

★ The Spanish Civil War

★ The Rome–Berlin Axis and the Anti-Comintern Pact

A vital question to consider is why Britain and France were unable to contain Nazi Germany and Japan. The impact of the Great Depression is one reason, but as you read through the chapter, you may come to the conclusion that lack of unity among the former victorious powers in the years 1930–6 was also important, as was the disastrous mishandling of the Abyssinian crisis.

Key dates

1929	Oct.	Wall Street Crash	1935	March	Hitler reintroduced conscription	
1929–33		Great Depression		April	Stresa Conference	
1933	Jan. 30	Hitler appointed Chancellor of Germany		May	Franco-Soviet Pact	
				June	Anglo-German Naval Agreement	
	Oct.	Germany left both League of Nations and the Disarmament Conference		Oct.	Abyssinia invaded by Italy	
			1936	March	Rhineland remilitarised	
1934	Jan.	German–Polish Non-aggression Pact		July	Start of Spanish Civil War	
				Oct.	Rome–Berlin Axis	
	July	Nazi uprising in Austria failed		Nov.	Anti-Comintern Pact	

The Great Depression 1929–33

▶ *What impact did the Great Depression have on the international situation?*

Wall Street Crash The 1929 collapse of share prices in the US stock exchange, located in Wall Street, New York.

The Great Depression, triggered by the **Wall Street Crash**, marked a turning point in inter-war history. Not only did it weaken the economic and social stability of the world's major powers, but it also dealt a devastating blow to the progress made since 1924 towards creating a new framework for peaceful international co-operation. It has been called by historian Robert Boyce 'the third global catastrophe of the century' (along with the two world wars). It is hard to exaggerate its international impact. To a great extent the economic recovery in Europe after 1924 had been dependent on short-term US loans, of which $4 billion went to Germany. After the Wall Street stock exchange crash, US investors abruptly terminated these loans and no more were forthcoming. This was a devastating blow to the European and world economies. Between 1929 and 1932 the volume of world trade fell by 70 per cent. Unemployment rose to 13 million in the USA, to 6 million in Germany and to 3 million in Britain. Japan was particularly hard hit: some 50 per cent of its mining and heavy industrial capacity was forced to close and the collapse of the US market virtually destroyed its large and lucrative export trade in silk.

Inevitably, an economic crisis on this scale had a decisive political impact:

- In Germany it helped to bring Hitler to power in January 1933.
- In Japan it strengthened the hand of an influential group of army officers who argued that only by seizing Manchuria could Japan recover from the slump.
- In Italy it prompted Mussolini to have plans drawn up for the conquest of Abyssinia.
- The Great Depression's long-term impact on the politics of the three democracies – Britain, France and USA – was equally disastrous. It delayed their rearmament programmes and created an international climate in which each of the three suspected the others of causing its financial and economic difficulties. It thus prevented any effective collaboration between them at a time when it was vital both to deter the aggressive nationalism of Japan and Germany and to deal with the global economic crisis.

As international trade collapsed, the Great Powers erected tariff barriers and attempted to make themselves economically self-sufficient. The British and the French with their huge empires had a decisive advantage over the Germans, Italians and Japanese, who increasingly began to assert their right to carve out their own empires, spheres of interest, or *Lebensraum* as Hitler called it.

SOURCE A

What is the intended message of Source A?

German soldiers serving out food from their soup kitchen to unemployed and destitute civilians in 1931. The Nazi Party (see next section) successfully exploited the Great Depression to gain political support.

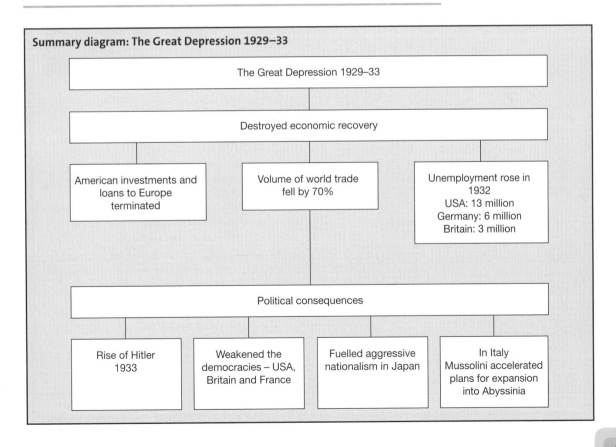

Summary diagram: The Great Depression 1929–33

The Great Depression 1929–33

Destroyed economic recovery

American investments and loans to Europe terminated

Volume of world trade fell by 70%

Unemployment rose in 1932
USA: 13 million
Germany: 6 million
Britain: 3 million

Political consequences

Rise of Hitler 1933

Weakened the democracies – USA, Britain and France

Fuelled aggressive nationalism in Japan

In Italy Mussolini accelerated plans for expansion into Abyssinia

KEY FIGURES

Franz von Papen (1879–1969)

German chancellor, May–November 1932; vice-chancellor 1933–4.

Kurt von Schleicher (1882–1934)

German chancellor, December 1932 to January 1933. Murdered by Hitler in 1934.

KEY TERMS

Putsch Takeover of power.

Élites The ruling classes.

2 Hitler's rise to power

▶ *What legacy in foreign policy did Brüning, Papen and Schleicher leave Hitler?*

▶ *What were the aims of Nazi foreign policy and what had Hitler achieved by 1935?*

The foreign policy of Hitler's predecessors 1930–3

In March 1930 Heinrich Brüning (see page 124) was appointed chancellor of a minority government supported by the German Nationalist Party (DNVP), which was later to cooperate closely with the Nazi Party. Although he and his two successors, **Franz von Papen** and **General von Schleicher**, failed to revive the German economy and so prepared the way for Hitler's rise in power in January 1933, they achieved two great successes, which assisted Hitler.

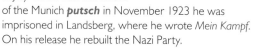

Adolf Hitler

1889	Born in Braunau am Inn, Austria-Hungary (now in Austria)
1914–18	Served in the German army
1921	Chairman of the NSDAP (Nazi Party)
1923	Played a key role in the Munich *putsch*, for which he was imprisoned for a year
1925–9	Rebuilt the Nazi Party
1933	Appointed chancellor of the German *Reich*
1936	Launched the Four-Year Plan to prepare the German economy for war
1939	Germany invaded Poland and unleashed the Second World War
1945	Killed himself in his bunker in Berlin

Adolf Hitler's father, Alois, was an Austrian customs official. Hitler left school without any qualifications in 1905 and, convinced of his artistic gifts, tried unsuccessfully to gain a place at the Academy of Fine Arts in Vienna. Up to 1914 he lived the life of an increasingly penniless artist in Vienna and Munich. He showed great interest in the current social Darwinistic, nationalist and racist thinking, which was to form the basis of his future foreign policy.

In August 1914 Hitler joined a Bavarian regiment and fought for the next four years with considerable personal bravery, winning the Iron Cross (First Class). In 1919 he joined the German Workers' Party, subsequently renamed the NSDAP, and became chairman in July 1921. After the failure of the Munich **putsch** in November 1923 he was imprisoned in Landsberg, where he wrote *Mein Kampf*. On his release he rebuilt the Nazi Party.

The Great Depression made the NSDAP the largest party in the *Reichstag*. Hitler came to power in 1933 because the Conservative–Nationalist **élites** were convinced wrongly that they could control him. By August 1934 Hitler had destroyed all opposition and was able to combine the post of chancellor and president and call himself 'Führer of the German *Reich*'.

By 1937 Hitler had laid the foundations for 'rearmament in depth' and had dismantled the Versailles system. From 1938 onwards his foreign, domestic and racial policies became increasingly radical. He annexed Austria and Czechoslovakia and invaded Poland, which caused war with Britain and France. In June 1941 he made a major error of attacking the USSR and then in December of declaring war on the USA while leaving Britain undefeated in the west. Hitler killed himself on 30 April 1945 when the Red Army had reached Berlin.

The German government managed to persuade the Western democracies effectively to abolish reparations at the Lausanne Conference in July 1932. It also achieved another success at the World Disarmament Conference, which met in February 1932, when the Great Powers agreed to concede to Germany 'equality of rights' within a 'system which would provide security for all nations'. As a result of this concession, in November 1932 the German war ministry finalised plans for large increases in military spending by 1938.

Hitler's long-term aims

The tempo of the German campaign against Versailles quickened once Hitler came to power in 1933, although for two years, at least, he appeared to pursue the same policy as his three predecessors, albeit somewhat more vigorously and unconventionally. Was he, then, just following the traditional policy of making Germany 'the greatest power in Europe from her natural weight by exploiting every opportunity that presented itself', as the historian A.J.P. Taylor argued?

In his book *Mein Kampf* (*My Struggle*), written in 1924, Hitler was quite specific about the main thrust of Nazi foreign policy. Germany was to turn its 'gaze towards the land in the east', which meant above all Russia. Was this still an aim in 1933 or was it just a pipe dream long since forgotten? Like Taylor, Hans Mommsen, a German historian, doubts whether Hitler had a consistent foreign policy of 'unchanging … priorities' and argues that it was usually determined by economic pressures and demands for action from within the Nazi Party itself. Other historians, particularly those of the '**programme school**', take a diametrically opposed line and argue on the strength of *Mein Kampf* and *Hitler's Secret Book* (published in 1928) that he had a definite programme or systematic plan. First of all Hitler planned to defeat France and Russia, and then after building up a large navy, to make a determined bid for world power, even if it involved war against both Britain and the USA.

The history of Nazi foreign policy generates such controversy because Hitler's actions were so often ambiguous and contradictory. Despite this, there is currently a general consensus among historians that Hitler did intend to wage a series of wars which would ultimately culminate in a struggle for global hegemony. As the historian Alan Bullock has argued, the key to understanding Hitler's foreign policy is that he combined 'consistency of aim with complete **opportunism** in method and tactics'.

Hitler's immediate priorities

In 1933 Hitler's first priority was to consolidate the Nazi takeover of power and to rebuild Germany's military strength. This would eventually put him in a position to destroy what remained of the Versailles system. However, while rearming, he had to be careful not to provoke an international backlash. He therefore followed a cautious policy of avoiding risks and defusing potential opposition, while gradually withdrawing Germany from any

KEY TERMS

Programme school
Historians who believe that Hitler had a specific programme to carry out.

Opportunism Seizing the opportunity when it occurs.

multilateral commitments, such as being a member of the League of Nations, which might prevent him from pursuing an independent policy. He hoped particularly to isolate France by negotiating alliances with Britain and Italy.

Hitler's immediate aim was to extricate Germany from the World Disarmament Conference, but he was careful to wait until the autumn of 1933 before he risked withdrawing from both the conference and the League of Nations. He had first skilfully reassured Britain and Italy of his peaceful intentions by signing in June 1933 the Four-Power Pact, proposed by Mussolini, which aimed at revising Versailles through joint agreement of the Great Powers. Although on the face of it this seemed to limit Germany's freedom of action, Hitler calculated, correctly as it turned out, that the French would never ratify it.

The German–Polish Non-aggression Pact

Hitler's first major initiative in foreign policy was the conclusion of the German–Polish **Non-aggression Pact**. He decided on this despite opposition from the German foreign office, the foreign office preferred to maintain good relations with the USSR, and the Soviets regarded Poland as a hostile pro-French state. The pact seriously weakened France's security system in eastern Europe (see page 126), as it had relied on its alliance with Poland to put pressure on Germany's eastern frontiers. Nevertheless, Germany still remained very vulnerable. Hitler was warned about this danger in August 1934 by a senior German diplomat, B.W. von Bülow (see Source B).

SOURCE B

German diplomat B.W. von Bülow writing to Hitler in August 1934, quoted in J. Noakes and G. Pridham, editors, *Nazism 1919–1945*, volume 3, Liverpool University Press, 2001, p. 662.

*In judging the situation we should never overlook the fact that no kind of rearmament in the next few years could give us military security. Even apart from our isolation, we shall for a long time yet be hopelessly inferior to France in the military sphere. A particularly dangerous period will be 1934–5 on account of the re-organisation of the **Reichswehr**. Our only security lies in a skilful foreign policy and in avoiding provocation.*

In doing so we must, of course, not only prevent the taking of military measures against Germany … In views of our isolation and our present weakness … our opponents … can place us in the most difficult situation by setting up a financial and economic blockade against us … within the framework of the economic sanctions in Article 16 [of the League of Nations Charter].

The attempted Nazi coup in Austria, July 1934

Hitler was certainly aware of Germany's vulnerability, but over Austria he adopted a more provocative line, possibly because he assumed that Austria was

KEY TERMS

Multilateral commitments Membership of international organisations.

Non-aggression pact An agreement between two or more countries not to resort to force.

Reichswehr The German army 1919–35.

Study Source B. Why does von Bülow advise Hitler to avoid 'provocation' in his foreign policy?

a domestic German affair. He also believed passionately in uniting the Germans in one state. In June 1934 he met Mussolini, in Venice, and tried to convince him that Austria should become a German satellite. When Mussolini rejected this, Hitler gave the Austrian Nazis strong unofficial encouragement to stage a month later what turned out to be a disastrously unsuccessful uprising in Vienna. Mussolini, determined to keep Austria as a **buffer state** between Italy and Germany, immediately mobilised troops on the Brenner frontier and forced Hitler to disown the coup. The incident brought about a sharp deterioration in German–Italian relations and appeared to rule out any prospect of an alliance.

German rearmament 1933–5

Germany did begin to rearm as soon as Hitler seized power. In February 1933 Hitler announced a long-term plan for increases in the armed forces. Ultimately, his intention was to mobilise the whole German economy and society for war. In July 1933 the decision was taken to create an independent *Luftwaffe* and a year later the July programme was unveiled, which envisaged the construction of some 17,000 aeroplanes. The majority of these were training planes to familiarise future pilots with flying so that the *Luftwaffe* could be greatly increased in size in the near future.

On 18 December 1933 the defence ministry unveiled a new programme that aimed to create a peacetime army of 300,000 men. In March 1935 Hitler announced the reintroduction of **conscription**, despite the fears of his advisers that this would lead to French intervention.

Even though naval rearmament was not initially one of Hitler's priorities, as he hoped for at least a temporary alliance with Britain, a naval programme was drawn up which would produce a moderate-sized German fleet of eight battleships, three aircraft carriers, eight cruisers, 48 destroyers and 72 submarines by 1949.

The Stresa Conference

In April the British, French and Italian heads of government met at Stresa in Italy to discuss forming a common front against Germany, in view of Hitler's rejection of the clauses of Versailles limiting Germany's armaments. They all condemned German rearmament and resolved to maintain the peace settlements.

Hitler, however, quickly launched a diplomatic offensive to reassure the powers of his peaceful intentions. In a speech that in places appeared to echo the language of Stresemann and Briand he proposed a series of non-aggression pacts with Germany's neighbours, and promised to observe Locarno and accept an overall limitation on armaments. He also offered Britain an agreement limiting the German fleet to 35 per cent of the total strength of the Royal Navy.

> **KEY TERMS**
>
> **Buffer state** A small state positioned between two much larger ones.
>
> **Luftwaffe** The German air force.
>
> **Conscription** Compulsory military service.

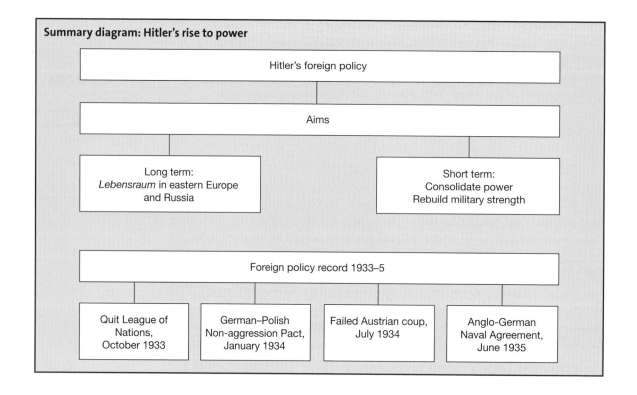

Summary diagram: Hitler's rise to power

Hitler's foreign policy

Aims

Long term:
Lebensraum in eastern Europe and Russia

Short term:
Consolidate power
Rebuild military strength

Foreign policy record 1933–5

Quit League of Nations, October 1933

German–Polish Non-aggression Pact, January 1934

Failed Austrian coup, July 1934

Anglo-German Naval Agreement, June 1935

3 # Reaction of the Great Powers to Nazi Germany 1933–5

▶ *How did the Great Powers respond to the rise of Hitler 1933–5?*

For the Great Powers 1933–5 was a period in which they had to come to terms with the reality of Nazi Germany. In 1933, even though Germany was only just beginning to rearm, its strength was potentially far greater than in 1914, as it was enhanced by a ring of weak states which had been created in 1919 out of the ruins of the Austrian and Russian Empires around its eastern and southern frontiers.

France

By 1934 France had long since lost the diplomatic leadership of Europe which it had exercised in the immediate post-war years. France's economy had been belatedly hit by the Great Depression and its **social cohesion** threatened by a wave of rioting sparked off in February 1934 by the exposure of a series of financial scandals. French society was deeply divided as the **right** wanted to negotiate with Hitler and Mussolini, while the **left** wanted to fight fascism and looked to Russia as an ally.

🔑 **KEY TERMS**

Social cohesion The social unity of a country.

Right Term used to denote parties stretching from Conservative to Nazi or Fascist (extreme right).

Left Term used to denote parties stretching from Social Democrat to Communist.

Even if France had still possessed the will to intervene militarily in Germany, the Locarno Treaties prevented it from reoccupying the Rhineland. Neither could it rely on Poland after the German–Polish Non-aggression Pact of January 1934. France's response to the new Nazi Germany was therefore hesitant and sometimes contradictory. The French sought to contain Germany, as they had done since 1919, through a network of alliances and pacts but, like the British, they also tried to negotiate with Hitler.

Although ultimately Britain remained France's major European partner, it was not ready in 1935 to commit itself to an alliance with France. The French therefore attempted to strengthen the Little *Entente* (see page 126) and negotiate agreements with Italy and Russia. However, this was by no means an easy task as in 1933 its relations with both powers were strained.

Franco-Italian negotiations and the Rome Agreement

In its attempts to negotiate an Italian alliance, France was greatly assisted by the abortive Nazi coup in Vienna, which more than anything convinced Mussolini that a military agreement with France was essential.

In January 1935 both countries signed the Rome Agreement by which they undertook not to meddle in the affairs of their Balkan neighbours and to act together in the event of unilateral German rearmament or another threat to Austrian independence. In June direct Franco-Italian military staff talks started to discuss joint action in the event of a German attack on Austria, Italy or France.

Franco-Russian negotiations

In parallel with these negotiations, talks were proceeding between the French and the Soviets. Paris did not show the same enthusiasm for a Soviet alliance as it did for one with Italy. This was partly because the USSR had been regarded as scarcely less of a threat to the west than Germany and partly because it no longer had a common border with Germany.

The French intended to enmesh the USSR in an elaborate treaty of regional assistance or, in other words, an eastern European version of the Locarno Treaty, which would be signed not only by the USSR but also by Germany, Poland, Czechoslovakia and the Baltic states. This was to be strengthened by a separate Franco-Soviet agreement which would associate Russia with the Locarno Agreements in western Europe and France with the proposed eastern pact.

But the whole plan came to nothing as both Germany and Poland refused to join. The Poles were more suspicious of the Russians than of the Germans. France had therefore little option but to pursue a mutual assistance pact with the USSR alone. In May 1935, the Franco-Soviet Treaty of Mutual Assistance was signed, but Paris refused to follow up the treaty with detailed military staff talks between the two armies. The main aim of the pact was to restrain the USSR from moving closer to Germany, as it had done in 1922 with the signature of the Rapallo Agreement (see page 109).

Franco-German negotiations

Meanwhile the French government attempted to negotiate a settlement with Germany. Both in the winter of 1933–4 and in the summer of 1935, immediately after the signature of the Franco-Soviet Treaty, attempts were made to open up a Franco-German dialogue. These efforts were doomed as the French attempted to draw the Germans into negotiating agreements essentially aimed at preserving the Versailles system. Hitler was ready, when it suited him, to lower the political temperature through cordial diplomatic exchanges, but he was not ready to tolerate the restrictions with which French – and British – diplomacy was attempting to entangle him.

Great Britain

Like France, Britain's reaction to Nazi Germany was conditioned by its military, economic and strategic vulnerability. In 1933 it faced a growing threat not only from Germany in Europe, but also from Japan in the Far East. Consequently, the main aim of British policy towards Germany was to blunt Hitler's aggression by continuing to modify the Treaty of Versailles peacefully while simultaneously drawing Germany back into the League, where it could be tied down in multilateral agreements on security. Sir John Simon (1873–1954), the foreign secretary, summed up this policy in a letter to King George V in February 1935 (see Source C).

SOURCE C

Foreign Secretary Sir John Simon writing to King George V in February 1935, quoted in H. Nicolson, *King George the Fifth: His Life and Reign*, Constable, 1952, p. 522.

*… the practical choice is between a Germany which continues to rearm without any regulation or agreement and a Germany which, through getting a recognition of its rights and some modification of the peace treaties, enters into the **comity of nations** and contributes, in this and other ways, to European stability. As between these two courses, there can be no doubt which is wiser.*

According to Simon in Source C, what choice concerning Germany confronted the British government?

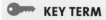 **KEY TERM**

Comity of nations Nations which mutually respect each other's laws and institution.

Britain also worked hard for an overall settlement with Germany. Despite the reintroduction of German conscription in March, Simon went to Berlin later in the month to explore the possibility of a comprehensive settlement with Germany involving German recognition of Austrian independence, its participation in an 'eastern Locarno' and return to the League. British ministers attended the Stresa meeting on 8 April, but they were determined at that stage not to join any alliances or pacts directed against Germany as they were convinced that the pre-1914 alliance system (see page 55) had been a major cause of the very war it had aimed to prevent. In June this policy seemed to be rewarded with success when the Anglo-German Naval Agreement was signed (see above).

Italy

Mussolini, who had extensive territorial aims in the Balkans and North Africa, at first attempted to maintain a special position as mediator between Germany on the one hand and Britain and France on the other, hoping that this would in time bring him concessions from both sides. However, the increasing German threat to Austria began to convert Mussolini from a critic and potential revisionist of the Treaty of Versailles to an upholder of the territorial *status quo*. As early as August 1933 Mussolini met **Engelbert Dollfuss**, the Austrian chancellor, at Rimini and discussed arrangements for Italian military support in case of German intervention in Austria.

Mussolini's conversion to a defender of the existing territorial settlement was accelerated by the abortive Nazi *putsch* in Vienna in July 1934 (see pages 147–8) and by the German announcement of conscription the following March. By the spring of 1935 Italy appeared to have aligned itself firmly with Britain and France in their desire to preserve what was left of the Versailles settlement.

The USSR

Stalin, the Soviet leader (see his profile on page 154), like the other European leaders, reacted cautiously to the Nazi takeover of power. His distrust of the West was at least as great as his fear of Nazi Germany. Consequently, even though he negotiated a defensive agreement with the French and sought collective security by joining the League of Nations in September 1934, he also attempted to maintain good relations with Germany despite such setbacks as the German–Polish Non-aggression Pact (see page 147).

The Soviet negotiations with the French in the spring of 1935 were also accompanied by a series of secret talks with the Germans, which mirrored the French tactics of trying for a settlement with Hitler as an alternative to a Franco-Soviet Pact (see page 151). Nazi–Soviet talks continued intermittently right up to February 1936. Only with the ratification of the Franco-Soviet Treaty of Mutual Assistance by the French parliament were they broken off, but were renewed in the summer of 1939 (see page 182).

The USA

In 1933 there was considerable sympathy in the USA for the economic hardships that Germany was suffering as a result of the Depression, while both Britain and France were viewed with some suspicion on account of their huge colonial empires. However, with the coming to power of Hitler and beginning of the persecution of the Jews, public opinion in the USA began to become more hostile to Germany; nevertheless, US foreign policy remained firmly isolationist.

KEY FIGURE

Engelbert Dollfuss (1892–1934)

A devout Catholic who became chancellor of Austria in 1932. He admired Fascist Italy and suspended the Austrian parliamentary constitution in 1933.

Joseph Stalin

1879	Born Jozef Djugashvili in what is present-day Georgia. His father worked as a cobbler. Adopted the name Stalin, meaning 'man of steel'
1903	Joined the Bolshevik Party
1917	Assisted Lenin in the Russian Revolution
1922	Secretary of the Communist Party
1929	Effectively dictator of the USSR and introduced a policy of 'socialism in one country'
1936–8	Conducted the great purge of his enemies
1939	Signed the Nazi–Soviet Pact
	Ordered the Soviet occupation of eastern Poland
	Ordered the invasion of Finland
1941–5	Supreme director of the Soviet war effort
1953	Died

Stalin was originally going to become a priest but was expelled from the seminary in 1899 for being a revolutionary. He was twice exiled to Siberia but each time managed to escape. At various times he was in exile in Paris and Vienna, and in 1912 became the Bolshevik Party's expert on racial minorities. He edited the Communist Party's newspaper, *Pravda*, in 1917 and became commissar for nationalities in the first Soviet government. In 1922 he became secretary of the Bolshevik Party.

By 1929 Stalin had defeated his rivals for the control of the Bolshevik Party, and was in a position to launch the first of the Five-Year Plans involving the collectivisation of agriculture and the massive expansion of heavy industry. He defended himself from the criticism, which followed the ruthless implementation of these policies, through purges, show trials and 'the terror'. In May 1941 he became chairman of the council of ministers, and during the Great Patriotic War (the Second World War) against Germany took over supreme control of the Soviet war effort. The Soviet victory in 1945 was celebrated as his supreme achievement, and enabled the USSR to control most of eastern Europe. After 1945, until his death, Stalin's position in the USSR was unchallenged.

In the Far East, the USA was alarmed by the Japanese occupation of Manchuria (see page 198), but did no more than make diplomatic protest. Indeed, the Temporary Neutrality Act of 1935, by empowering **President Roosevelt** to ban the supply of arms to all belligerents – whether aggressors or victims of aggression – in the event of the outbreak of war, strengthened the US policy of non-involvement.

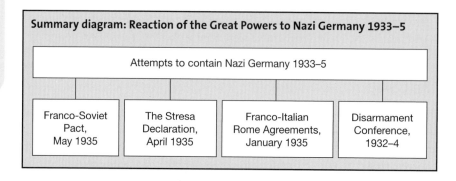

Summary diagram: Reaction of the Great Powers to Nazi Germany 1933–5

Attempts to contain Nazi Germany 1933–5

Franco-Soviet Pact, May 1935	The Stresa Declaration, April 1935	Franco-Italian Rome Agreements, January 1935	Disarmament Conference, 1932–4

The Abyssinian crisis 1935

▶ *Why was the conquest of Abyssinia not stopped by Britain and France?*

▶ *Why did attempts to find a compromise over Abyssinia fail?*

Mussolini had for a long time wanted to build up a large empire in North Africa which would have the added advantage of distracting his people from the impact of the Great Depression on the Italian economy. By 1932 he had begun to plan in earnest the annexation of Abyssinia. Not only would Abyssinia provide land for Italian settlers, but it would also connect Eritrea with Italian Somaliland and thus put most of the Horn of Africa under Italian control (see the map on page 156). In December 1934 a clash occurred between Italian and Abyssinian troops at the small oasis of Wal-Wal, some 80 km on the Abyssinian side of the border with Italian Somaliland. The following October the long-expected invasion of Abyssinia began.

The failure of Anglo-French attempts to compromise

Mussolini was convinced that neither Britain nor France would raise serious objections. In January 1935 French Foreign Minister Laval had verbally promised Mussolini a free hand, while the British foreign office was desperate to avert the crisis either by offering him territorial compensation elsewhere or by helping to negotiate an arrangement, comparable to Britain's own position in Egypt, which would give Italy effective control of Abyssinia without **formal annexation**.

SOURCE D

Sir Robert Vansittart, a senior British diplomat, writing in 8 June 1935, quoted in R. Lamb, *Mussolini as Diplomat*, Fromm International, 1999, p. 121.

*The position is as plain as a pikestaff [that is, completely obvious]. Italy will have to be bought off – let us use and face ugly words – in some form or other, or Abyssinia will eventually perish. That might in itself matter less, if it did not mean that the League would also perish (and that Italy would simultaneously perform another **volte-face** into the arms of Germany).*

Why then could such a compromise not be negotiated? The scale and brutality of the Italian invasion confronted both the British and French governments with a considerable dilemma. The British government was facing an election in November 1935 and was under intense pressure from the electorate to support the League. In an unofficial peace ballot in June 1935 organised by the League of Nations Union, which was formed in 1918 to win public support for the League, 10 million out of 11 million replies backed the use of economic sanctions by the League in a case of aggression. In France, public opinion was more divided, with the left supporting the League and the right supporting Italy. However, both powers feared the diplomatic consequences of alienating Italy over Abyssinia.

 KEY TERMS

Formal annexation Taking over full control of a territory by another power.

Volte-face An about-turn; a sudden and complete change of policy.

According to Vansittart in Source D, why was it so important to appease Italy?

In particular, Britain's persistent refusal to join France in guaranteeing the *status quo* in central and eastern Europe inevitably increased the importance for the French of their friendly relations with Italy.

On 18 October the League condemned the Italian invasion of Abyssinia, and voted for a gradually escalating programme of sanctions. In the meantime both Britain and France continued to search for a compromise settlement. In December **Pierre Laval** and the British foreign minister, Sir Samuel Hoare, produced a plan which involved placing some two-thirds of Abyssinia under Italian control. There was a strong possibility that it would have been acceptable to Mussolini, but it was leaked to the French press and an explosion of rage among the British public forced Hoare's resignation and the dropping of the plan.

The failure of diplomacy did not then ensure vigorous action against Mussolini. The League put no embargo on oil exports to Italy, and Britain refused to close the Suez Canal to Italian shipping on the grounds that this might lead to war. Mussolini was thus able to step up his campaign and by May 1936 had overrun Abyssinia.

KEY FIGURE

Pierre Laval (1883–1945)

French Socialist and prime minister 1931–2. He was chief minister in Vichy France and was executed in 1945.

? What changes were being proposed to the frontiers of Abyssinia and which state would benefit from these changes?

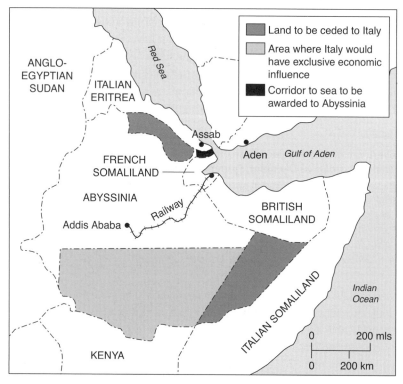

The Hoare–Laval Plan for the partition of Abyssinia. It was eventually dropped in the face of opposition from public opinion and the press in Britain.

The consequences of the Abyssinian War

The crisis was a crucial turning point in the 1930s. Not only did it irreparably weaken the League and provide Hitler with an ideal opportunity for the illegal remilitarisation of the Rhineland (see below), but it also effectively destroyed the Franco-Italian friendship and ultimately replaced it with the Rome–Berlin 'Axis' (see page 162). This eventually enabled Hitler in 1938 to absorb Austria without Italian opposition. The Axis was also to threaten vital British and French lines of communication in the Mediterranean with the possibility of hostile naval action and thus seriously weaken their potential response to future German – or indeed Japanese – aggression.

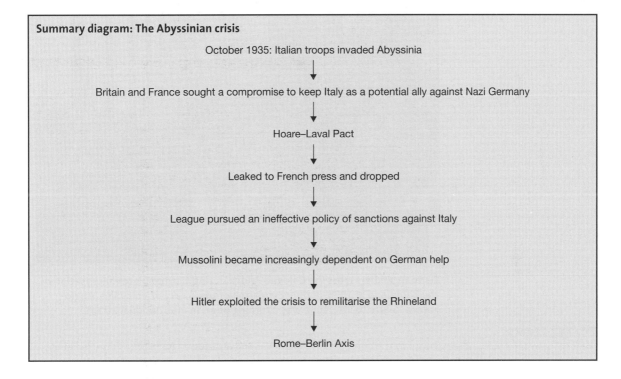

Summary diagram: The Abyssinian crisis

October 1935: Italian troops invaded Abyssinia
↓
Britain and France sought a compromise to keep Italy as a potential ally against Nazi Germany
↓
Hoare–Laval Pact
↓
Leaked to French press and dropped
↓
League pursued an ineffective policy of sanctions against Italy
↓
Mussolini became increasingly dependent on German help
↓
Hitler exploited the crisis to remilitarise the Rhineland
↓
Rome–Berlin Axis

⑤ Remilitarisation of the Rhineland

▶ *Why, despite the Locarno Agreements, was there no effective opposition when Hitler broke the Treaties of Versailles and Locarno and remilitarised the Rhineland?*

The remilitarisation of the Rhineland marked an important stage in Hitler's plans for rebuilding German power. The construction of strong fortifications there would enable him to stop any French attempts to invade Germany. Hitler had originally planned to reoccupy the Rhineland in 1937, but a combination of the favourable diplomatic situation created by the Abyssinian crisis and the need to distract domestic attention from German economic problems brought about by the speed of the rearmament programme persuaded him to act in March 1936. In December 1935 the German army was ordered to start planning the reoccupation, while Hitler's diplomats began to manufacture a legal justification for such action by arguing that the Franco-Soviet Pact (see page 151) was contrary to the Locarno Agreement.

SOURCE E

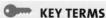
What message does Source E give about Hitler's foreign policy?

German soldiers cross the Cologne Bridge during Germany's remilitarisation of the Rhineland in 1936, in direct violation of the Treaty of Versailles. Anglo-French failure to intervene was a turning point in international affairs.

Crucial to the success of his plan was the attitude of Italy. Mussolini, isolated from the other **Stresa Powers** because of his Abyssinian policy, had little option but to reassure Germany that he would not co-operate with the British and French to enforce Locarno if German troops entered the Rhineland.

German troops marched into the Rhineland on 7 March 1936. In order to reassure France that they did not intend to violate the Franco-German frontier they were initially, at any rate, few in number and lightly equipped. So why did the French army not immediately intervene? The French general staff, which since the late 1920s had been planning for a defensive war against Germany based on the fortifications of the **Maginot line** on France's eastern frontier, refused to invade the Rhineland unless they had full backing from the British.

🔑 KEY TERMS

Stresa Powers The powers who attended the Stresa Conference in 1935.

Maginot line A line of concrete fortifications, which France constructed along its borders with Germany. It was named after André Maginot, the French minister of defence.

The most the British government was ready to do was to promise France that, in the event of an unprovoked German attack on French territory, it would send two divisions of troops across the Channel. Essentially, British public opinion was convinced that Hitler was merely walking into 'his own back garden'.

The remilitarisation of the Rhineland was a triumph for Hitler, as it marked a decisive shift in power from Paris to Berlin (see Source F).

SOURCE F

From an internal French foreign office memorandum of 12 March 1936 on the consequences of the German action, quoted in J. Néré, *The Foreign Policy of France from 1914–1945*, Routledge, 1975, p. 337.

A German success would likewise not fail to encourage elements which, in Yugoslavia, look towards Berlin … In Roumania this will be a victory of the elements of the Right which have been stirred up by Hitlerite propaganda. All that will remain for Czechoslovakia is to come to terms with Germany. Austria does not conceal her anxiety. 'Next time it will be our turn' … Turkey, who has increasingly close economic relations with Germany, but who politically remains in the Franco-British axis, can be induced to modify her line. The Scandinavian countries … are alarmed.

What, according to Source F, are the consequences of the German remilitarisation of the Rhineland?

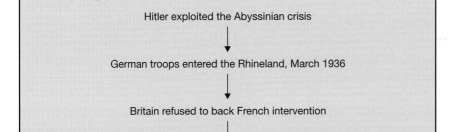

Summary diagram: Remilitarisation of the Rhineland

Hitler exploited the Abyssinian crisis

↓

German troops entered the Rhineland, March 1936

↓

Britain refused to back French intervention

↓

Consequences: Destruction of Locarno settlement and strengthening of Nazi Germany

 # 6 The Spanish Civil War

▶ *How did the Great Powers react to the Spanish Civil War?*

The Spanish Civil War was essentially a domestic matter which rapidly became an international issue threatening to involve the major powers in a European conflict. It began in July 1936 with a Nationalist revolt led by the army against the Spanish Republican government. When the rebels were defeated in a number of cities by the workers, both sides appealed to the international community for help. The Nationalists, led by **General Franco**, looked to Germany and Italy, while the Republicans approached Britain, France and the USSR.

German and Italian intervention

Hitler quickly agreed to provide a fleet of transport aircraft to fly Franco's men across to Spain. He then followed this up with the dispatch of some 6000 troops. Hitler certainly wanted to stop Spain becoming Communist but he also wanted to distract the Western powers so that he could continue to rearm without fear of intervention. He was aware too of the advantages of having a friendly government in Madrid which would not only supply Germany with Spanish mineral resources but also in wartime possibly provide bases for German submarines.

Mussolini also agreed to assist Franco for the same mixture of ideological and strategic reasons: he hoped to defeat the left in Spain, gain a new ally in Franco, who might grant Italy a naval base on one of the Balearic islands, and 'strengthen' the Italian character by exposure to war.

The non-intervention policy of Britain and France

With both Germany and Italy openly helping Franco there was a real danger of a European war, should France and Britain be drawn in on the Republican side. When the French prime minister, **Léon Blum**, whose power rested on a left-wing coalition, was first asked for help by the Republic, he was tempted to give it, if only to deny potential allies of Germany a victory in Spain. However, two factors forced him to have second thoughts. First, the actual dispatch of French military aid to the Republicans would have polarised French society, which was already deeply divided between right and left, and run the risk of plunging France into a civil war of its own; and secondly, the British government came out strongly against intervention. The British ambassador in Paris even threatened neutrality should French assistance to the Republicans lead to war with Germany. Despite the strategic dangers for Britain's position in the Mediterranean in the event of a Nationalist victory, the cabinet viewed the civil war as essentially a side issue which must not be allowed to prevent its continued search for a lasting settlement with Germany. In addition, there were powerful voices within the Conservative Party who actively sympathised with Franco.

In an attempt to prevent the war spreading, Britain and France proposed a non-intervention agreement. This was signed by the other European powers, but Germany and Italy ignored it and continued to assist Franco.

Soviet intervention

The Republican government therefore had little option but to approach the USSR for help. In September 1936 Stalin sent hundreds of military advisers and large quantities of military equipment, while the **Comintern** was made responsible for recruiting brigades of international volunteers. Stalin, like Hitler, saw the civil war as a way of dividing his enemies.

A conflict between the Western powers and Germany would certainly have suited Stalin's policy, but he was also anxious to prevent a Nationalist victory in Spain since this would strengthen the forces of international fascism and make a German attack on the USSR more likely. However, by early 1937, when he realised that the Republicans could not win, he reduced the flow of arms to a level that was just sufficient to prolong the conflict. In this he was successful, as it was not until March 1939 that Franco at last occupied Madrid.

The consequences of the civil war

For the democracies the Spanish Civil War could not have come at a worse time. It polarised public opinion between right and left, threatened France with encirclement and cemented the Italian–German *rapprochement*. It may also have helped to convince the USSR of the weakness of the West and prepare the way for the Nazi–Soviet Pact of September 1939 (see page 182). As with the Abyssinian crisis, it was undoubtedly Germany who benefited most from the conflict since it diverted the attention of the powers during the crucial period 1936–7 away from the Nazi rearmament programme.

KEY TERM

Comintern The Communist international movement set up in 1919 to organise worldwide revolution.

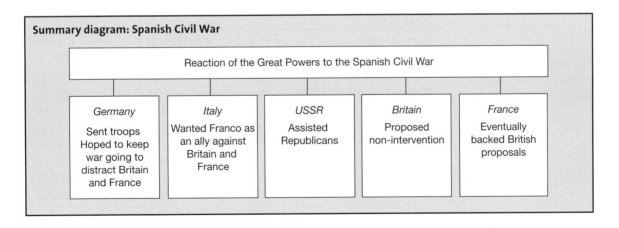

Summary diagram: Spanish Civil War

Reaction of the Great Powers to the Spanish Civil War

Germany	Italy	USSR	Britain	France
Sent troops Hoped to keep war going to distract Britain and France	Wanted Franco as an ally against Britain and France	Assisted Republicans	Proposed non-intervention	Eventually backed British proposals

7 The Rome–Berlin Axis and the Anti-Comintern Pact

▶ *Why and how did Japan, Germany and Italy draw closer together in the period 1936–7?*

The summer of 1936 saw increasingly cordial relations between Berlin and Rome. While Britain pointedly refused to recognise the King of Italy as the 'Emperor of Abyssinia', Germany rapidly did so. Hitler and Mussolini co-operated in blocking a new British initiative to update the Locarno Treaty. Italy's growing hostility towards Britain, France and especially the USSR, with whom until the Spanish Civil War it had enjoyed good relations, also ensured that it had to be more tolerant of German influence in Austria. In January 1936 Mussolini assured the German ambassador in Rome that 'If Austria, as a formerly independent state, were … in practice to become a **German satellite**, he would have no objection.' On 11 July Germany and Austria signed an agreement whereby Austria remained independent but followed a pro-German foreign policy.

KEY TERM

German satellite A state completely dominated by Germany.

The October Protocols: the Rome–Berlin Axis

The understanding between Italy and Germany over Austria prepared the way for a German–Italian agreement, the October Protocols, which were signed in Berlin in October 1936. Mussolini announced this new alignment to the world at a mass meeting in Milan in November (see Source G).

? According to Mussolini in Source G, what have the Berlin conversations with Hitler resulted in?

SOURCE G

Extract from Mussolini's speech in Milan, 1 November 1936, quoted in J. Noakes and G. Pridham, editors, *Nazism 1919–1945*, volume 3, Liverpool University Press, 2001, p. 672.

The meeting at Berlin [between the Nazi legal expert, Hans Frank and the Italian foreign minister] resulted in an agreement between the two countries on certain questions, some of which are particularly interesting in these days. But these agreements which have been included in special statements and duly signed – this vertical line between Rome and Berlin is not a partition, but rather an axis around which all the European states animated by the will to collaboration and peace can also collaborate. Germany, although surrounded and solicited, did not adhere to sanctions. With the agreement of 11 July [on Austria's relations to Germany] there disappeared any element of dissension between Berlin and Rome, and I may remind you that even before the Berlin meeting Germany had practically recognised the Empire of Rome.

The Anti-Comintern Pact

Three weeks later Hitler overrode advice from his professional diplomats and signed the Anti-Comintern Pact with Japan. This was more of symbolic than practical importance as it was aimed against the Comintern rather than the USSR itself, although, of course, the Comintern was run by the Soviets. For Hitler, coming so soon after the Rome–Berlin Axis, the pact trumpeted to the world that Germany was no longer isolated, as it had appeared to be in the spring of 1935. In November 1937 the pact was further strengthened by Italy's accession.

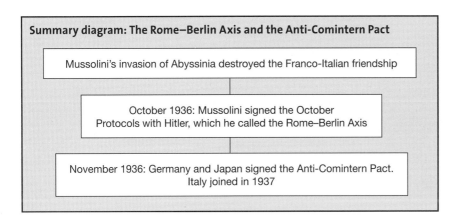

Summary diagram: The Rome–Berlin Axis and the Anti-Comintern Pact

Mussolini's invasion of Abyssinia destroyed the Franco-Italian friendship

October 1936: Mussolini signed the October Protocols with Hitler, which he called the Rome–Berlin Axis

November 1936: Germany and Japan signed the Anti-Comintern Pact. Italy joined in 1937

Chapter summary

In 1930 Britain and France still dominated Europe. Germany was committed to co-operation with Britain and France, and Italy remained a friendly power. By 1937 all this had changed. The Great Depression had economically weakened Britain, France and the USA, and brought Hitler to power in Germany, as well as strengthening the power of the army in Japan. Hitler immediately began to rearm Germany. He also supported an unsuccessful Nazi coup in Austria. To counter these threats, France, Britain and Italy attempted to form a common front at Stresa in 1935, and France and Russia also negotiated a security pact. The Stresa Front was first weakened by the Anglo-German Naval Agreement and then destroyed by the Abyssinian crisis, which drove a wedge between Italy and Britain and France. Hitler exploited the crisis to remilitarise the Rhineland in March 1936. Once this was fortified, the Western powers were no longer able to threaten Germany with military sanctions, as they had done 1923–4 (see pages 109–10). In July 1936 Italy and Germany intervened on behalf of the Nationalists in the Spanish Civil War, and in November the October Protocols and the Anti-Comintern pact were signed. It was now the democracies and not Germany who were on the defensive.

Refresher questions

Use these questions to remind yourself of the key material covered in this chapter.

1 What were Hitler's immediate priorities as far as foreign policy went?

2 Why did the German–Polish Non-aggression Pact weaken France's security system?

3 Why was the Stresa Conference called?

4 How did France respond to the rise of Hitler 1933–5?

5 What was the main aim of British policy towards Germany?

6 Why had Italy by the spring of 1935 aligned itself with Britain and France in an attempt to defend the Versailles settlement?

7 What was the USSR's reaction to the rise of Hitler?

8 How isolationist was US foreign policy up to 1936?

9 What were the consequences of the Abyssinian War?

10 Why did Britain and France not intervene to stop the German remilitarisation of the Rhineland in 1936?

11 Why did the Germans and Italians support General Franco?

12 Why did Stalin decide to help the Republicans in the Spanish Civil War?

13 What was the value for Germany of the Anti-Comintern Pact with Japan?

14 In what ways, and for what reasons, was the diplomatic situation in Europe transformed between 1930 and 1937?

 Question practice

ESSAY QUESTIONS

1 Assess the consequences for the international situation from 1930 to 1936 of the Great Depression.

2 How successfully did France seek closer links with Italy and Russia 1933–5?

3 Which of the following was the greater challenge to Britain and France 1933–6: i) the Abyssinian crisis or ii) the remilitarisation of the Rhineland? Explain your answer with reference to both i) and ii).

INTERPRETATION QUESTIONS

1 Read the interpretation and then answer the question that follows. 'Appeasement was an acceptable strategy only as long as it matched what were perceived as British interests' (from R. Overy, *Origins of the Second World War*, Longman, 1987). Evaluate the strengths and limitations of this interpretation, making reference to other interpretations that you have studied.

2 Read the interpretation and then answer the question that follows. '[With] the reoccupation of the Rhineland in March 1936 ... Hitler scored a great diplomatic victory at the expense of Britain and France and at no cost to himself' (from W. Carr, *Arms, Autarky and Aggression*, Arnold, 1979). Evaluate the strengths and limitations of this interpretation, making reference to other interpretations you have studied.

SOURCE ANALYSIS QUESTION

1 With reference to Sources 1, 2 and 3 (page 165), and your understanding of the historical context, assess the value of these sources to a historian studying German foreign policy 1933–6.

SOURCE 1

German diplomat B.W. von Bülow writing to Hitler in August 1934, quoted in J. Noakes and G. Pridham, editors, *Nazism 1919–1945*, volume 3, Liverpool University Press, 2001, p. 662.

In judging the situation we should never overlook the fact that no kind of rearmament in the next few years could give us military security. Even apart from our isolation, we shall for a long time yet be hopelessly inferior to France in the military sphere. A particularly dangerous period will be 1934–5 on account of the re-organisation of the Reichswehr. Our only security lies in a skilful foreign policy and in avoiding provocation.

In doing so we must, of course, not only prevent the taking of military measures against Germany … In views of our isolation and our present weakness … our opponents … can place us in the most difficult situation by setting up a financial and economic blockade against us … within the framework of the economic sanctions in Article 16 [of the League of Nations Charter].

SOURCE 2

From US Senator Borah's address to a US radio station, 22 February 1936, quoted in R. Birley, editor, *Speeches and Documents in American History, 1914–1939*, volume IV, Oxford University Press, 1951, pp. 176–7.

The United States in pursuing a course of neutrality not only consults and serves the interests of her own people, but under no reasonable rule of international conduct can be regarded as doing an injustice to other people … We should be neutral. We should remain free of European controversies. We have our own problems. They are distinct from the problems abroad. A democracy must remain at home in all matters which affect the nature of her institutions. They are of a nature to call for the undivided energy of the whole nation. We do not want racial antipathies or national antagonisms of the Old World transplanted to this continent, as they will, should we become a part of European politics. The people of this country are overwhelmingly for a policy of neutrality.

SOURCE 3

From Mussolini's speech in Milan, 1 November 1936, quoted in J. Noakes and G. Pridham, editors, *Nazism 1919–1945*, volume 3, Liverpool University Press, 2001, p. 672.

The meeting at Berlin [between the Nazi legal expert, Hans Frank and the Italian foreign minister] resulted in an agreement between the two countries on certain questions, some of which are particularly interesting in these days. But these agreements which have been included in special statements and duly signed – this vertical line between Rome and Berlin is not a partition, but rather an axis around which all the European states animated by the will to collaboration and peace can also collaborate. Germany, although surrounded and solicited, did not adhere to sanctions. With the agreement of 11 July [on Austria's relations with Germany] there disappeared any element of dissension between Berlin and Rome, and I may remind you that even before the Berlin meeting Germany had practically recognised the Empire of Rome.

CHAPTER 8

Countdown to war in Europe 1937–41

The core of this chapter covers the crucial period from March 1938 to September 1939. It begins with Hitler's plans for expansion and then looks at the succession of crises which started with the *Anschluss* and ended with Britain's and France's declaration of war on Germany. It then briefly traces the spreading conflict in Europe up to June 1941.

In dealing with these events this chapter focuses on:

★ Hitler's options

★ Arms race: Britain, France and Germany 1936–9

★ Britain, France and appeasement

★ The *Anschluss* and the destruction of Czechoslovakia

★ Anglo-French guarantees and attempts to construct a peace front

★ Gaining the support of the USSR

★ Outbreak of the Second World War 1939

★ The spreading conflict: October 1940 to June 1941

The key debate on *page 190* of this chapter asks the question: What were the causes of the Second World War?

Key dates

1938	March 12	German occupation of Austria (*Anschluss*)	1939	May 22	Pact of Steel signed in Berlin
	Sept. 8	Sudeten Germans broke off negotiations with Prague		Aug. 23	Nazi–Soviet Pact
				Sept. 1	Germany invaded Poland
	Sept. 29–30	Four-Power Conference at Munich		Sept. 3	Britain and France declared war on Germany
1939	March 15	Germany occupied Bohemia and Moravia	1940	June 10	Italy declared war on Britain and France
	March 31	Anglo-French guarantee of Poland		June 22	Fall of France
				Sept. 27	Tripartite Pact signed by Germany, Italy and Japan
	April 13	Anglo-French guarantee of Greece and Romania	1941	June 22	German invasion of Russia

Hitler's options

▶ *What light does the Hossbach Memorandum shed on the aims of Hitler's foreign policy?*

By the autumn of 1937 Hitler had virtually dismantled the Europe created by the Locarno and Versailles treaties. The Spanish Civil War (see page 159) and the Sino-Japanese War (see pages 201) distracted his potential enemies, while Italy was drawing ever closer to Germany. In August 1936 he had initiated the Four-Year Plan for preparing the German economy for war by 1940. He was thus in a favourable position to consider options for a new and more aggressive phase of foreign policy.

The Hossbach Memorandum

On 5 November 1937 Hitler called a special meeting which was attended by his commanders-in-chief and foreign and war ministers. The account of the meeting was written down by Hitler's **adjutant**, Colonel Hossbach (1894–1980). Hitler told them that what he had to say was so important that it was to be regarded as 'his last will and testament'. He stressed that his overriding aim was to acquire *Lebensraum* within Europe rather than colonies in Africa, at the latest by 1943–5, but indicated that he would move against Czechoslovakia and Austria before this date if France were distracted either by a civil war or by hostilities with Italy.

At the **Nuremberg trials** after the war in 1946 the Allies claimed that Hossbach's memorandum showed that Hitler had drawn up a detailed timetable for war, but the historian A.J.P. Taylor was more sceptical. He argued that the meeting was not really about foreign policy but about the allocation of armaments between the German armed services. Today, few historians agree with Taylor's conclusions that Hitler's exposition was for the most part

🔑 **KEY TERMS**

Adjutant Military assistant.

Nuremberg trials The trials of war criminals in Nuremberg after the Second World War.

SOURCE A

Extract from *Documents on German Foreign Policy*, series D, volume 1, HMSO, 1957–66, pp. 29–38.

The aim of German policy was to make secure and to preserve the racial community and to enlarge it. It was therefore a question of space [Lebensraum] … The question for Germany was: Where could she achieve the greatest gain at the lowest cost? German policy had to reckon with two hate inspired antagonists, Britain and France, to whom a German colossus in the centre of Europe was a thorn in the flesh … Germany's problem could only be solved by the use of force … If the resort to force with its attendant risks is accepted … there then remains still to be answered the questions 'When'? and 'How'?

Study Source A. According to Hitler, what were the key questions facing German foreign policy in 1937?

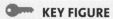

KEY FIGURE

Alfred Jodl (1890–1946)

Chief of the operations staff of the German Armed Forces High Command. At the Nuremberg trials in 1946, he was sentenced to death and hanged as a war criminal.

'day-dreaming unrelated to what followed in real life' and that he was in fact 'at a loss what to do next even after he had the power to do it'. The consensus of research still favours the historian William Carr's view that Hitler was warning his generals 'that a more adventurous and dangerous foreign policy was imminent'. It was significant, for instance, that a month later **General Jodl**, the chief of the operations staff, drew up plans for an offensive rather than a defensive war against Czechoslovakia.

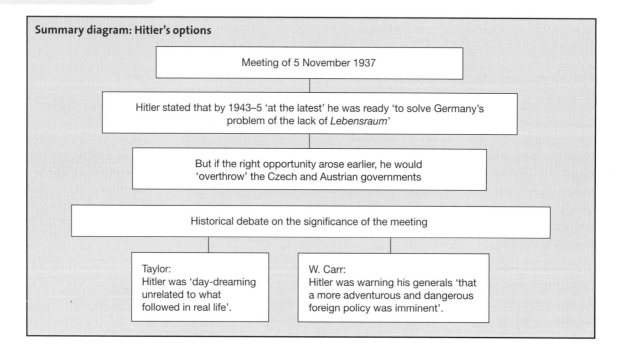

Summary diagram: Hitler's options

Meeting of 5 November 1937

Hitler stated that by 1943–5 'at the latest' he was ready 'to solve Germany's problem of the lack of *Lebensraum*'

But if the right opportunity arose earlier, he would 'overthrow' the Czech and Austrian governments

Historical debate on the significance of the meeting

Taylor:
Hitler was 'day-dreaming unrelated to what followed in real life'.

W. Carr:
Hitler was warning his generals 'that a more adventurous and dangerous foreign policy was imminent'.

② Arms race: Britain, France and Germany 1936–9

▶ *In what ways did the experiences of the First World War influence the arms race of the period 1936–9?*

▶ *What was the impact of the arms race on the diplomatic situation?*

It was not until 1935 that the scale of German rearmament became clear. Inevitably, this triggered an arms race with Britain and France. Unlike in 1914, there was no calm assumption that the next war would be soon over. All three countries, learning from the First World War, expected a long struggle.

Even though the tank and aeroplane had restored mobility to the battlefield, most military experts still thought in terms of First World War tactics. The French built the Maginot line, which was an enormous series of concrete fortifications along their frontier with Germany, while the Germans built the *Westwall* along the east bank of the Rhine.

An important lesson from the First World War was that the armed forces needed so much equipment that the economy and the workforce had to be totally mobilised in order to supply them. The nation which could most efficiently supply and finance its armed forces in a long, protracted struggle would in all probability win the war. In all three countries rearmament caused major financial problems.

Germany

By 1936 Germany was already finding it difficult to finance rearmament. Hitler, however, brushed aside complaints from **Hjalmar Schacht**, his economics minister, and appointed **Göring** to implement the Four-Year Plan which was to prepare Germany for war by 1940. Through raising taxes, government loans and cutting consumer expenditure, military expenditure nearly quadrupled between 1937 and 1939. An ambitious programme for the production of **synthetic materials** was also started to beat the impact of a British blockade. By August 1939 the *Luftwaffe* had 4000 frontline aircraft and the strength of the army had risen to 2,758,000 men. In January 1939 Hitler also announced plans for the construction of a major battle fleet to challenge Britain's.

Despite the initial target of 1940 set by the Four-Year Plan, the German rearmament programme was in reality planned to be ready by the mid-1940s. In the meantime, as historian Richard Overy observes, 'Hitler pursued a policy of putting as much as possible in the "shop window" to give the impression that Germany was armed in greater depth than was in fact the case.'

France and Britain

The pace of German military expansion created concern in both France and Britain, which in turn both embarked on major rearmament programmes.

France

In France rearmament caused considerable economic and social problems. Between 1936 and 1938 the franc had to be devalued three times to help pay for rearmament. In November 1938 a general strike was called in Paris in protest against wage cuts and the decline in living standards caused by diverting resources to rearmament. The pace of French rearmament was slowed by the weakness of their economy, but even so military expenditure had increased six times between 1936 and 1939.

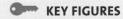 **KEY FIGURES**

Hjalmar Schacht (1877–1970)
As president of the *Reichsbank* and economics minister he played an important part in financing German rearmament 1933–5. After disagreements about the pace of rearmament he was dismissed in 1937.

Hermann Göring (1893–1946)
Nazi leader and First World War air ace. In charge of the *Luftwaffe* and the Four-Year Plan. Killed himself in May 1945.

 **KEY TERM**

Synthetic materials
Objects imitating a natural product but made chemically.

Britain

In Britain too rearmament caused considerable financial strain, which Neville Chamberlain (see page 172) feared might 'break our backs'. Nevertheless, in 1936 a four-year plan for rearmament was unveiled in which priority was given to the navy and air force. A key part of the programme was the construction of a bomber strike force. The programme was accelerated when Chamberlain became prime minister in 1937 and increased funds were also made available for the army. Between 1936 and 1939 expenditure on armaments increased from £185.9 million to £719 million. On 22 February 1939 the government authorised aircraft production 'to the limit', regardless of cost.

SOURCE B

Study Source B. What do these statistics show about the arms race in aircraft production 1935–40?

From R. Overy, *The Origins of the Second World War*, Longman, 1987, p. 49.

Aircraft production in Britain, France and Germany:

	Britain	France	Germany
1935	1,140	785	3,183
1936	1,877	890	5,112
1937	2,153	743	5,606
1938	2,827	1,382	5,235
1939	7,940	3,163	8,295
1940	15,049	2,113	10,247

The impact of the arms race on the diplomatic situation

The German rearmament programme would not be completed until the mid-1940s. This would not, however, stop Hitler from waging a limited war against Czechoslovakia or Poland if he believed that Britain and France would stand aside.

The British and French programmes, on the other hand, were planned to be ready by 1939–40. Neither Britain nor France wanted war, and both were ready to seek agreement with Nazi Germany to prevent it, but if there was no option but war, then 1939–40 was the best possible date for it to occur. Beyond that date both countries would find it increasingly difficult to maintain the high level of spending that their armament programmes demanded.

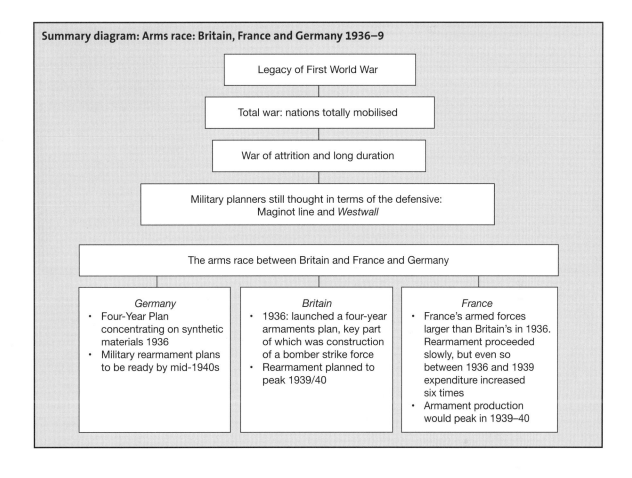

③ Britain, France and appeasement

▶ *Why and how did Chamberlain launch a policy of appeasement in the autumn of 1937?*

▶ *What did Chamberlain hope that his appeasement policies would achieve?*

Appeasement: the historical debate

Essentially, appeasement was a realistic policy for the rulers of the large and vulnerable British Empire. It was based on the assumption that a willingness to compromise would avert conflict and protect the essential interests of the empire (see page 7). With Hitler, however, it completely failed to achieve any lasting settlement and appeared in retrospect to be a cowardly policy of surrender.

Neville Chamberlain

1869	Born in Birmingham
1915–18	Lord Mayor of Birmingham
1918	Entered parliament
1923–9	Minister of health
1931–7	Chancellor of the exchequer
1939–40	Prime minister
1940	Died

Chamberlain was an energetic politician, who had been a very successful minister of health and chancellor of the exchequer. When he became prime minister he was determined to solve the German problem and avoid plunging Europe into war. He took control of British foreign policy and marginalised the foreign office.

Chamberlain hoped that he would be able to come to an agreement by a direct man-to-man discussion with Hitler and that German grievances could be met through a policy of appeasement. Even though he reluctantly realised that war was probable after Hitler's seizure of Bohemia in March 1939, Chamberlain never completely abandoned appeasement.

KEY TERM

Dunkirk In May 1940 the British Expeditionary Force in France was compelled to retreat to Dunkirk and was only rescued by a risky sea evacuation.

In the first twenty years after the defeat of Hitler, historians on both the right and left scornfully dismissed Chamberlain's appeasement policy. They were heavily influenced not only by Winston Churchill's memoirs, but also by a brilliant book, *Guilty Men*, which was written by three left-wing journalists, including Michael Foot, later a leader of the Labour Party. It was published in July 1940, just a few weeks after the fall of France and the evacuations from **Dunkirk**. It bitterly accused Chamberlain of pursuing a disastrous policy that had left Britain unprepared militarily to face the dictators. In the eyes of the general public and for historians on both the left and right, Neville Chamberlain rapidly became the scapegoat – and not only for his own countrymen. French historians and politicians claimed that he bullied them into appeasement, while some Germans were tempted to excuse their own support for Hitler by blaming Chamberlain for not standing up to the Nazis.

Only with the opening up of the British and French archives in the 1960s and 1970s did it gradually become possible to reassess the whole policy of appeasement and place Chamberlain's decisions in the context of Britain's slow economic decline as well as the global challenges facing the British Empire. R.P. Shay, in his study of British rearmament in the 1930s, argues that Chamberlain had to maintain a balance between rearming and balancing the budget, so that if war came Britain would have enough money to buy vital materials and equipment from the USA. By the end of the 1980s revisionist historians were arguing that Chamberlain's policy was essentially determined by Britain's economic weakness and that he had no other option but to attempt to appease Germany if the empire was to be preserved. John Charmley even argued that Churchill was the real 'guilty man' by fighting a war that could only end in the dissolution of the empire and bankruptcy. This revisionist line was, however, strongly challenged by R.A.C. Parker, who insisted that 'after the *Anschluss* [see page 174] in March 1938 Chamberlain could … have secured sufficient support in Britain for a close alliance with France, and a policy of containing and encircling Germany, more or less shrouded under the League of Nations covenant'.

Chamberlain and appeasement

In the autumn of 1937 Chamberlain launched a major initiative aimed at achieving a settlement with Hitler. He hoped to divert German expansion in eastern Europe by offering to return African colonies to Germany. In late November an Anglo-French summit was held in London where this policy was more fully explored. Chamberlain won over the French to this policy and by March 1938 he was ready to negotiate a package of colonial concessions with Berlin, but the gathering pace of German expansion signalled first by the *Anschluss* and then by the destruction of Czechoslovakia made this approach irrelevant.

SOURCE C

From Neville Chamberlain's letter to Mrs Morton Prince, an American citizen, 16 January 1938, quoted in J. Joll, *Britain and Europe*, Oxford University Press, 1967, p. 322.

… as a realist I must do what I can to make this country safe … [The British people] are perfectly aware that until we are fully rearmed our position will be one of great anxiety. They realise that we are in no position to enter light-heartedly upon a war with such a formidable power as Germany, much less if Germany were aided by Italian attacks on our Mediterranean possessions and communications. They know that France, though her army is strong, is desperately weak in some vital spots …

According to Source C, what are Chamberlain's reasons for appeasement?

Summary diagram: Britain, France and appeasement

Appeasement essentially a traditional British policy to avoid damaging conflict

Failure in 1938–9 led to Chamberlain becoming a scapegoat for Anglo-French failures 1939–40. Since the 1970s revisionist historians have defended Chamberlain's policies

In November 1937 Chamberlain launched a major initiative aimed at achieving settlement with Hitler by offering Germany return of its colonies

The *Anschluss* and the destruction of Czechoslovakia

▶ *Why did Hitler decide to invade Austria?*

▶ *What did Hitler hope to achieve by exploiting the nationalism of the Sudeten Germans?*

In November 1937 Hitler had outlined a possible scenario involving civil war in France or a Franco-Italian war (see page 167), which would enable him to annex Austria and dismember Czechoslovakia without fear of international intervention. He was able to achieve these aims in 1938–9, even though the circumstances that he had predicted never in fact came about. Both the *Anschluss* and the eventual destruction of Czechoslovakia do indeed show Hitler's ability to adapt his tactics to the prevailing circumstances while steadily pursuing his overall aims.

The *Anschluss*

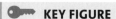 **KEY FIGURE**

Kurt von Schuschnigg (1897–1977)

Chancellor of Austria 1934–8. He was imprisoned by the Nazis after the *Anschluss*.

The annexation of Austria had long been a key aim of Nazi foreign policy, but Hitler did not plan the actual events that enabled him to achieve it. The crisis was ultimately triggered when **Schuschnigg**, the Austrian chancellor, alarmed by the activities of the Austrian Nazis, requested an interview with Hitler. Hitler welcomed the chance to achieve an easy diplomatic success by imposing on Schuschnigg an agreement which would not only have subordinated Austrian foreign policy to Berlin but also have given the Austrian Nazi Party complete freedom. However, Schuschnigg then decided unexpectedly to regain some room for manoeuvre by asking his countrymen to vote in a referendum, which he planned to hold on Sunday 14 March, for a 'free and German, independent and social, Christian and united Austria'.

The German army occupies Austria

The immediate danger for the German government was that if Schuschnigg's appeal was endorsed by a large majority, he would be able to renounce his agreement with Hitler. Confronted by this challenge, Hitler rapidly dropped his policy of gradual absorption of Austria and not only forced Schuschnigg to cancel the referendum but on 12 March ordered the German army to occupy Austria. Then Hitler decided, apparently on the spur of the moment after a highly successful visit to the Austrian city of Linz, where he had attended secondary school as a boy, to incorporate Austria into the *Reich* rather than install a satellite Nazi government in Vienna.

The reaction of Italy, Britain and France

Besides violating the Versailles and St Germain treaties which specifically forbade the union of Germany and Austria (see page 101), Hitler had for the first time invaded an independent state, even though the Austrian army did not oppose him, and put himself in a position from which to threaten Czechoslovakia. Why then did this not bring about a repetition of the Stresa Front that was briefly formed in 1934 against German aggression (see page 149)? Although Chamberlain was in contact with the Italian government, and in April concluded an agreement aimed at lowering the tension in the Mediterranean, essentially Mussolini had decided as long ago as 1936 that Austria was a German sphere of interest (see page 162). Not surprisingly therefore, on 11 March, he backed Hitler's decision to invade Austria. Both Britain and France protested to Berlin but neither had any intention of going to war over Austria. Indeed, the French were paralysed by an internal political crisis caused by the resignation of **Chautemps'** ministry, and between 10 and 13 March did not even have a government.

The initial reaction of the British government was to hope that the storm would blow over and that talks could resume with Berlin on a package of possible colonial concessions, which had already been handed to the German government on 3 March. These concessions were, after all, aimed at distracting Berlin from pursuing its ambitions in central Europe. Whether Chamberlain really believed that Hitler could be bought off is hard to say. Privately he wrote that 'it was now clear' that force was the only argument that Germany understood, but publicly he was not yet ready to draw the logical conclusion from this and confront Hitler. Was he gaining time for his country to rearm or was he seriously giving peace one more chance?

KEY FIGURE

Camille Chautemps (1885–1963)

Served in several French governments and was prime minister three times.

To what extent does this map show that Hitler had effectively reversed the territorial clauses of the Treaty of Versailles by August 1939?

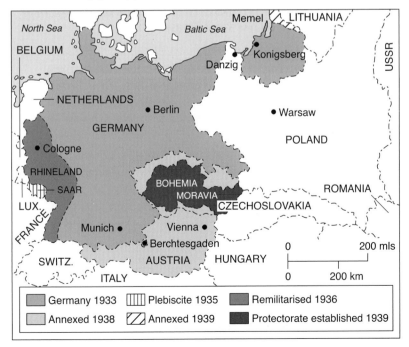

Central Europe showing German expansion from 1935 to August 1939. It was an impressive achievement, which increased Hitler's popularity in the *Reich*.

The Sudeten crisis

The annexation of Austria with the minimum of international protest greatly increased the vulnerability of Czechoslovakia to Nazi pressure, as it was now surrounded on three sides by German territory. Hitler had long regarded Czechoslovakia, with its alliances with both France and Russia, as a strategic threat to Germany which would eventually have to be eliminated. It is, however, arguable that in April 1938 Hitler was by no means sure how he was to carry out this aim. He certainly played with the idea of launching a sudden attack on Czechoslovakia if a major crisis were to be triggered, for instance by the assassination of the German ambassador in Prague. An easier and safer way to bring about the disintegration of Czechoslovakia was to inflame the nationalism of the **Sudeten Germans**. Czechoslovakia was a fragile state undermined by an ethnically divided population. Its unity was particularly threatened by the 3 million Sudeten Germans (see page 101) and the 2 million Slovaks. Hitler therefore specifically instructed **Konrad Henlein**, the Sudeten German leader, to keep making demands for concessions which the Prague government could not possibly grant if it wanted to preserve the unity of Czechoslovakia.

In the aftermath of the *Anschluss* both Britain and France were acutely aware of the growing threat to Czechoslovakia. Britain was unwilling to guarantee Czechoslovakia and yet realised that it might well not be able to stand aloof from the consequences of a German attack on it.

KEY TERM

Sudeten Germans Ethnic Germans who had been settled in the Sudetenland since the thirteenth century.

KEY FIGURE

Konrad Henlein (1898–1945)

Leader of the Sudeten German Nazis and later Nazi *Gauleiter* of the Sudetenland.

? What, according to Source D, were the likely consequences of a German attack on Czechoslovakia?

SOURCE D

From Chamberlain's speech to the House of Commons on 24 March 1938, from *House of Commons Debates*, **volume 333, cols 1399–407.**

[I]t would be well within the bounds of possibility that other countries, besides those which were parties to the original dispute, would almost immediately become involved. This is especially true in the case of two countries like Great Britain and France, with long associations of friendship, with interests closely interwoven, devoted to the same ideals of democratic liberty and determined to uphold them.

The French, unlike the British, were pledged by two treaties signed in 1924 and 1925 to consult and assist Czechoslovakia in the event of a threat to their common interests (see page 126). In reality, the French were in no position to help the Czechs. The chief of the French air staff, who was in charge of operational planning, made no secret of his fears that the French air force would be wiped out within fifteen days after the outbreak of war with Germany. The French government was therefore ready to follow the British lead in seeking a way of defusing the Sudeten crisis before it could lead to war.

The May crisis

The urgency of solving the Sudeten war crisis was underlined by the war scare of the weekend of 20–21 May 1938, when the Czech government suddenly partially mobilised its army in response to false rumours that a German attack was imminent. Hitler, warned by both Britain and France of the dangerous consequences of any military action, rapidly proclaimed the absence of any mobilisation plans. Yet far from making Hitler more reasonable, this incident appears to have had the opposite effect, as he immediately stepped up military preparations for an invasion and set 1 October as a deadline for 'smashing Czechoslovakia'. Taylor sees this as bluff and argues that 'Hitler did not need to act. Others would do his work for him.' There were certainly, as we have seen, powerful forces working for the disintegration of the Czech state, but most historians do not dismiss Hitler's plans so lightly. It is more likely that he was just keeping his options open, as Bullock argues, to the 'very last possible moment'.

Meanwhile, France and Britain were redoubling their efforts to find a peaceful solution. The Anglo-French peace strategy aimed to put pressure on both the Czechs and the Sudeten Germans to make concessions, while continuing to warn Hitler of the dangers of a general war. In early September, **Beneš**, the Czech prime minister, responded to this pressure by granting almost all Henlein's demands. As this threatened the justification for Hitler's campaign against Czechoslovakia, Hitler immediately instructed Henlein to provoke a series of incidents which would enable him to break off the talks with Beneš.

Chamberlain intervenes

On 12 September 1938 Hitler's campaign moved into a new phase when, in a speech at the Nuremberg rally, he violently attacked the Czechs and assured the Sudetens of his support. Both Britain and France desperately attempted to avoid war. **Daladier**, the French prime minister, suggested that he and Chamberlain should meet Hitler, but Chamberlain seized the initiative and flew to see Hitler on 15 September at Berchtesgaden. There he agreed, subject to consultation with the French, that Czechoslovakia should cede to Germany all areas which contained a German population of 50 per cent or over. This would be supervised by an international commission. Hitler also demanded that Czechoslovakia should renounce its pact with the USSR, which it had signed in 1935 as a consequence of the France-Soviet Treaty (see page 151). When Chamberlain again met Hitler at Bad Godesberg on 22 September, after winning French backing for his plan, Hitler demanded that the German occupation of the Sudetenland should be speeded up so that it would be completed by 28 September. Nor was it to be supervised by any international commission. Why Hitler should suddenly have changed his mind has puzzled historians. Taylor argued that Hitler was anxious to avoid accepting Chamberlain's plan in the hope that the Hungarians and Poles would formulate their own demands for Czechoslovakian territory, and that he would then be able to move in and occupy the whole state under the pretext of being 'a peacemaker creating a new order'. On the other hand, it is possible that Hitler had no such elaborate plan in mind and merely wanted to eliminate Czechoslovakia once and for all through war. At this stage Chamberlain's peace initiative seemed to have failed. France and Britain reluctantly began to mobilise, although both powers still continued to seek a negotiated settlement.

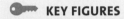

KEY FIGURES

Edvard Beneš (1884–1948)

A leader of the Czechoslovak independence movement before 1918, then minister of foreign affairs and president 1935–8 and 1945–8.

Édouard Daladier (1884–1970)

A radical French politician and prime minister 1938–41.

The Munich Agreement

In retrospect it is often argued that the French and British should have gone to war and called Hitler's bluff. Chamberlain's critics particularly stress that the USSR was ready to come to the help of Czechoslovakia, but at the time offers of Soviet help seemed to the British, French and even the Czechs to be unconvincing. As neither Poland nor Romania would allow Soviet troops through their territory, how could they help Czechoslovakia? It is thus not surprising that Chamberlain and Daladier warmly welcomed Mussolini's last-minute proposal on 28 September for a four-power conference in Munich.

The next day, under pressure from his generals and from Mussolini, who both dreaded a premature war, Hitler reluctantly agreed to delay the occupation of the Sudetenland until 10 October and to allow an international commission to map the boundary line. He also consented, together with Britain, France and Italy, to guarantee what remained of the independence of Czechoslovakia and signed a declaration which affirmed the desire of Britain and Germany 'never to go to war with one another again'. This was supplemented by a similar declaration signed by Ribbentrop, Hitler's foreign minister, in Paris in December.

It is too simple to call Munich a triumph for Hitler. He had, it is true, secured the Sudetenland, but arguably he had been cheated of his real aim, the destruction of Czechoslovakia, which apparently was now about to be protected by an international guarantee. Germany seemed to be in danger of being enmeshed in just the sort of international agreement Hitler had always hoped to avoid. However, even the most revisionist of historians would be hard put to call Munich a great victory for Chamberlain. Arguably, he did buy more time for rearmament, but to the outside world Munich seemed to be a major defeat for Britain and France. The British ambassador in Tokyo reported that 'the Japanese reaction … is that we are prepared to put up with almost any indignity rather than fight. The result is that, all in all, our prestige is at a low ebb in the East … .'

The destruction of Czechoslovakia

The argument that Hitler merely responded to events is hard to sustain when his foreign policy from October 1938 to March 1939 is analysed. His main priority remained the destruction of Czechoslovakia. On 21 October 1938 the German army was ordered to draw up fresh plans for military action. Simultaneously, Hitler dangled the bait of territorial gains at the expense of the Czechs in front of the Hungarians, Poles and Romanians in order to enlist their support. German agents were also sent into Slovakia to fuel agitation against Prague. In practice, Britain and France were already beginning to recognise Czechoslovakia as a German sphere of influence. The German representatives were allowed to dominate the international commission that was to map out the new frontiers after the secession of the Sudetenland and neither power protested when Germany refused to participate in finalising the terms of the joint guarantee of Czechoslovakia in February 1939.

On 6 March 1939 the Germans were given the opportunity finally to dismember Czechoslovakia. When the Czechs suddenly moved troops into Slovakia to crush local demands for independence, which the Nazis of course had helped to stir up, Hitler persuaded the Slovaks to appeal to Berlin for assistance. On 14 March 1939 the Czech president, Emil Hácha, was ordered to travel to Berlin, where he was ruthlessly bullied into entrusting the future of his country to 'the hands of the *Führer*'. The next day German troops occupied Prague, and Bohemia and Moravia became a German protectorate. Slovakia remained nominally independent, but in reality was a German satellite. This action was to precipitate a major diplomatic revolution in Europe.

Summary diagram: The *Anschluss* and the destruction of Czechoslovakia

Eruption of Austrian and Czech crises 1938

Anschluss
- Faced with threat of referendum on Austro-German Agreement, Germany annexed Austria, 12 March
- Chamberlain accepted *Anschluss* and hoped talks with Germany on a comprehensive settlement would go ahead

Sudeten crisis
- Hitler intended to exploit Sudeten demands for independence to 'smash' Czechoslovakia
- Fearing war, Chamberlain negotiated Munich Agreement with Hitler: Sudetenland ceded to Germany; rest of Czechoslovakia guaranteed by Britain, France, Italy and Germany (29 September)

German occupation of Prague, March 1939 marked total failure of appeasement policy

---

5 Anglo-French guarantees and attempts to construct a peace front

▶ *Why did Britain and France guarantee Poland, Greece and Romania?*

▶ *Why did Hitler decide that Poland had to be destroyed?*

In 1925 the British foreign minister had declared that the defence of the Polish corridor was not worth the bones of one British grenadier (see page 120), yet on 31 March 1939 Britain broke decisively with its traditional foreign policy of avoiding a Continental commitment, and, together with France, guaranteed Poland against a German attack. In many ways it appeared a foolhardy and contradictory gesture as both Britain and France lacked the military power to defend Poland and had already tacitly written off eastern Europe as a German sphere of influence. What caused this U-turn was the speed and brutality of the German occupation of the Czech province of Bohemia, which clearly indicated that Hitler could no longer be trusted to respect treaties and guarantees. It is also important to stress that, in the spring of 1939, the French economy and with it French self-confidence had made a strong recovery. Thus, a tougher policy towards Hitler increasingly appeared to the French government to be a realistic option.

Britain was initially stampeded into this revolutionary new policy by panic-stricken rumours on 17 March that Hitler was about to occupy Romania and seize the oil wells there. Access to these would greatly strengthen the German war industry and enable it to survive any future British naval blockade. At first, Britain aimed to contain Germany by negotiating a four-power pact with France, Russia and Poland, but given the intense suspicion with which Russia was viewed by Poland and the other eastern European states this was not a practical policy. Yet when Hitler went on to force Lithuania to hand back the former German city of Memel to the *Reich* on 23 March, it became even more vital to deter Hitler by any means possible. Thus, Chamberlain and Daladier had little option but to announce on 31 March 1939 an immediate Anglo-French guarantee of Poland against external attack. The Polish guarantee was, however, seen as merely the first step towards constructing a comprehensive security system in eastern Europe. Chamberlain hoped to buttress it with a series of interlocking security pacts with other eastern European and Baltic states.

When, on 7 April, Mussolini invaded Albania a similar wave of panic among the eastern Mediterranean states galvanised Britain and France to guarantee both Greece and Romania. In May, Britain considerably strengthened its position in the eastern Mediterranean by negotiating a preliminary agreement with Turkey for mutual assistance 'in the event of an act of aggression leading to war in the Mediterranean area'. By July both Bulgaria and Yugoslavia were beginning to gravitate towards the Anglo-French '**peace bloc**'.

The German reaction to the British guarantee

In October 1938, and then again in January and March 1939, Hitler unsuccessfully sounded out the Poles about the return of Danzig, the construction of a road and rail link through the corridor and joining the Anti-Comintern Pact. In return, the Poles were offered the eventual prospect of acquiring land in Ukraine. Essentially, Hitler wanted to turn Poland into a reliable satellite, but given the fate of Czechoslovakia it was precisely this status that the Poles finally rejected in March 1939. The Anglo-French guarantee of Poland, far from deterring Hitler, convinced him that Poland would have to be eliminated, even if this meant war with Britain and France.

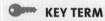
KEY TERM

Peace bloc A group of states committed to opposing aggressor powers.

SOURCE E

From Hitler's message to his generals, 23 May 1939, quoted in *Documents on German Foreign*, series D, volume VI, no. 433, HMSO, 1957–66.

Poland will always be on the side of our adversaries … Danzig is not the objective. It is a matter of expanding our living space in the east … We cannot expect a repetition of Czechoslovakia. There will be fighting. The task is to isolate Poland … Basic principle: conflict with Poland, beginning with the attack on Poland, will be successful only if the West keeps out. If that is impossible, then it is better to attack the West and finish off Poland at the same time. It will be a task of dexterous diplomacy to isolate Poland …

According to Source E, what were Hitler's plans towards Poland?

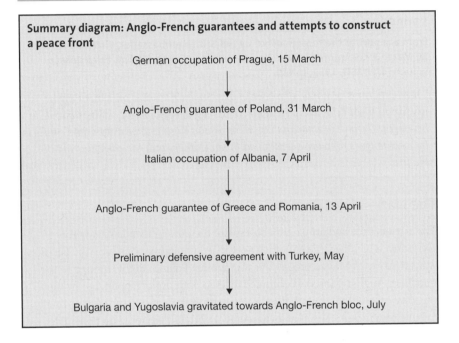

Summary diagram: Anglo-French guarantees and attempts to construct a peace front

German occupation of Prague, 15 March

↓

Anglo-French guarantee of Poland, 31 March

↓

Italian occupation of Albania, 7 April

↓

Anglo-French guarantee of Greece and Romania, 13 April

↓

Preliminary defensive agreement with Turkey, May

↓

Bulgaria and Yugoslavia gravitated towards Anglo-French bloc, July

6 Gaining the support of the USSR

▶ *Why did Britain, France and Germany begin negotiations with the USSR in the summer of 1939?*

▶ *Why did Germany want an alliance with the USSR?*

Origins of the Nazi–Soviet Pact

Once war against Poland seemed inevitable, it made good sense for Hitler to ensure the support or at least neutrality of the USSR. As soon as victory was assured over Poland and the Western democracies, the USSR could in due course be dealt with. Britain and France also needed a pact with the USSR to build up their 'peace front'. Stalin was now in the enviable position of being able to play off Hitler against Chamberlain and Daladier.

Protracted negotiations between the USSR, Britain and France began in April 1939, but both sides deeply mistrusted each other. Stalin's demand that the USSR should have the right militarily to intervene in the affairs of the small states on its western borders if they were threatened with internal subversion by the Nazis, as Austria and Czechoslovakia had been in 1938, was rejected outright by the British. They feared that the Soviets would use the threat of Nazi indirect aggression as an excuse to seize the territories for themselves. Stalin, on the other hand, was equally suspicious that the democracies were attempting to manoeuvre the Soviets into a position where they would have to do most of the fighting against Germany. A report to the foreign office in 1939 by the British ambassador to Moscow, Sir William Seeds (1882–1973), is quoted in Source F.

SOURCE F

? What does Source F reveal about the state of Anglo-Russian relations?

From a report to the foreign office by the British ambassador, Sir William Seeds, 20 March 1939, quoted in *Documents on British Foreign Policy*, third series, volume 4, HMSO, 1951, p. 419.

Those innocents at home who believe that Soviet Russia is only awaiting an invitation to join the Western democracies should ponder M. Stalin's advice to his party: 'To be cautious and not allow Soviet Russia to be drawn into conflicts by warmongers who are accustomed to have others pull the chestnuts out of the fire.'

The Nazi–Soviet Pact

The Soviets thus had ample time to explore the possibility of a pact with Germany, which became genuinely interested in negotiations once the decision was taken on 23 May to prepare for war against Poland. Right through to the middle of August, Moscow continued to keep both options open, but by then the slow pace of the military discussions with Britain and France seems finally to have convinced Stalin that an agreement with Hitler would be preferable. With only days to go before the start of the military campaign against Poland, Hitler was ready to accept Stalin's terms and the Nazi–Soviet Pact was signed on 23 August.

Not only did the pact commit both powers to benevolent neutrality towards each other, but in a secret protocol it outlined the German and Soviet spheres of interest in eastern Europe: the Baltic states and Bessarabia in Romania fell within the Soviet sphere, while Poland was to be divided between the two. Above all, by neutralising the USSR, the pact made an attack on Poland a much less risky policy for Hitler, even if Britain and France did try to come to its rescue.

The pact shocked and surprised Britain and France, but given the deep and often justified suspicions of the USSR in Britain, France and the eastern European states, the Nazi–Soviet Pact was arguably the most likely outcome from the tangle of negotiations that took place in the summer of 1939. It did, however, make a German attack on Poland almost inevitable.

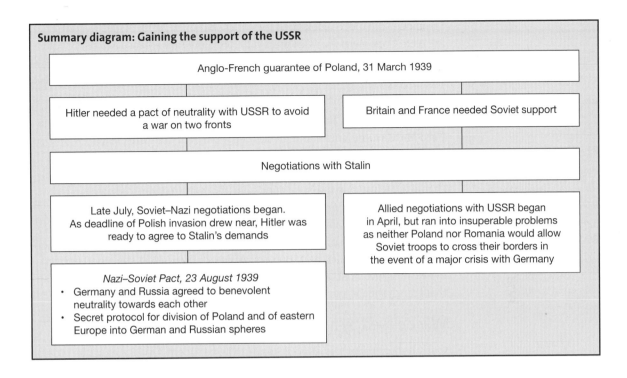

Summary diagram: Gaining the support of the USSR

Anglo-French guarantee of Poland, 31 March 1939

Hitler needed a pact of neutrality with USSR to avoid a war on two fronts

Britain and France needed Soviet support

Negotiations with Stalin

Late July, Soviet–Nazi negotiations began. As deadline of Polish invasion drew near, Hitler was ready to agree to Stalin's demands

Allied negotiations with USSR began in April, but ran into insuperable problems as neither Poland nor Romania would allow Soviet troops to cross their borders in the event of a major crisis with Germany

Nazi–Soviet Pact, 23 August 1939
- Germany and Russia agreed to benevolent neutrality towards each other
- Secret protocol for division of Poland and of eastern Europe into German and Russian spheres

7 Outbreak of the Second World War 1939

▶ *What signs were there that appeasement was not yet dead?*

▶ *Why was Mussolini unable to avert the war?*

On the eve of the signature of the Nazi–Soviet Pact, Hitler boasted of his plans in a speech to his military commanders as quoted in Source G.

SOURCE G

From a speech made by Hitler to his military commanders on 22 August 1939, quoted in A.P. Adamthwaite, *The Making of the Second World War*, Allen & Unwin, 1979, p. 219.

*To be sure a new situation has arisen. I experienced those poor worms, Daladier and Chamberlain, in Munich. They will be too cowardly to attack. They won't go beyond a blockade. Against that we have **autarchy** and the Russian raw materials. Poland will be depopulated and settled with Germans. My pact with the Poles was merely conceived of as a gaining of time … After Stalin's death – he is a very sick man – we will break the Soviet Union. Then there will begin the dawn of German rule of the earth.*

Why, according to Source G, does Hitler think that Germany will be able to defeat Poland in isolation?

 KEY TERM

Autarchy Economic self-sufficiency.

The omens did indeed look good for Hitler. Although he had failed to convert the Anti-Comintern Pact (see page 163) into a military alliance against Britain and France, he had in May concluded the Pact of Steel with Italy by which Mussolini rashly agreed to support Germany militarily. Privately, Mussolini had been assured that Hitler had no intention of going to war for at least three years!

Neither did it appear that appeasement in Britain and France was dead. In June, **Lord Halifax**, the British foreign secretary, stressed that while Britain would defend Poland against any threat to its independence, this did not necessarily mean that its existing frontiers could not be altered or the status of Danzig changed. He went on to repeat a message that was frequently to come out of London in the summer of 1939; namely that, once trust was re-established, 'any of Germany's claims are open to consideration round a table'. In June and July there were also sporadic talks between British and German officials on economic collaboration in Europe and Africa. In France, too, the mood seemed increasingly defeatist, and **Bonnet**, the French foreign minister, was suggesting that France should 'push Warsaw into a compromise'.

War delayed by a week

Overall then, Hitler had good grounds to be confident. On 23 August he ordered the army to prepare to attack Poland on the 26th, but then two days later, on the 25th, these orders were cancelled because, contrary to his expectations, Britain had reacted to the news of the Nazi–Soviet Pact by ratifying its guarantee of Poland. Mussolini also announced that he could not fight without impossibly large deliveries of German armaments and equipment. Was there now a chance for a compromise? Superficially, it might seem that there was. During the next few days the British and French used all the diplomatic channels they could to avoid war. Theoretically, some sort of compromise on Poland might eventually be possible, but in the final analysis they were not ready to sacrifice Poland's independence to achieve it. They were unwilling to repeat Munich. They wanted, as the historian A.P. Adamthwaite has stressed, 'détente, but negotiated from strength'.

Hitler's position was diametrically opposed to this. He was insistent on first destroying Poland and only then negotiating with Britain and France. On 25 August he even offered Britain an alliance and a guarantee of its empire provided it consented to the destruction of Poland and to German supremacy in eastern Europe. The response from London continued to be that only after a freely negotiated Polish–German agreement could the future of Anglo-German relations be discussed.

Belatedly, it looked as if Hitler was making some concession to this position when, on 29 August, he suddenly demanded that the British should instruct the Poles to send a minister with full negotiating powers to Berlin by the following day. Fearing that Hitler would treat him as he had Schuschnigg and

KEY FIGURES

Lord Halifax (1881–1959)

Viceroy of India 1926–31 and British foreign minister 1938–40.

Georges Bonnet (1889–1973)

French foreign minister 1938–9, and a leading spokesmen for French appeasement.

Hácha (see pages 174 and 179), the British government refused to press the Poles to send a negotiator to Berlin, and instead argued that such a deadline was impracticable since time was needed to prepare for negotiations. Was a last-minute chance to save the peace lost? Taylor argues that war began simply because Hitler launched 'on 29 August a diplomatic manoeuvre which he ought to have launched on 28 August'. It is more likely, however, that Hitler was aiming to isolate the Poles and to manoeuvre them into a position where their 'stubbornness' could be blamed for starting the war, and so give Britain and France an excuse not to back them.

SOURCE H

German troops demolish a Polish frontier barrier during the invasion of Poland, which began in September 1939. Poland was rapidly defeated and partitioned between Germany and the USSR.

War breaks out

Even when, on 1 September 1939, Germany at last invaded Poland, frantic efforts to avert war still continued. Mussolini urged a Four-Power European Conference, and only when it was absolutely clear that Hitler would not withdraw his troops from Poland did Britain and France declare war on Germany on 3 September. Italy, despite the Pact of Steel, remained neutral, until France was defeated in June 1940, as Mussolini was initially unsure of a speedy German victory and wanted to hedge his bets.

Study Source H. What message is the photo communicating to the German people?

Summary diagram: Outbreak of war

Hitler's position strengthened through Pact of Steel (23 May) and Nazi–Soviet Pact (23 August)

↓

23 August, Hitler ordered German army to prepare to invade Poland on 26 August

↓

Cancelled on 25 August because Britain reacted to Nazi–Soviet Pact by ratifying Polish guarantee. Mussolini also informed Hitler that Italy was not ready for war

↓

25 August, Hitler attempted to bribe Britain to give up Polish guarantee by offering German support for the British Empire and an alliance

↓

29 August, Hitler sent demand to Britain that Poland should send a negotiator to Berlin with full powers. London refused to press the Poles and demanded more time

↓

31 August, German army given orders to attack at 04.45 hours on 1 September

↓

1 September, German troops invaded Poland

↓

3 September, Britain and France declared war

 8

The spreading conflict: October 1939 to June 1941

▶ *How did Stalin exploit the 'phoney war' to achieve his aims?*

▶ *What were the immediate consequences for Continental Europe of Hitler's victories in 1940?*

Stalin exploits the 'phoney war', October 1939 to March 1940

German troops completed the occupation of Poland within six weeks and Soviet forces rapidly moved into the areas allocated to them by the Nazi–Soviet Pact. Hitler offered Britain and France, who had made hardly any effort to assist Poland, peace on the basis of setting up a small Polish state, which would in reality be a German satellite. When both states rejected this offer, Hitler had little option but to prepare to extend the war westwards. Inevitably, he became more dependent on Soviet neutrality and supplies of raw materials to defeat the British blockade.

Stalin was not slow to exploit the USSR's favourable position during this '**phoney war**'. He persuaded Hitler to transfer Lithuania, which by the Nazi–Soviet Pact of August had originally been assigned to the German sphere of influence, to the Soviet sphere. He also rapidly negotiated pacts with the Baltic states, which reduced them to the status of satellites. When Finland refused to cede the USSR a naval base and agree to the revision of its frontier, the Soviet army invaded in November 1939 and by March 1940 had forced the Finns to comply with Stalin's demands.

German victory in the west

In April, German troops rapidly occupied both Norway and Denmark to prevent a British attempt to interrupt the flow of iron ore from Sweden to Germany by seizing the Norwegian ports and mining the waters around Narvik. Then, on 10 May the Germans turned west and within six weeks Belgium, France and the Netherlands were defeated and Britain was driven from the Continent.

The sheer scale of these victories in May 1940 at last persuaded Mussolini in June to take the plunge and declare war on Britain and France. The defeat of France radically changed the balance of power on a global scale. British and US assumptions that France would be able to hold the line against Germany while they would have time to build up their armaments were now destroyed, as was Stalin's calculation that Germany and the Western powers would fatally weaken themselves in a replay of the most bloody campaigns of the First World War.

Britain's refusal to make peace

By defeating France, Hitler had removed the most immediate threat to his Continental policies. Hitler's next step was to attempt to negotiate a peace with Britain. On 25 June he made an optimistic declaration, as quoted in Source I.

SOURCE I

Extract from a statement by Hitler on 25 June 1940, quoted in H.W. Koch, 'Hitler's "Programme" and the Genesis of Operation "Barbarossa"', *The Historical Journal*, volume 26, no. 4, December 1983, Cambridge University Press, pp. 896–7.

The war in the west has ended, France has been conquered, and I shall come, in the shortest possible time, to an understanding with England. There still remains the conflict with the east. That, however, is a task which throws up worldwide problems, like the relationship with Japan and the distribution of power in the Pacific; one might perhaps tackle it in 10 years' time, perhaps I shall leave it to my successor. Now we have our hands full for years to come to digest and to consolidate what we have obtained in Europe.

KEY TERM

Phoney war The period from October 1939 to March 1940 when there was no fighting in western Europe.

According to Hitler in Source I, what problems confront Germany after the end of the war with France?

Yet despite this relaxed, almost statesman-like view of the future, within a year Hitler had attacked the USSR. Why did he do so? Historians disagree as to whether Hitler was carrying out a long-term ideological programme or whether, in H.W. Koch's words, 'Hitler could only act and react within the context of the changing political constellation'.

SOURCE J

? Study Source J. To what extent was this victory parade justified by events?

German troops parade down the Champs-Elysées in Paris after the fall of France in 1940. Paris fell to the German army on 14 June without any fighting.

KEY TERM

Triad A group of three.

The biggest blow to Hitler's plans came when Churchill (see page 68), convinced that with US aid Britain could still wage a war that would eventually wear down the German economy through, to quote historian David Reynolds, 'the **triad** of blockade, bombing and propaganda', refused to react to Hitler's peace-feelers in June 1940.

This was totally unexpected and forced Hitler to consider several options for bringing Britain to the conference table. In September 1940 pressure on Britain was intensified when a new Tripartite Pact was signed by Italy, Japan and Germany. In a key clause that was aimed at the USA they agreed 'to assist one another with all political, economic and military means' should one of them be attacked by a power not yet at war in Europe or China. In November, Hungary, Romania and Slovakia signed the pact, but significantly, attempts to bring in the USSR failed. The Soviet price for membership was too high, as Stalin demanded not only that Bulgaria should be recognised as a Soviet satellite, but also that he should receive German backing for setting up a chain of bases in the Dardanelles and the Persian Gulf.

It is therefore possible to argue that a combination of British intransigence and mounting Soviet ambitions forced Hitler to bring forward his plans for war against the USSR. The historian G.L. Weinberg argues, for instance, that the 'decision to attack the Soviet Union was Hitler's answer to the challenge of England – as it had been Napoleon's'. This interpretation would certainly seem to be supported by Hitler's assessment of the military and diplomatic situation delivered to his generals at a conference on 31 July 1940. After stressing the difficulties involved in the invasion of the British Isles at a time when 'our small navy is only 15 per cent of [the] enemy's', Hitler went on as quoted in Source K.

SOURCE K

From Hitler's speech to a meeting of military and naval chiefs, 31 July 1940, quoted in J. Noakes and G. Pridham, editors, *Nazism, 1919–1945*, Liverpool University Press, 2001, volume 3, p. 790.

Russia is the Far Eastern sword of Britain and the United States pointed at Japan … Japan, like Russia, has her programme which she wants to carry through before the end of the war … With Russia smashed, Britain's last hope would be shattered. Germany will then be master of Europe and the Balkans. Decision: Russia's destruction must therefore be made part of this struggle. Spring 1941. The sooner Russia is crushed, the better.

According to Source K, why is it important to defeat the USSR?

On the other hand, many historians remain unconvinced that Hitler attacked the USSR merely as an extension of the war against Britain. They point out that if the defeat of Britain had really been Hitler's chief priority, then he would surely have concentrated on building up sufficient naval forces and on weakening Britain in the Mediterranean. The Nazi–Soviet Pact was, of course, fragile and likely to break down when the balance of advantages favoured either of the parties sufficiently, but in June 1941 there is absolutely no evidence that Stalin was planning an imminent war against Germany. On balance, it seems more likely that Hitler's long-term ideological hatred of Bolshevism and his determination to gain *Lebensraum*, both of which are amply documented, played the key role in his decision to attack the USSR in June 1941.

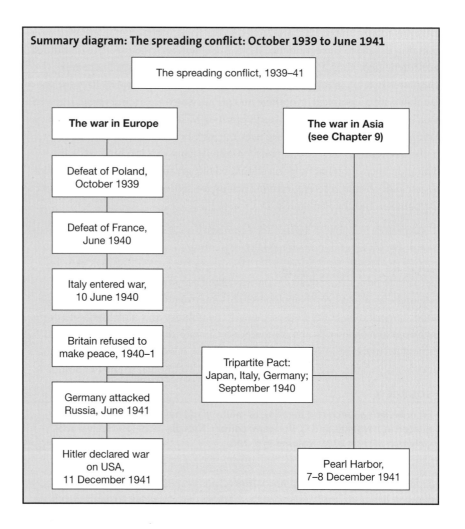

Summary diagram: The spreading conflict: October 1939 to June 1941

9 The key debate

▶ *What were the causes of the Second World War?*

From 1945 to the early 1960s it was accepted that Hitler was the main, if not sole, cause of the Second World War. In 1961 this view was challenged by A.J.P. Taylor in Britain and Fritz Fischer in Germany. Taylor argued that Hitler's foreign policy aims were similar to his predecessors both before 1914 and in the 1920s, while Fischer argued that there existed a continuity of expansionist ambitions from Imperial Germany to the Third Reich. Both books caused furious debates, which ultimately resulted in a deeper understanding of the causes of the Second World War.

The Versailles Treaty as the main cause of the Second World War

Was the Second World War inevitable? Was it essentially a continuation of the First World War or an entirely different conflict which competent diplomacy could have prevented? In 1918 the Germans were defeated but not destroyed. Germany still remained potentially strong and ultimately capable of making a second attempt at dominating Europe. In that sense, the Treaty of Versailles, which humiliated but did not permanently weaken Germany, could well be seen as the 'seed bed' of the Second World War. Arguably, the chain of crises that started with the German remilitarisation of the Rhineland and ended in the German attack on Poland, owed its origins to the Versailles settlement. Does it therefore follow that Versailles made the Second World War inevitable?

Opposition to this argument

On the other hand, as we have already noted, it was a humiliating but not actually a **Carthaginian peace**. Stresemann, Briand and Austen Chamberlain appeared for a time to be able to make the settlement work after modifying the reparation clauses. Nevertheless, it was clear that a revived Germany would still demand its drastic revision, as indeed Stresemann was already beginning to do by the late 1920s. But would this necessarily have produced another world war? Germany was not alone in believing that Versailles needed revision. Certainly, the dominant mood in 1928, as indicated by the Kellogg–Briand Pact and Briand's proposals for a European customs union, was for compromise rather than confrontation.

The Great Depression as a catalyst

EXTRACT 1

From R. Boyce, 'World Depression, World War: Some Economic Origins of the Second World War', quoted in R. Boyce and E. Robertson, editors, *Paths to War*, Macmillan, 1989, p. 55.

So dramatic and complex are the events surrounding the two World Wars that, perhaps inevitably, they tend to obscure the impact on international affairs of the third global catastrophe of the [twentieth century] – the world economic depression which occurred midway between the wars. Beginning in 1929, the depression wreaked havoc on currencies, trade and employment throughout the world, brought down governments, undermined political systems and scarred the lives of nearly everyone who survived its depredations.

The Great Depression at the very least made the outbreak of the Second World War more likely. It weakened the democracies, helped to bring Hitler to power in Germany and strengthened militant nationalism in Japan.

KEY TERM

Carthaginian peace
A peace aimed at destroying the enemy. The term derives from the peace imposed on Carthage by Rome in 146BC.

The revisionist view

Yet how accurate is it to argue that once Hitler came to power, war was inevitable? Taylor argues that Hitler was not essentially different from his predecessors in Germany, and that he lacked any precise programme, despite the so-called Hossbach Memorandum.

EXTRACT 2

From A.J.P. Taylor, *The Origins of the Second World War*, Hamish Hamilton, 1961, p. 68.

In one sphere alone he changed nothing. His foreign policy was that of his predecessors, of the professional diplomats at the foreign ministry, and indeed of virtually all Germans. Hitler too wanted to free Germany from the restrictions of the peace treaty; to restore a great German army; and then to make Germany the greatest power in Europe from her natural weight.

Taylor's critics

Despite Taylor's attempts to portray Hitler as a politician whose foreign policy was relatively traditional, his coming to power in January 1933 did make a crucial difference, as historians such as Michael Burleigh, Ian Kershaw and Richard Evans have shown. He gave a new and powerful impetus not only to German revisionism but to German demands for *Lebensraum* in eastern Europe based on the doctrine of racial superiority. It was this that prompted him to invade the USSR in 1941, leaving an undefeated Britain supplied by the USA on his other front. Historian Adam Tooze also argues that Hitler saw the USA, with its immense financial strength allegedly controlled by the Jews in New York's Wall Street, as a dangerous long-term opponent who would ultimately seek to destroy Nazi Germany.

EXTRACT 3

From A. Tooze, *The Wages of Destruction: The Making and Breaking of the Nazi Economy*, Penguin, 2007, p. xxv.

Why did Hitler take this epic gamble [of starting the Second World War?] … It was ideology which provided Hitler with the lens through which he understood the international balance of power in Europe and the Spanish Civil War in the summer of 1936. In Hitler's mind, the threat posed to the Third Reich by the United States was not just that of conventional superpower rivalry. The threat was existential and bound up with Hitler's abiding fear of the world Jewish conspiracy, manifested in the shape of 'Wall Street Jewry'.

The roles of Britain and France

EXTRACT 4

From R. Overy, *The Origins of the Second World War*, Longman, 1987, p. 65.

The evidence suggests that Britain and France were determined to take some sort of action, and had been building up to that point since the spring of 1938 when rearmament was set fully in motion. At least some of the change in public opinion was engineered by the government and not the other way around. Both populations had to be persuaded over the summer that Danzig was a cause worth fighting for where the Sudetenland was not. Of course Danzig was not the cause of the conflict for the Allies either, but was the instrument whereby public opinion could be shown the intransigent and evil nature of German ambitions. This gave a moral gloss to what was in fact a decision about when was the best time to fight for Britain and France, not for Poland.

How useful are the opinions of the historians quoted in Extracts 1, 2, 3 and 4 for assessing the causes of the Second World War?

The horrendous figure of Adolf Hitler with his well-documented aims for territorial expansion, as the historian Richard Overy argues, obscures the fact that the British and French governments went to war to maintain their independence as Great Powers in Europe and indeed in the world rather than to wage a crusade against the evil force of Nazism. There is no doubt that Hitler's successes in eastern Europe in 1938–9 did threaten to destabilise the whole continent. After the German occupation of Bohemia, the British and French governments believed that they had no choice but to oppose Hitler if they wished to maintain any influence in Europe. Of course, they still kept the door open to negotiations, and pursued the increasingly vain hope of a general settlement with Germany, but essentially Britain and France were ready to risk war in 1939. Indeed, the British Treasury was beginning to argue that Britain's financial position would decline after 1939, and that if war had to come, it was preferable sooner rather than later. In France, Daladier had steadied the economy and the aeronautical industry was rapidly expanding in early 1939.

It does seem, therefore, that Britain and France went to war in 1939, as they did in 1914, to contain Germany and safeguard their own Great Power status. Arguably, it was for the Western powers a continuation of the same struggle, even though Italy and Japan were later to join Germany, and the USSR only became an ally of Britain after the German invasion of June 1941. As in 1917, the USA again became Britain's key ally, but only entered the war as a result of the Japanese attack on Pearl Harbor in December 1941 (see page 206).

Chapter summary

By 1936 Britain, France and Germany had all embarked on major rearmament plans. In November 1937 Hitler, after his success in destroying the Locarno and Versailles treaties, considered his options for expansion within Europe, even though German rearmament would not be completed until the mid-1940s. Taking advantage of Chamberlain's attempts to solve the German problem through appeasement, Hitler first of all annexed Austria and then went on to exploit the nationalism of the Sudeten Germans in an attempt to break up Czechoslovakia. Chamberlain's intervention produced a grudging compromise from Hitler after pressure from both the German generals and Mussolini, who all dreaded war: the Sudetenland was awarded to Germany and rump Czechoslovakia was placed under a four-power guarantee. In March 1939 Germany occupied Bohemia and Moravia, which led to Anglo-French plans to contain Germany and Italy by guaranteeing Poland, Greece and Romania. An attempt to negotiate a defensive treaty with the USSR failed when Stalin signed the Nazi–Soviet Pact. The Second World War started with Germany's invasion of Poland in September 1939. By the summer of 1940 Hitler had defeated France and driven the British from the Continent. Italy joined Germany in June. A year later Hitler invaded the USSR, leaving an undefeated Britain to his rear.

Refresher questions

Use these questions to remind yourself of the key material covered in this chapter.

1 What problems did the French and British rearmament programmes face 1936–9?

2 How did Germany, France and Britain prepare for war 1936–9?

3 What are the historical arguments about appeasement?

4 What did Hitler initially hope to achieve in his talks with Schuschnigg in February 1938?

5 What was the reaction of Italy, Britain and France to the *Anschluss*?

6 What was the significance of the May crisis of 1938?

7 Why did it appear that Chamberlain's peace initiative had failed after the Bad Godesberg meeting of 22–23 September 1938?

8 Was the Munich Agreement a triumph for Hitler?

9 Why was Hitler allowed by Britain and France to destroy Czechoslovakia?

10 Was the Anglo-French guarantee of Poland essentially an act of bluff?

11 Why was the Nazi–Soviet Pact signed?

12 Why did Hitler cancel his invasion plans for Poland on 25 August 1939?

13 What problems did Britain's refusal to make peace in 1940 create for Hitler?

14 Why did Hitler attack the USSR in June 1941?

Question practice

ESSAY QUESTIONS

1 To what extent were the policies pursued by the Nazi government responsible for the outbreak of the Second World War?

2 Assess the consequences of the policy of appeasement for the continent of Europe 1937–8.

3 Which was the more responsible for the outbreak of the Second World War: i) the destruction of Czechoslovakia or ii) the Nazi–Soviet Pact? Explain your answer with reference to both i) and ii).

4 To what extent was appeasement to blame for the outbreak of war in Europe in 1939?

INTERPRETATION QUESTIONS

1 Read the interpretation and then answer the question that follows. 'Hitler may have projected a great war all along yet it seems from the record that he became involved in war through launching on 29 August [1939], a diplomatic manoeuvre which he ought to have launched on 28 August' (adapted from A.J.P. Taylor, *The Origins of the Second World War*, 1961). Evaluate the strengths and limitations of this interpretation, making reference to other interpretations that you have studied.

2 Read the interpretation and then answer the question that follows. 'It was largely because of recent history of deep suspicion and mutual hostility [between the USSR and the Western powers] that common cause was never recognized in confronting Hitler before the war' (from J. Haslam, *Russia's Cold War*, 2011). Evaluate the strengths and limitations of this interpretation, making reference to other interpretations.

SOURCE ANALYSIS QUESTION

1 With reference to Sources 1, 2 and 3 (below), and your understanding of the historical context, assess the value of these sources to a historian studying German–Soviet relations 1933–41.

SOURCE 1

From Hitler's Memorandum on the Four-Year Plan, quoted in J. Noakes and G. Pridham, editors, *Nazism, 1919–1945*, volume 2, Liverpool University Press, 2000, pp. 281–2.

Germany will always have to be regarded as the focus of the western world against attacks of Bolshevism. I do not regard this as an agreeable mission but as a serious handicap and burden for our national life, regrettably resulting from our disadvantageous position in Europe. We cannot escape this destiny. At the moment there are only two countries in Europe which can be regarded as standing firm against Bolshevism – Germany and Italy …

It is not the aim of this memorandum to prophesy the moment when the untenable situation in Europe will reach the stage of an open crisis. I only want in these lines to express my conviction that this crisis cannot and will not fail to occur, and that Germany has the duty of securing her existence by every means in the face of this catastrophe … For a victory of Bolshevism over Germany would lead not a Versailles treaty but to the final destruction, indeed to the annihilation of the German people.

SOURCE 2

From the Nazi–Soviet Pact, 23 August 1939, quoted in R. Overy, *The Origins of the Second World War*, Longman, 1987, pp. 106–7.

Guided by the desire to strengthen the cause of peace between the USSR and Germany and proceeding from the fundamental stipulations of the neutrality treaty concluded in April 1926, the Government of the USSR and the Government of Germany have come to the following agreement:

Article 1. The two contracting parties undertake to refrain from any act of force, any aggressive act, or any attack against each other, either individually or in conjunction with other Powers.

Article 2. If one of the contracting parties should become the object of hostilities on the part of a third Power, the other contracting party will give no support of any kind to that third power.

Secret Additional Protocol

On the occasion of the signature of the non-aggression treaty … the undersigned plenipotentiaries [diplomats with full powers] of the two parties discussed in strictly confidential conversations the delimitation of their respective sphere of interest in eastern Europe.

SOURCE 3

From Hitler's order of 31 July 1940, quoted in J. Noakes and G. Pridham, editors, *Nazism, 1919–1945*, volume 3, Liverpool University Press, 2001, p. 790.

… In the event that invasion [of Britain] does not take place, our action must be directed to eliminate all factors that let England hope for a change in the situation. To all intents and purposes the war is won … Britain's hope lies in Russia and the United States. If Russia drops out of the picture, America too is lost for Britain, because elimination of Russia would tremendously increase Japan's power in the Far East. Russia is the Far Eastern sword of Britain and the United States pointed at Japan … Japan, like Russia, has her programme which she wants to carry through before the end of the war … With Russia smashed, Britain's last hope would be shattered. Germany will then be master of Europe and the Balkans. Decision: Russia's destruction must therefore be made part of this struggle. Spring 1941. The sooner Russia is crushed, the better.

CHAPTER 9

Countdown to war in Asia 1931–41

Japanese expansion into Manchuria and China had a major impact on the situation in Europe during the decade after 1941. Ultimately, through the attack on Pearl Harbor, the Japanese turned a predominantly European war into a global war. The nature of this impact, from 1931 to 1941, is studied under the following headings:

★ The Manchurian Crisis 1932

★ The Sino-Japanese War

★ The road to Pearl Harbor 1940–1

Key dates

1931	Sept.	Mukden incident	1941	July		Japan occupied southern Indo-China
1933	Feb.	Japan left the League of Nations		Dec. 7–8		Japan attacked Pearl Harbor
1936	Nov.	Anti-Comintern Pact signed		Dec. 8		USA declared war on Japan
1937	July	Japan attacked China		Dec. 11		Germany declared war on the USA
1940	Sept. 27	Tripartite Pact signed by Germany, Italy and Japan				

1   The Manchurian Crisis 1932

▶ *Why did Japan occupy Manchuria?*

▶ *What was the League's initial response to the occupation of Manchuria by Japan?*

Arguably, the Japanese occupation of Manchuria in 1931 was a continuation of policies followed by Japanese governments since the defeat of Russia in 1905 (see page 34), when Japan had been awarded the lease of the South Manchurian Railway and the right to protect it with some 15,000 troops. In the late 1920s these concessions were threatened by the turmoil caused by the Chinese Civil War, which broke out in 1927 and was fought between the Nationalists and Communists.

Japanese occupation of Manchuria 1931

The failure of the Japanese government to deal with the impact of the Great Depression on the economy convinced the Japanese officer corps that it would have to act decisively and occupy the whole of Manchuria. This would then enable Japan to control the region's valuable coal and iron resources at a time when economic nationalism was already making it difficult for it to purchase these vital raw materials elsewhere. Consequently, Japanese officers in Manchuria decided to devise an incident which would provide the pretext for intervention. On 18 September 1931 a bomb exploded on the railway line just outside Mukden, where both Chinese and Japanese troops were stationed. This was immediately blamed on the Chinese and provided the Japanese forces with the desired excuse to occupy not only Mukden but the whole of southern Manchuria.

The response of the League of Nations

China immediately appealed to the League of Nations, but the Council responded cautiously. It first asked Japan to withdraw its troops back into the railway zone and, when this was ignored, sent a commission of inquiry under the chairmanship of **Lord Lytton**. The Japanese were able to complete the occupation of Manchuria and turned it into the satellite state of Manchukuo while the Lytton Commission was conducting a leisurely fact-finding operation in the spring of 1932.

Refusal of Britain and the USA to use force

It is easy to criticise the League for not acting more decisively, but without the commitment of the Great Powers it was not in a position to take effective action. Neither of the two most important naval powers, Britain and the USA, was ready to use force against Japan. From the Japanese point of view, the timing of the Mukden incident could not have been better. On 15 September, a minor mutiny at the naval base at Invergordon, which was caused by a cut in the sailors' wages, threatened temporarily to paralyse the Royal Navy; and five days later Britain was forced off the **gold standard**. The USA, shell-shocked by the Great Depression, was unwilling to do more than denounce Japanese aggression. President Hoover, for instance, argued that economic sanctions would be like 'sticking pins in tigers' and would run the risk of leading to war.

It is sometimes argued that the British government and powerful financial interests in the City of London secretly supported Japan. It is true that Britain did have some sympathy with Japanese action in Manchuria. Like Japan it had commercial interests in China, which it felt were threatened by the chaos and civil war there. Britain also appreciated Japan's potential role in providing a barrier against the spread of Bolshevism from the USSR into northern China. Nevertheless, the real reason why Britain was not ready to urge more decisive

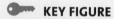

KEY FIGURE

Lord Lytton (1876–1947)

British governor of Bengal 1922–7. In 1931 he chaired the Lytton Commission in Manchuria.

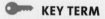

KEY TERM

Gold standard A system by which the value of a currency is defined in terms of gold. The value of the pound was linked to gold. On 20 September 1931 the pound was forced off the gold standard and its value fell from $4.86 to $3.49.

action against Japan was that neither the government nor the people desired to fight a war on an issue that was not central to British interests (see Source A).

SOURCE A

From Sir John Simon's speech to the House of Commons, February 1933, quoted in F.S. Northedge, *The League of Nations*, Leicester University Press, 1988, p. 163.

I think I am myself enough of a pacifist to take the view that however we handle the matter, I do not intend my own country to get into trouble about it … There is one great difference between 1914 and now and it is this: in no circumstances will this government authorise this country to be party to this struggle.

What does Source A reveal about British policy towards Manchuria?

Report of the Lytton Commission

It was not until September 1932 that the League received the Commission's report. Although it conceded that the treaty rights, which Japan had enjoyed in Manchuria since 1905, had made Sino-Japanese friction unavoidable, it nevertheless observed that 'without a declaration of war a large area of what was indisputably Chinese territory had been forcibly seized and occupied by the armed forces of Japan and has in consequence of this operation been separated from and declared independent of the rest of China'. It proposed that Japanese troops should withdraw back into the railway zone, and then both China and Japan should negotiate not only a treaty guaranteeing Japan's rights in Manchuria but also a non-aggression pact and a trade agreement.

Essentially, the report was mistakenly based on the assumption that the Japanese had no territorial designs in China and were ready to compromise over Manchuria. When it was adopted unanimously, with the single exception of Japan, by the League Assembly on 24 February 1933, Japan withdrew from the League in protest. It was obvious that only armed intervention by the Great Powers would now be able to force Japan out of Manchuria, and that option was not politically realistic in 1933.

Consequences of the occupation

The Japanese occupation of Manchuria changed the balance of power in the Pacific. Japan had broken free from the restraints that had been imposed on it at the Washington Conference in 1922 by Britain and the USA (see page 137) and had guaranteed it access to valuable coal and iron ore resources. Above all, Japan was now in a favourable strategic position to plan a large-scale military invasion of China. The Manchurian incident is often seen as the first link in a chain of events that led to the Second World War. Later, a Liberal British MP, Sir Geoffrey Mander (1882–1962), argued that the 'pathway to the beaches of Dunkirk lay through the waste of Manchuria'.

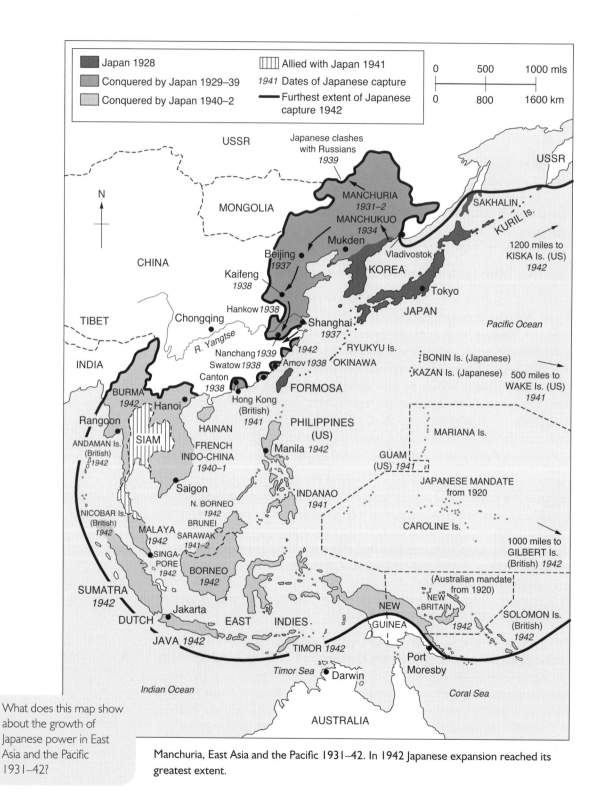

Japan 1928

Conquered by Japan 1929–39

Conquered by Japan 1940–2

Allied with Japan 1941

1941 Dates of Japanese capture

Furthest extent of Japanese capture 1942

| 0 | 500 | 1000 mls |
| 0 | 800 | 1600 km |

USSR

Japanese clashes with Russians *1939*

USSR

MONGOLIA

MANCHURIA *1931–2*

MANCHUKUO *1934*

Mukden

SAKHALIN

KURIL Is.

1200 miles to KISKA Is. (US) *1942*

CHINA

Beijing *1937*

Kaifeng *1938*

Vladivostok

KOREA

Tokyo

JAPAN

Pacific Ocean

TIBET

Chongqing

R. Yangtse

Hankow *1938*

Shanghai *1937*

1942

RYUKYU Is.

OKINAWA

BONIN Is. (Japanese)

KAZAN Is. (Japanese)

500 miles to WAKE Is. (US) *1941*

INDIA

Nanchang *1939*

Swatow *1938*

Canton *1938*

Amoy *1938*

FORMOSA

BURMA *1942*

Hanoi

Hong Kong (British) *1941*

PHILIPPINES (US)

MARIANA Is.

Rangoon

ANDAMAN Is. (British) *1942*

SIAM

HAINAN

FRENCH INDO-CHINA *1940–1*

Manila *1942*

GUAM (US) *1941*

JAPANESE MANDATE from 1920

Saigon

INDANAO *1941*

N. BORNEO *1942*

CAROLINE Is.

NICOBAR Is. (British) *1942*

MALAYA *1942*

BRUNEI

SARAWAK *1941–2*

1000 miles to GILBERT Is. (British) *1942*

SINGA-PORE *1942*

BORNEO *1942*

(Australian mandate from 1920)

SUMATRA *1942*

Jakarta

DUTCH   EAST   INDIES

NEW BRITAIN

NEW GUINEA *1942*

SOLOMON Is. (British) *1942*

JAVA *1942*

TIMOR *1942*

Port Moresby

Indian Ocean

Timor Sea   Darwin

Coral Sea

AUSTRALIA

? What does this map show about the growth of Japanese power in East Asia and the Pacific 1931–42?

Manchuria, East Asia and the Pacific 1931–42. In 1942 Japanese expansion reached its greatest extent.

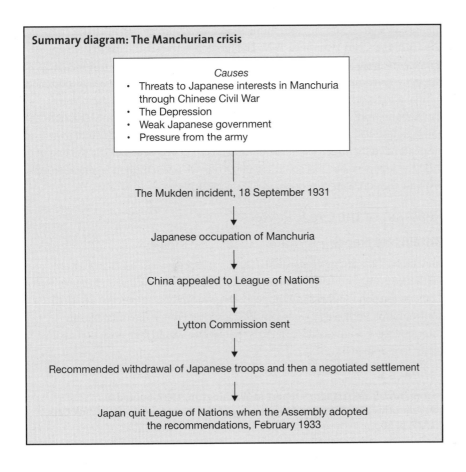

Summary diagram: The Manchurian crisis

Causes
- Threats to Japanese interests in Manchuria through Chinese Civil War
- The Depression
- Weak Japanese government
- Pressure from the army

↓

The Mukden incident, 18 September 1931

↓

Japanese occupation of Manchuria

↓

China appealed to League of Nations

↓

Lytton Commission sent

↓

Recommended withdrawal of Japanese troops and then a negotiated settlement

↓

Japan quit League of Nations when the Assembly adopted the recommendations, February 1933

② The Sino-Japanese War

▶ *What impact did the Sino-Japanese War have on the Great Powers?*

The war in the Pacific, which ended with the dropping of atom bombs on Hiroshima and Nagasaki in 1945, began when a minor incident involving Japanese and Nationalist Chinese troops occurred at the Marco Polo Bridge near Beijing on 7 July 1937, and then rapidly escalated into full-scale hostilities. Japan was determined to turn northern China into an economic and political satellite and progressively to extend its influence throughout the whole of South-east Asia at the cost of the US and European colonial empires.

The course of the war until 1941

By 1938 the most fertile area of China, including the valleys of the Yellow and Yangtze rivers, was in Japanese hands. Nanking and the old capital of China, Beijing, were also occupied and the leader of the Chinese Nationalists, **General Chiang Kai-shek**, was forced to retreat to Chongqing and negotiate an uneasy

 **KEY FIGURE**

Chiang Kai-shek (1887–1975)

Leader of the Chinese Nationalists. After the defeat of Japan in 1945, his forces were destroyed by the Communists in 1949 and he retreated to Taiwan.

alliance with the Chinese Communists, against whom he had been waging the **Chinese Civil War** since 1927. The territories they managed to hold on to were the least advanced economically in China. The Japanese installed a puppet government in Beijing in 1938, but it attracted little loyalty in unoccupied China, and its officials were subjected to guerrilla attacks by the nationalists. By 1940 the front between the two forces extended some 3000 km. Although the Japanese had achieved considerable military success, they had militarily overextended themselves and the fighting had reached deadlock. By the end of 1941 the Japanese had lost some 185,000 troops. Up to a million Japanese troops with air support were tied down in China until 1945.

Reaction of the Great Powers

Britain and France

Inevitably, the war emphasised the fragility of British and French power as neither country could afford simultaneous hostilities in Europe and the Far East. Thus, as tension mounted in Europe, both governments in practice avoided confrontation with the Japanese. In 1937 a senior French diplomat bluntly informed the US ambassador in Paris that France would take no action against Japan (see Source B).

? What does Source B show about the problems facing French foreign policy in 1937?

SOURCE B

From the US ambassador's report to Washington, 1937, quoted in A. Adamthwaite, *France and the Coming of the Second World War*, **Frank Cass, 1977, p. 60.**

*… as long as the present tension existed in Europe it would be impossible for France to take part in any common action in the Far East, which might imply at some stage the **furnishing** of armed forces … It was regrettable that this situation existed … but the situation was a fact and had to be faced.*

The USA

Although the USA was equally reluctant to take military measures against Japan, the spreading conflict did enable President Roosevelt to begin the slow process of realigning the USA with the democracies against the Rome–Berlin Axis and Japan. In December 1937, when British and US ships on the Yangtze river were attacked by Japanese planes, Roosevelt, despite immediate Japanese apologies and offers of compensation, took the potentially important step of sending a US naval officer to discuss possible future co-operation between the British and US fleets; but when Congress found out, there was an explosion of anger and Roosevelt was severely criticised for compromising US neutrality. No wonder that Chamberlain observed that 'It is always best and safest to count on nothing from the Americans but words.'

The USSR

Like Roosevelt, Stalin had no wish to become embroiled in the Sino-Japanese war. Stalin consequently rejected Chiang Kai-shek's request for a Soviet invasion of Manchukuo, as he feared that Nazi Germany would exploit the opportunity to attack in the west. The USSR was also weakened by **the purges**, which had eliminated most of the Red Army's senior officers on the spurious grounds that they were traitors to communism. On the other hand, Stalin did not want Japan to dominate China and threaten Soviet-controlled Mongolia (see the map on page 200). He therefore urged the Chinese Communists and Nationalists to create a united front against the Japanese and continued to supply Chiang Kai-Shek with weapons and aircraft. In 1938 Soviet efforts to reinforce the USSR–Mongolian border led to an armed clash lasting for two weeks at Lake Khason. In May 1939, tension escalated when Japanese troops occupied disputed territory on the border near the river Khalkin-Gol in eastern Mongolia. This led to a major confrontation involving tanks and aircraft and only ended when a truce was signed on 15 September 1939.

KEY TERM

The purges The elimination of about 7 million people alleged to be traitors in the USSR in 1936–8.

SOURCE C

What information does Source C convey about the Japanese in China?

Japanese infantry advance while displaying their rising sun flag in China, 1938. The bitter fighting in China was on a huge scale. By the beginning of 1938 the front stretched hundreds of kilometres.

KEY FIGURE

Joachim von Ribbentrop (1893–1946)

German ambassador to Britain, 1936–8, and foreign minister, 1938–45.

Germany

The new Nazi foreign minister, **Joachim von Ribbentrop**, urged Hitler to create what he called a 'world triangle' by forging alliances with Japan and Italy that would place maximum pressure on the French and British Empires. The Japanese welcomed this policy in the hope that it would discourage both US and Russian intervention in China. In Ribbentrop's eyes a start to this policy of creating a 'world triangle' had been made in December 1936, when Germany and Japan had signed the Anti-Comintern Pact, which was joined a year later by Italy (see page 163).

In 1938 Japan's policy of drawing closer to Nazi Germany paid off when the Nazi government cancelled all military aid to Chiang Kai-shek and recognised Manchukuo, but a year later the Nazi–Soviet Pact appeared to undo the propaganda advantages of the Anti-Comintern Pact for the Japanese. However, after the German victories in Europe in 1940 the Japanese saw the chance of taking over the French and Dutch colonies in the Far East and were anxious to gain German support. These aims were welcomed by Hitler and especially Ribbentrop, who saw it as the realisation of his 'world triangle' concept, which would force Britain to make peace. On 27 September 1940 the Tripartite Pact with Italy and Japan was negotiated (see page 189).

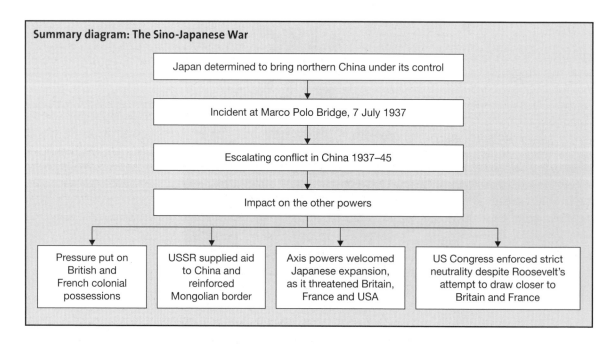

Summary diagram: The Sino-Japanese War

Japan determined to bring northern China under its control

↓

Incident at Marco Polo Bridge, 7 July 1937

↓

Escalating conflict in China 1937–45

↓

Impact on the other powers

- Pressure put on British and French colonial possessions
- USSR supplied aid to China and reinforced Mongolian border
- Axis powers welcomed Japanese expansion, as it threatened Britain, France and USA
- US Congress enforced strict neutrality despite Roosevelt's attempt to draw closer to Britain and France

The road to Pearl Harbor 1940–1

▶ *Why did US–Japanese relations deteriorate in 1940–1?*

One historian, J.G. Utley, has stressed that 'the Japanese–American conflict grew out of two mutually exclusive views of world order':

- Japan, regarding itself as a 'have-not power', attempted to guarantee its access to markets and raw materials by gradually dominating, economically and politically, not only China but the whole of South-east Asia by creating the 'Greater Asia Co-Prosperity Sphere'.
- To the Americans, as was made clear in the **Atlantic Charter**, it was an article of both faith and practical economics that they should be able to trade and invest freely in China and elsewhere.

With Germany having established a self-sufficient siege economy in Europe, it became even more imperative from the US point of view to stop Japan from doing the same in Asia. Washington responded to each fresh extension of Japanese power not only by building up its naval forces in the Pacific, but also by restricting more and more tightly the exports of potential war materials to Japan, a measure which in fact only intensified the Japanese drive for economic self-sufficiency. The USA also agreed to extend financial aid to Chiang Kai-shek's government.

Japan and the USA seemed therefore to be on a collision course. But history is never that simple. There were sufficiently ambiguous and conflicting signals coming out of Tokyo to encourage Roosevelt and the US state department sometimes to believe that, if sufficient economic pressure were applied, Japan would be forced to pull out of China and the Japanese army would lose influence with its government.

In June 1940 Hitler's victories strengthened the hand of the 'hawks' in Tokyo who advocated the occupation of the European colonies in South-east Asia. A relatively moderate government, which wished to avoid confrontation with the USA, was replaced by a more anti-Western regime under **Konoe Fumimaro**, which openly proclaimed its aim of creating a Japanese-dominated Asia and advocated closer co-operation with the victorious Nazi Germany. Washington responded by suspending exports of vital aviation fuel and lubricating oil. To neutralise growing US opposition the Japanese then tried to negotiate a Four-Power pact with the Axis states and the USSR. They succeeded in reaching an agreement with Germany and Italy in September (the Tripartite Pact). And they signed a five-year treaty of neutrality with Stalin the following spring. But the German invasion of the USSR in June 1941 terminated any prospect of a grand four-power alliance against Britain and the USA.

In response to Germany's invasion of the USSR, Konoe urged that Japan should come to an agreement with Britain and the USA, but he was overruled by his

 KEY TERM

Atlantic Charter
Statement of basic principles issued jointly by Roosevelt and Churchill in 1941.

 KEY FIGURE

Konoe Fumimaro (1891–1945)
Japanese prime minister in 1937–40 and from July 1940 to October 1941.

foreign minister and the armed services, who all believed that Hitler would quickly defeat the Soviets. Thus, Tokyo and Washington remained on a collision course.

Pearl Harbor

In July 1941 the Japanese occupied the southern half of French Indo-China and the Americans responded by imposing a comprehensive oil embargo on Japan. The embargo confronted the Japanese with the alternative of either seeing their war machine paralysed through lack of oil or launching, within a few months at the latest, a pre-emptive strike against their enemies.

In early December they received verbal assurances from Ribbentrop that, in the event of a Japanese attack, Germany would also declare war against the USA, even though strictly speaking the Tripartite Pact did not commit Germany to such an action as it was a defensive alliance only. Thus, at dawn on 7 December, the Japanese felt sufficiently confident to launch their attack on the US naval base at Pearl Harbor in the Hawaiian islands.

Hitler's declaration of war on the USA on 11 December can in retrospect be seen as a major error since one cannot with certainty say that Roosevelt, confronted with war in the Far East, would have been able to persuade Congress to declare war on Germany as well. However, it could be argued that informally the Americans were already at war with Germany, as they were committed to supplying Britain with all it needed to survive. In that sense, Hitler's declaration of war was therefore both a recognition of reality and a politically calculated gesture of solidarity aimed at encouraging the Japanese to tie down the Americans in the Pacific so that they could not assist the British in the Atlantic and Europe.

SOURCE D

> What, according to Konoe in Source D, are the options facing Japanese foreign policy in September 1941?

From a statement by Prime Minister Konoe Fumimaro to the Japanese Imperial Conference of 6 September 1941, quoted in M.L. Hanneman, *Japan Faces the World, 1925–1952*, Pearson, 2001, pp. 130–1.

As you all know, the international situation in which we are involved has become increasingly strained; and in particular, the United States, Great Britain and the Netherlands have come to oppose our Empire with all available means. There has emerged the prospect that the United States and the Soviet Union will form a united front against Japan, as the war between Germany and Japan becomes prolonged.

… Under these circumstances our Empire must, of course, quickly prepare to meet any situation that may occur, and at the same time it must try to prevent the disaster of war by resorting to all possible diplomatic measures. If the diplomatic measures should fail to bring about favourable results within a certain period, I believe we cannot help but to take the ultimate step to defend ourselves.

SOURCE E

The USS *Arizona* sinks in Pearl Harbor following the Japanese air attack on
7 December 1941. It was this attack that brought the US into the war.

Study Source E. What
message would this photo
have given the US public?

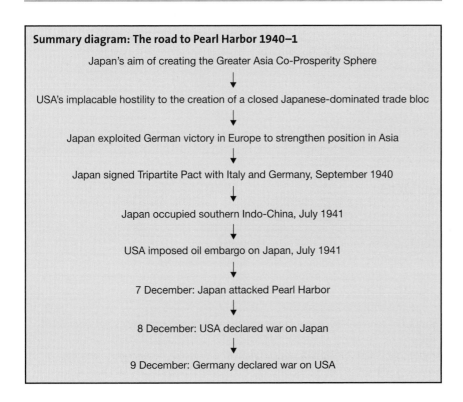

Summary diagram: The road to Pearl Harbor 1940–1

Japan's aim of creating the Greater Asia Co-Prosperity Sphere

↓

USA's implacable hostility to the creation of a closed Japanese-dominated trade bloc

↓

Japan exploited German victory in Europe to strengthen position in Asia

↓

Japan signed Tripartite Pact with Italy and Germany, September 1940

↓

Japan occupied southern Indo-China, July 1941

↓

USA imposed oil embargo on Japan, July 1941

↓

7 December: Japan attacked Pearl Harbor

↓

8 December: USA declared war on Japan

↓

9 December: Germany declared war on USA

Chapter summary

The Japanese occupation of Manchuria was a consequence of the impact of the Great Depression. Convinced that Japan needed the valuable minerals in Manchuria, the Japanese army devised an incident which gave them an excuse to seize southern Manchuria. China immediately appealed to the League of Nations. It dispatched a commission of inquiry under Lord Lytton, but its proposals were rejected by Japan, which promptly quit the League. No Western power was ready to intervene militarily. In 1937 Japan used the excuse of another minor incident to launch a full-scale war against China. Japanese expansion into China posed a threat to the French, Dutch and British empires as well as to the USSR and USA at a time when Nazi Germany and Italy were expanding. In 1940 the defeat of France and of the Netherlands made French Indo-China and the Dutch colonial empire vulnerable to Japanese occupation. The aim of creating a Japanese-dominated Asia was opposed by the USA. When Japanese troops invaded Indo-China in 1941, the USA immediately imposed an oil embargo on Japan, which was to lead to Pearl Harbor on 7 December, the US declaration of war on Japan and then the declaration of war on the USA by Germany.

Refresher questions

Use these questions to remind yourself of the key material covered in this chapter.

1 Why was neither Britain nor the USA ready to use force in the Manchurian crisis?
2 What were the recommendations of the Lytton report?
3 What were the consequences of the Japanese occupation of Manchuria?
4 What did Japan hope to gain from waging war in China?
5 What did Japan gain from the Anti-Comintern Pact?
6 What were the causes of the Japanese attack on Pearl Harbor?
7 Were Germany and Japan 'natural allies'?
8 What were Japan's relations with the USSR?
9 To what extent was Japanese expansion in Asia influenced by events in Europe?
10 How did great powers react to the Sino-Japanese War 1937–41?
11 Why did Japan attack Pearl Harbor?

Question practice

ESSAY QUESTIONS

1 To what extent did the Manchurian crisis weaken the Western powers?
2 'The USA's entry into the war in December 1941 was inevitable.' How far do you agree?
3 'Only the USA could have halted Japanese aggression before the attack on Pearl Harbor.' Assess the validity of this view.
4 To what extent did Japan co-operate with the Axis powers?
5 Assess the reasons for the growth of tensions between Japan and the Western democracies between 1931 and 1941.
6 Which of the following did more to increase tension between Japan, the Western democracies and the USSR: i) the Japanese occupation of Manchuria or ii) the Sino-Japanese war 1937–40? Explain your answer with reference to both i) and ii).

CHAPTER 10

Interpreting international relations 1890–1941

This chapter concentrates on the main issues to consider when studying the period 1890–1941. The following key topics are analysed:

★ Causes of the First World War

★ Peace treaties

★ The new global balance of power

★ The fragile stabilisation 1924–9

★ Road to war in Europe and Asia 1931–41

1 Causes of the First World War

▶ *To what extent was Germany the root cause of the First World War?*

In retrospect, the coming of the First World War dominates the history of the period 1890–1914. The war's causes were complex. Certainly the alliance system, nationalism, militarism, imperialism, economic rivalry and the arms race were all key factors, but at the heart of the problem that led to war was the question of German military and economic power.

Germany after the fall of Bismarck was a clumsy and often aggressive power. The construction of a modern navy, the attempt to destroy the Anglo-French *Entente* during the Moroccan crisis of 1906 and then the humiliation of Russia during the Bosnian crisis of 1908 all helped to isolate it and make it more dependent on Austro-Hungary. On the other hand, Germany was the strongest military and economic power in Europe, and arguably its demands 'for a place in the sun' were, by the nationalist and imperialist standards of the time, justified.

In 1914, Britain, Russia and France went to war to protect their own positions and ensure that Germany did not dominate Europe, and by extension the world, by claiming its 'place in the sun'. Germany too went to war for defensive reasons. The hostile alliance system, which its own power and policies had brought into being, forced it on to the defensive.

Bethmann Hollweg saw the Sarajevo crisis as a window of opportunity. If it could be successfully resolved to Austria's advantage, without the *Entente* backing Russia, then Germany's position in Europe would be greatly strengthened, the Franco-Russian alliance ruptured, and a way opened for future colonial expansion. If the *Entente* stood by Russia, 'the war was better sooner than later'. Ironically, if Germany had pursued a more subtle and less aggressive policy, its economic power would in time have peacefully secured it a predominant position in Europe without the need for war.

 # Peace treaties

▶ *How open to criticism are the peace treaties?*

After 1945 the peace treaties of 1919–20 were blamed for the rise of Hitler and the Second World War. In its millennium issue, a prestigious London weekly, *The Economist*, described the Treaty of Versailles as a major 'crime of the twentieth century … whose harsh terms would ensure a second world war'. Yet in so many ways Versailles was a compromise peace: the German *Reich*, which had only been created in 1871, was left intact, and with the disintegration of the Austro-Hungarian and Russian Empires in eastern Europe, its position was in fact, in the medium to long term, actually strengthened.

The other peace treaties are arguably even harder to defend. Sèvres had to be revised, under threat of war, with a revived nationalist Turkey led by Kemal. St Germain, Neuilly and Trianon aimed to form a series of states in the Balkans and south-eastern Europe, along the lines suggested in the Fourteen Points. This involved, however, attempting to create nation states where there was no ethnic unity.

 # The new global balance of power

▶ *How stable was the new balance of power created by the peace treaties?*

In 1919 the USA emerged from the First World War as the dominant world financial power. At this stage the USA still lacked the will to play the role of a Great Power. The refusal of the Republican-dominated Senate to ratify the Treaty of Versailles ensured that the USA remained on the sidelines of international politics until 1941. This placed France in a paradoxical position. As a consequence of Germany's defeat and the USA's return to isolation, it had become by default the world's greatest military power, but it was not a role that it could sustain.

In 1919, Russia, like Germany, had been a defeated power. The peace treaties had, in effect, been imposed on it as they were on Germany, Austria, Hungary, Bulgaria and Turkey. Russia had not been consulted about the borders of Turkey or of Poland. After the Bolshevik victory in the civil war, the Soviet Union's greatest priority was to defend the revolution and modernise the economy.

Like France in 1919, Britain still outwardly appeared to be a Great Power, but it was a status that it could not sustain. The British economy, already declining before 1914, had been seriously weakened in the war. Britain's empire too was increasingly being challenged by the rise of nationalism in India and the Middle East.

Japan made considerable gains at Versailles, where it was able to increase its influence in China and in the Pacific at Germany's expense, and Japan was also given a permanent seat on the Council of the League of Nations. However, as the Washington Naval Convention (see page 137) showed, Japan was still regarded as an inferior power to the USA and Britain in the Far East.

Apart from benefiting from the destruction of the Austro-Hungarian Empire, which dominated its northern frontiers, Italy gained little from the peace treaties. It could not achieve its territorial ambitions in Africa and the Balkans until it could play off the Western powers against Germany, a situation which was only possible after Hitler's rise to power.

 # The fragile stabilisation 1924–9

▶ *Why was the period of stabilisation, 1924–9, so short lived?*

At the end of the First World War European prosperity could not be rebuilt until the USA partially re-emerged from isolation to assist in restoring European finances, after the French occupation of the Ruhr had triggered hyperinflation in Germany and also seriously weakened the franc. The brief stabilisation of the European economy that occurred between 1924 and 1929 had some similarities with the stabilisation of the western European economy after 1948. In 1924 a fragile economic and diplomatic equilibrium was created as a consequence of the Dawes Plan and the Locarno Agreements. As in 1948, US money did flow into Germany and help to revive the economy. Confidence was further strengthened by a growing trust between France and Germany symbolised by the Briand–Stresemann relationship and the increasing talk about a European union, which to some extent anticipated the debates of the 1950s.

Are historians, then, correct to see the 1920s as a 'darkening twilight of the liberal era'? One US scholar, Charles S. Maier, points out that this period was in fact a time of new ideas for economic and political co-operation, which could have provided an escape from Great Power conflict. Indeed, he argues that if it was a 'twilight decade, the 1920s was one of morning as well as dusk'. The crucial difference, however, between the two post-war periods is that in the 1920s the financing of the European economy was left to private investors,

mainly American, while in the late 1940s, through the **Marshall Plan**, investment was guaranteed by the US state itself and was therefore more secure.

 # Road to war in Europe and Asia 1931–41

▶ *Why was the impact of the Great Depression on international politics so disastrous?*

The Great Depression was instrumental in pushing the USA back into isolation just when Europe most needed it. German and Japanese expansion in the 1930s was facilitated by US inactivity in the Far East and the failure of the Anglo-French policy of appeasement in Europe. Only in March 1939, when Hitler occupied Bohemia and Moravia, and when Britain and France guaranteed Poland, did it become quite clear that they could not tolerate unlimited German expansion in eastern Europe.

The last chance of deterring Hitler was destroyed when Stalin opted for the Nazi–Soviet Pact, rather than a military alliance with Britain and France, in order to regain some of Russia's former Polish territory. Were the events that led to war in 1938–9 inevitable? What role did miscalculation or just bad luck play in their unfolding? If you are convinced that Hitler was determined on war, then you will clearly be very sceptical of Taylor's argument that there was nothing inevitable about the outbreak of the European war in September 1939. On the other hand, would a crucial difference have been made if Britain and France had managed to keep Italy on their side or to negotiate a successful alliance with the USSR? Is there any truth in the argument that the British feared Stalin more than they did Hitler? An even more important question is the role of appeasement. Was it, as many of the revisionist historians argue, the only rational policy open to Britain and France, given the hostility of Italy and Japan, or could Chamberlain have pursued a different policy, as R.A.C. Parker has indicated, of building up an alliance against Nazi Germany in the name of the League of Nations?

Until 1941 the Second World War consisted of several distinct wars that only gradually merged into one great war. It is arguable that President Roosevelt's determination to supply Britain with all necessary war material and the ever more serious clashes between the US navy and German U-boats in the summer of 1941 would in time have brought the USA into the war, but it was the massive miscalculation of the Japanese at Pearl Harbor, and Hitler's declaration of war on the USA on 11 December, that finally brought about this crucial event.

Summary diagram: Interpreting international relations 1890–1941

	1914	1919	1941
Germany	The most powerful state in Europe, but felt deprived of colonies and wanted 'a place in the sun'	Defeated in First World War, but position in Europe potentially strengthened through collapse of Austria	Hitler gained power in 1933 and rearmed Germany. In 1940 Germany had conquered Continental Europe, but by December 1941 faced a war she could not win against Britain, the USSR and the USA
Italy	The least powerful of the Great Powers. Entered war on Allied side in 1915	Claimed that it was cheated of its just gains by the Allies in the peace treaties	1940 entered the war on German side. Only saved from defeat by German assistance in 1941. Mussolini overthrown 1943
Japan	August, declared war on Germany and seized German territory in China	Kept most of this territory despite American opposition	1929–31 hard hit by Depression … Embarked on programme of expansion: Manchuria, 1931. Attacked China, 1937. Occupied southern Indo-China, 1941. Attacked Pearl Harbor, December 1941
France	Recovered from defeat of 1871, built up large colonial empire. Through alliance with Russia and *Entente* with Britain escaped from isolation imposed by Bismarck	Severely weakened by war, but emerged victorious, yet lacking an Anglo-American guarantee, was vulnerable to a German revival	Defeated in 1940 by Germany
Britain	Possessed huge colonial empire. Went to war to maintain its position as a world power	Emerged victorious from war, but also weakened by cost of war	After failure to appease Hitler, Britain with France declared war on Nazi Germany in September 1939. By December 1941 junior partner of USA and USSR in Grand Alliance
Russia	Potentially a Great Power but weakened by internal divisions	Revolution of 1917 temporarily eliminated Russia as a major power	Nazi–Soviet Pact of August 1939 brought USSR back as a major player. Nearly destroyed by German invasion of 1941, but USSR emerged in 1945 as victor and superpower
USA	Economically the strongest global power. Only entered the war in 1917	Played key role in peace treaty, but Senate refused to ratify the Treaty of Versailles. Retreated to isolationism	1924–9, played a major part in financial reconstruction of Europe, but driven back into isolation by the Great Depression. Supported Britain economically in 1940–1. Opposed Japanese expansion. Brought into war by Japanese attack on Pearl Harbor in 1941
Austria	Her declaration of war on Serbia led to outbreak of First World War	Austrian Empire dissolved in 1918	1938, rump Austria was absorbed by Germany
Turkey	Joined Central Powers in October. Had lost almost all its Balkan territory by 1913	By the Treaty of Sèvres lost Middle Eastern provinces, but forced revision of Treaty at Lausanne in 1923	Remained neutral during Second World War

OCR A level History

Essay guidance

The assessment of OCR Units Y218 and Y248 International Relations 1890–1941 depends on whether you are studying it for AS or A level:

- for the AS exam, you will answer one essay question from a choice of two, and one interpretation question, for which there is no choice
- for the A level exam, you will answer one essay question from a choice of two, and one shorter essay question also from a choice of two.

The guidance below is for answering both AS and A level essay questions. Guidance for the shorter essay question is at the end of this section. Guidance on answering interpretation questions is on page 218.

For both OCR AS and A level History, the types of essay questions set and the skills required to achieve a high grade for Unit Group 2 are the same. The skills are made very clear by both mark schemes, which emphasise that the answer must:

- focus on the demands of the question
- be supported by accurate and relevant factual knowledge
- be analytical and logical
- reach a supported judgement about the issue in the question.

There are a number of skills that you will need to develop to reach the higher levels in the marking bands:

- understand the wording of the question
- plan an answer to the question set
- write a focused opening paragraph
- avoid irrelevance and description
- write analytically
- write a conclusion which reaches a supported judgement based on the argument in the main body of the essay.

These skills will be developed in the section below, but are further developed in the 'Period Study' chapters of the *OCR A level History* series (British Period Studies and Enquiries).

Understanding the wording of the question

To stay focused on the question set, it is important to read the question carefully and focus on the key words and phrases. Unless you directly address the demands of the question you will not score highly. Remember that in questions where there is a named factor you must write a good analytical paragraph about the given factor, even if you argue that it was not the most important.

Types of AS and A level questions you might find in the exams	The factors and issues you would need to consider in answering them
1 Assess the reasons for the failure of appeasement to prevent the outbreak of the Second World War.	Weigh up the relative importance of a range of factors as to why appeasement failed to prevent the outbreak of war.
2 To what extent did the alliance system cause the First World War?	Weigh up the relative importance of a range of factors, including comparing the importance of the alliance system with other causes of the war.
3 'The Versailles Treaty was a failure on almost every count.' How far do you agree?	Weigh up the relative importance of the terms of the treaty to see whether all or some of them can be regarded as a failure to reach a balanced judgement.

Planning an answer

Many plans simply list dates and events – this should be avoided as it encourages a descriptive or narrative, rather than an analytical, answer. The plan should be an outline of your argument; this means you need to think carefully about the issues you intend to discuss and their relative importance before you start writing your answer. It should therefore be a list of the factors or issues you are going to discuss and a comment on their relative importance.

For question 1 in the table, your plan might look something like this:

- Aims of appeasement.
- Explain why it failed to satisfy the aims of the Axis powers.
- An analysis of the key situations where appeasement was applied and failed – link to key crises such as Abyssinia and Sudetenland.
- Rejection of appeasement by British public opinion and eventually government.

The opening paragraph

Many students spend time 'setting the scene'; the opening paragraph becomes little more than an introduction to the topic – this should be avoided. Instead, make it clear what your argument is going to be. Offer your view about the issue in the question – what was the most important reason for the failure of appeasement? – and then introduce the other issues you intend to discuss. In the plan it is suggested that the aims and attitude of the Axis powers were the most important factors. This should be made clear in the opening paragraph, with a brief comment as to why – perhaps that the aims of the Axis powers were such that compromise was impossible. This will give the examiner a clear overview of your essay, rather than it being a 'mystery tour' where the argument becomes clear only at the end. You should also refer to any important issues that the question raises. For example:

There are a number of reasons why appeasement failed to prevent the outbreak of the Second World War, including its limited aims, lack of consistent support by British public opinion and abandonment by the British and French governments.[1] However, the most important reason was the attitude of the Axis powers,

especially Germany, which in the end ensured that there was no distinction between appeasement and surrender.[2] This was particularly so with German policy in 1939.[3]

1 The student is aware that there were a number of important reasons.
2 The student offers a clear view as to what he or she considers to be the most important reason – a thesis is offered.
3 There is a brief justification to support the thesis.

Avoid irrelevance and description

Hopefully, the plan will stop you from simply writing indiscriminately all you know about appeasement and force you to weigh up the role of a range of factors. Similarly, it should also help prevent you from simply writing about the diplomacy of appeasement . You will not lose marks if you do that, but neither will you gain any credit, and you will waste valuable time.

Write analytically

This is perhaps the hardest, but most important skill you need to develop. An analytical approach can be helped by ensuring that the opening sentence of each paragraph introduces an idea, which directly answers the question and is not just a piece of factual information. In a very strong answer it should be possible to simply read the opening sentences of all the paragraphs and know what argument is being put forward.

If we look at the second question on the alliance system (see page 214), the following are possible sentences with which to start paragraphs:

- The alliance system ensured that Austro-Russian tension in the Balkans could not remain isolated.
- The emergence of the Triple Entente led to a German feeling of hostile encirclement.
- The alliance system alone did not cause the First World War, but it ensured that all the major crises that erupted were linked, and affected each Great Power.
- Developments after the assassination of Franz Ferdinand illustrate clearly the crucial part the

alliance system played in the outbreak of the First World War.

- It was the arms race, imperialism and nationalism that were the root causes of the First World War, rather than the alliance system.
- The alliance system was not the really the key cause of the First World War as it was a consequence of deep divisions between the powers.

You would then go on to discuss both sides of the argument raised by the opening sentence, using relevant knowledge about the issue to support each side of the argument. The final sentence of the paragraph would reach a judgement on the role played by the factor you are discussing. This approach would ensure that the final sentence of each paragraph links back to the actual question you are answering. If you can do this for each paragraph you will have a series of mini-essays which discuss a factor and reach a conclusion or judgement about the importance of that factor or issue. For example:

The alliance system was an important factor in the causes of the First World War, but it alone did not cause the war.[1] The intractable problems in the Balkans caused by the decline of Turkish power, the consequences of the unification of Germany and the defeat of France in 1871 by Prussia as well as imperialist rivalries and the arms race, were the basic causes of the First World War. The alliance system brought these factors all together, as we can see in the reaction of the Great Powers to the Sarajevo crisis.[2]

1 The sentence puts forward a clear view that the alliance system, while important, did not alone cause the First World War.
2 The claim that the alliance system was important is developed and some evidence is provided to support the argument.

The conclusion

The conclusion provides the opportunity to bring together all the interim judgements to reach an overall judgement about the question. Using the interim judgements will ensure that your conclusion

is based on the argument in the main body of the essay and does not offer a different view. For the essay answering question 1 (see page 214), you can decide what was the most important factor in the failure of appeasement, but for questions 2 and 3 you will need to comment on the importance of the named factor – the alliance system – as well as explaining why you think a different factor is more important, if that has been your line of argument. Or, if you think the named factor is the most important, you will need to explain why that was more important than the other factors or issues you have discussed.

Consider the following conclusion to question 2: to what extent did the alliance system cause the First World War?

In the decade before the First World War the alliance system had created two groups of potentially hostile nations in Europe, and was certainly one of the causes of the First World War. However, it did not cause the war by itself.[1] Major differences between the Great Powers existed. France resented the emergence of a unified Germany, while Austria and Russia were bitter rivals in the Balkans. The Germans resented the power of the British Empire and hoped to extract concessions from Britain by constructing a battle fleet, which led to intense Anglo-German naval rivalry. The Sarajevo assassinations brought together all these explosive tensions. Germany could not allow its only reliable ally to be humiliated by Serbia and Russia. Once Germany declared war on Russia, France could not stand back and see Russia defeated, while Britain, despite initial hesitations, could not afford to run the risk of a German victory.[2]

1 This is a strong conclusion because it considers the importance of the named factor – the alliance system – but weighs that up against a range of other factors to reach an overall judgement.
2 It is also able to show links between the other factors to reach a balanced judgement, which brings in a range of issues, showing the interplay between them.

How to write a good essay for the A level short answer questions

This question will require you to weigh up the importance of two factors or issues in relation to an event or a development. For example:

> Which of the following did more to divide Britain and France in the aftermath of the Versailles Treaty, 1920–4:
>
> (i) The territorial settlement
>
> (ii) The reparations question
>
> Explain your answer with reference to both (i) and (ii).

As with the long essays, the skills required are made very clear by the mark scheme, which emphasises that the answer must:

- analyse the two issues
- evaluate the two issues
- support your analysis and evaluation with detailed and accurate knowledge
- reach a supported judgement as to which factor was more important in relation to the issue in the question.

The skills required are very similar to those for the longer essays. However, there is no need for an introduction, nor are you required to compare the two factors or issues in the main body of the essay, although either approach can still score full marks. For example, an introduction could be:

Disagreement about the territorial clauses of the Treaty of Versailles had an important impact on Anglo-French relations in the aftermath of the treaty and resulted in growing bitterness between London and Paris, as both governments attempted unofficially to revise the treaty to suit their own interests.[1] The French attempted to engineer the secession of the Rhineland from Germany 1920–4, while Britain did all it could to thwart this aim. Similarly, in Danzig and the plebiscite regions, especially Upper Silesia, France did all it could to influence the vote in favour of the Danes and Poles in 1920, while Britain sympathised with

the Germans.[2] The impact of this disagreement was to weaken the Entente, enflame the reparation problem and to tempt France to 'go it alone' as in the Ruhr crisis.[3]

1 The answer explains the impact on Anglo-French relations of disagreement about the territorial clauses.
2 The implications of this development are considered.
3 The wider implications are hinted at and this could be developed with reference to the Ruhr crisis and Anglo-French disagreement over reparations.

The answer could go on to argue that the two problems were connected.

Most importantly, the conclusion must reach a supported judgement as to the relative importance of the factors in relation to the issue in the question. For example:

Both these issues were important in causing divisions between Britain and France in dealing with post-war Germany and were interlinked. The territorial settlement led to intense Anglo-French disagreements in implementing it and also had major implications for the reparation settlement.[1] The British argued that without Upper Silesia and economic control over the Rhineland, Germany would be unable to pay reparations. The French on the other hand were convinced that Germany would only pay if the Allies controlled the Ruhr. The Ruhr crisis of 1923 brought both these issues together and showed how deeply they divided London and Paris.[2]

1 The response explains the relative importance of the two factors and offers a clear view.
2 The response supports the view offered in the opening sentence and therefore reaches a supported judgement.

Interpretations guidance

The guidance below is for answering the AS interpretation question for OCR Y248 International Relations 1890–1941. Guidance on answering essay questions is on page 214.

The OCR specification outlines the two key topics from which the interpretation question will be drawn. For this book these are:

- Causes and nature of the First World War.
- Dictators and appeasers in Europe 1929–41.

The specification also lists the main debates to consider.

It is also worth remembering that this is an AS unit and not an A level historiography paper. The aim of this element of the unit is to develop an awareness that the past can be interpreted in different ways.

The question will require you to assess the strengths and limitations of a historian's interpretation of an issue related to one of the specified key topics.

You should be able to place the interpretation within the context of the wider historical debate on the key topic. However, you will *not* be required to know the names of individual historians associated with the debate or to have studied the specific books of any historians. It may even be counter-productive to be aware of particular historians' views, as this may lead you to simply describe their view, rather than analyse the given interpretation.

There are a number of skills you need to develop if you are to reach the higher levels in the mark bands:

- To be able to understand the wording of the question.
- To be able to explain the interpretation and how it fits into the debate about the issue or topic.
- To be able to consider both the strengths and weaknesses of the interpretation by using your own knowledge of the topic.

Here is an example of a question you will face in the exam:

Read the interpretation and then answer the question that follows:

> 'Hitler may have projected a great war all along; yet it seems from the record that he became involved in war through launching on 29 August [1939], a diplomatic manoeuvre which he ought to have launched on 28 August.'
>
> Adapted from A.J.P. Taylor, *The Origins of the Second World War*, 1961.

Evaluate the strengths and limitations of this interpretation, making reference to other interpretations that you have studied.

Approaching the question

There are several steps to take to answer this question:

1 Explain the interpretation and put it into context

In the first paragraph you should explain the interpretation and the view it is putting forward. This paragraph places the interpretation in the context of the historical debate and explains any key words or phrases relating to the given interpretation. A suggested opening might be as follows:

The interpretation puts forward the controversial view that Hitler did not intend to cause the outbreak of war at the end of August 1939. The author suggests that the war was an accident and caused by Hitler launching a diplomatic manoeuvre too late to stop the outbreak of hostilities.[1] In using the term 'diplomatic manoeuvre' Taylor is referring to his basic argument that Hitler hoped to gain all he wanted from Poland through diplomacy backed by threats. He hoped that the threat of war would frighten Britain and Poland to make concessions about Danzig and the Polish Corridor.[2] The interpretation suggests that he stumbled into war by mistake rather than by intention.[3]

1 The opening two sentences are clearly focused on the given interpretation. They clearly explain that there was more than one factor at work in Hitler's

foreign policy in August 1939, but there is no detailed own knowledge added at this point.

2 The third sentence explains what is meant by 'diplomatic manoeuvre' and this is developed in the following sentence.

3 The final sentence begins to place the concept of a failure in Hitler's diplomacy in the wider historical debate and suggests that this historian's emphasis on it might challenge the more frequent view that Hitler went to war intentionally.

To place Taylor's view in the context of the debate about the importance of various factors, you could go on to suggest there are a wide range of other factors to consider, such as Hitler's long-term plans, the Nazi–Soviet Pact and the Anglo-French guarantee of Poland.

2 Consider the strengths of the interpretation

In the second paragraph consider the strengths of the interpretation by bringing in your own knowledge that supports the given view. A suggested response might start as follows when considering the strengths of the view:

There is certainly some merit in Taylor's argument as it acknowledges that there were many factors motivating Hitler in August 1939.[1] Hitler did sometimes use diplomacy and bluff to achieve his ends, as can be seen over the Sudeten crisis of 1938. Hitler was an opportunist who would seize the chance to attain his objectives through any possible way.[2] The use of diplomacy and exploitation of chances at times were alternatives to force.[3]

1 The answer clearly focuses on the strength of the given interpretation.

2 The response provides some support for the view in the interpretation from the candidate's own knowledge. This is not particularly detailed or precise, but could be developed in the remainder of the paragraph.

3 The final sentence links together factors which support Taylor's arguments.

In the remainder of the paragraph you could explore how these two factors operated during the Polish crisis of August 1939.

3 Consider the weaknesses of the interpretation

In the third paragraph consider the weaknesses of the given interpretation by bringing in knowledge that can challenge the given interpretation and explains what is missing from the interpretation.

A suggested response might start as follows when considering the weaknesses of the view:

There are, however, a number of weaknesses in Taylor's interpretation.[1] Most importantly, it fails to take account of Nazi ideology and Hitler's failure to gain any concessions from the Poles in the period January to March 1939. Hitler was intent on expanding eastwards and creating Lebensraum for the German people. This meant war, eventually against the USSR and then any power that stood in Germany's way. Poland rejected an agreement over Danzig and the corridor in March 1939 and was strengthened by the Anglo-French guarantee.[2] The interpretation also fails to consider Hitler's scorn for diplomacy and the leaders of the Western democracies.[3]

1 The opening makes it very clear that this paragraph will deal with the weaknesses of the interpretation.

2 It explains clearly the weaknesses of the argument and provides evidence to support the claim. The evidence is not detailed and could be developed, but the answer focuses on explaining the weaknesses, rather than providing lots of detail.

3 Although more detail could have been provided about the aims of Hitler's foreign policy, the answer goes on to explain a third weakness in Taylor's argument, Hitler's deep scorn for diplomacy and democracy, and his belief that war was inevitable.

All three factors could be developed in the remainder of the paragraph.

Answers might go on to argue that Hitler had used diplomacy at certain stages between 1933 and 1939. It is also true that he did attempt to negotiate with the Poles during January to March 1939. Possibly, if they had been ready to make grovelling concessions in August, Hitler might have accepted them, but on the other hand he stated quite specifically several times that he wanted to destroy the Polish state. Thanks to the Nazi–Soviet Pact he was also in a strong position to wage war.

The paragraph might therefore suggest that the interpretation provides a partial answer which needs some modification.

There is no requirement for you to reach a judgement as to which view you find more convincing or valid.

Assessing the interpretation

In assessing the interpretation you should consider the following:

- Identify and explain the issue being discussed in the interpretation: did Hitler really intend to go to war over Poland?
- Explain the view being put forward in the interpretation: the interpretation is arguing that Hitler hoped to gain his objectives through diplomacy rather than war in 1939.
- The idea that Hitler blundered into war is just as important as the argument that he planned it.
- Explain how the interpretation fits into the wider debate about the issue: how seriously should the historian take what Hitler wrote or said. Did his actions indicate that he had plans that were intended to end in war?

In other interpretations you might need to:

- Consider whether there is any particular emphasis within the interpretation that needs explaining or commenting on, for example, if the interpretation says something is 'the only reason' or 'the single most important reason'.
- Comment on any concepts that the interpretation raises, such as 'Total War', 'authoritarian system', 'liberalisation'.
- Consider the focus of the interpretation, for example, if an interpretation focuses on an urban viewpoint, what was the rural viewpoint? Is the viewpoint given in the interpretation the same for all areas of society?

In summary: this is what is important for answering interpretation questions:

- Explaining the interpretation.
- Placing the interpretation in the context of the wider historical debate about the issue it considers.
- Explaining the strengths *and* weaknesses of the view in the extract.

AQA A level History

Essay guidance

At both AS and A level for AQA Component 2: Depth Study: International Relations and Global Conflict , *c*.1890–1941 you will need to answer an essay question in the exam. Each essay question is marked out of 25:

- for the AS exam, Section B: answer **one** essay question from a choice of two
- for the A level exam, Section B: answer **two** essay questions from a choice of three.

There are several question stems which all have the same basic requirement: to analyse and reach a conclusion, based on the evidence you provide.

The AS questions often give a quotation and then ask whether you agree or disagree with this view. Almost inevitably, your answer will be a mixture of both. It is the same task as for A level – just phrased differently in the question. Detailed essays are more likely to do well than vague or generalised essays, especially in the Depth Studies of Paper 2.

The AQA mark scheme is essentially the same for AS and the full A level (see the AQA website, www.aqa.org.uk). Both emphasise the need to analyse and evaluate the key features related to the periods studied. The key feature of the highest level is sustained analysis: analysis that unites the whole of the essay.

Writing an essay: general skills

- *Focus and structure.* Be sure what the question is asking and plan what the paragraphs should be about.
- *Focused introduction to the essay.* Be sure that the introductory sentence relates directly to the focus of the question and that each paragraph highlights the structure of the answer.
- *Use detail.* Make sure that you show detailed knowledge, but only as part of an explanation

being made in relation to the question. No knowledge should be standalone; it should be used in context.

- *Explanatory analysis and evaluation.* Consider what words and phrases to use in an answer to strengthen the explanation.
- *Argument and counter-argument.* Think of how arguments can be balanced so as to give contrasting views.
- *Resolution.* Think how best to 'resolve' contradictory arguments.
- *Relative significance and evaluation.* Think how best to reach a judgement when trying to assess the relative importance of various factors, and their possible interrelationship.

Planning an essay

Practice question 1

To what extent did the Locarno Agreements mark the beginning of a new era of conciliation?

This question requires you to analyse whether the Locarno Agreements initiated a new era of peace. You must discuss the following:

- How the agreements led to a new mood and optimism that the tension of the previous years had been overcome (your primary focus).
- What other factors contributed to this period of conciliation (your secondary focus).

A clear structure makes for a much more effective essay and is crucial for achieving the highest marks. You need three or four paragraphs to structure this question effectively. In each paragraph you will deal with one factor. One of these *must* be the factor in the question.

A very basic plan for this question might look like this:

- Paragraph 1: brief background as to why Stresemann proposed the Locarno Agreements.

- Paragraph 2: an analysis of the Agreements to show why they created a new atmosphere of trust and confidence.
- Paragraph 3: the impact of Locarno on Franco-German relations and Europe in general 1925–9.

It is a good idea to cover the factor named in the question first, so that you don't run out of time and forget to do it. Then cover the others in what you think is their order of importance, or in the order that appears logical in terms of the sequence of paragraphs.

The introduction

Maintaining focus is vital. One way to do this from the beginning of your essay is to use the words in the question to help write your argument. The first sentence of question 1, for example, could look like this:

The Locarno Agreements did mark a brief but genuine new era of conciliation between Germany and the members of the wartime entente, above all France.

This opening sentence provides a clear focus on the demands of the question.

Focus throughout the essay

Structuring your essay well will help with keeping the focus of your essay on the question. To maintain a focus on the wording in question 1, you could begin your first main paragraph with 'conciliation'.

Conciliation between France and Germany was vital if Europe was to recover from the bitterness of the war. The Dawes Plan had made the reparation problem more manageable, but it had not overcome France's deep distrust of Germany.

- This sentence begins with a clear point that refers to the primary focus of the question (Locarno and conciliation) while linking it to a factor (Franco-German distrust).
- You could then have a paragraph for each of your other factors.

- It will be important to make sure that each paragraph focuses on analysis and includes relevant details that are used as part of the argument.
- You may wish to number your factors. This helps to make your structure clear and helps you to maintain focus.

Deploying detail

As well as focus and structure, your essay will be judged on the extent to which it includes accurate detail. There are several different kinds of evidence you could use that might be described as detailed. These include correct dates, names of relevant people, statistics and events. For example, for question 1 you could use terms such as 'inviolability of frontiers' and 'Locarno spirit'. You can also make your essays more detailed by using the correct technical vocabulary.

Analysis and explanation

'Analysis' covers a variety of high-level skills including explanation and evaluation; in essence, it means breaking down something complex into smaller parts. A clear structure which breaks down a complex question into a series of paragraphs is the first step towards writing an analytical essay. The purpose of explanation is to provide evidence for why something happened, or why something is true or false. An explanatory statement requires two parts: a *claim* and a *justification*.

For example, for question 1, you might want to argue that one important reason was the agreement over the inviolability of the Franco-German and German–Belgian frontiers. Once you have made your point, and supported it with relevant detail, you can then explain how this answers the question. You could conclude your paragraph like this:

So the Locarno Agreements did in one key area mark the beginning of a new era of conciliation[1] because they guaranteed the Franco-German and German-Belgian frontiers from violation[2] by either France or Germany[3].

1 The first part of this sentence is the claim while the second part justifies the claim.
2 The relationship between the claim and the justification.
3 The justification.

Evaluation

Evaluation means considering the importance of two or more different factors, weighing them against each other, and reaching a judgement. This is a good skill to use at the end of an essay because the conclusion should reach a judgement which answers the question. For example, your conclusion to question 1 might read as follows:

Clearly, the Locarno Agreements did mark a new era in European diplomacy in that France, Germany and Britain began to co-operate in finding solutions to the problems left over by the war and Versailles. However, Stresemann was not ready to extend the Locarno system to eastern Europe and exploited the Locarno spirit to revise the Treaty of Versailles. Therefore, the spirit of conciliation introduced by Locarno did have its limits.

Words like 'clearly', 'however' and 'therefore' are helpful to contrast the importance of the different factors.

Complex essay writing: argument and counter-argument

Essays that develop a good argument are more likely to reach the highest levels. This is because argumentative essays are much more likely to develop sustained analysis. As you know, your essays are judged on the extent to which they analyse.

After setting up an argument in your introduction, you should develop it throughout the essay. One way of doing this is to adopt an argument–counter-argument structure. A counter-argument is one that disagrees with the main argument of the essay. This is a good way of evaluating the importance of the different factors that you discuss. Essays of this type

will develop an argument in one paragraph and then set out an opposing argument in another paragraph. Sometimes this will include juxtaposing the differing views of historians on a topic.

Good essays will analyse the key issues. They will probably have a clear piece of analysis at the end of each paragraph. While this analysis might be good, it will generally relate only to the issue discussed in that paragraph.

Excellent essays will be analytical throughout. As well as the analysis of each factor discussed above, there will be an overall analysis. This will run throughout the essay and can be achieved through developing a clear, relevant and coherent argument.

A good way of achieving sustained analysis is to consider which factor is most important.

Here is an example of an introduction that sets out an argument for question 1:

Despite the acceptance of the Dawes Plan, the situation was still tense in Europe in early 1925. The French refused to evacuate the Cologne zone in the Rhineland.[1] Hence, there was the danger that Franco-German relations could deteriorate again and that the French would never quit the Rhineland.[2] However, the Locarno Treaty was to solve this problem by guaranteeing the French–Belgian–west German frontiers. This guarantee was the single biggest contribution to the new era of conciliation.[3]

1 The introduction begins with a claim.
2 The introduction continues with another reason.
3 Concludes with an outline of argument of the most important reason.

- This introduction focuses on the question and sets out the key factors that the essay will develop.
- It introduces an argument about which factor was most significant.
- However, it also sets out an argument that can then be developed throughout each paragraph, and is rounded off with an overall judgement in the conclusion.

Complex essay writing: resolution and relative significance

Having written an essay that explains argument and counter-arguments, you should then resolve the tension between the argument and the counter-argument in your conclusion. It is important that the writing is precise and summarises the arguments made in the main body of the essay. You need to reach a supported overall judgement. One very appropriate way to do this is by evaluating the relative significance of different factors, in the light of valid criteria. Relative significance means how important one factor is compared to another.

The best essays will always make a judgement about which was most important based on valid criteria. These can be very simple, and will depend on the topic and the exact question.

The following criteria are often useful:

- Duration: which factor was important for the longest amount of time?
- Scope: which factor affected the most people?
- Effectiveness: which factor achieved most?
- Impact: which factor led to the most fundamental change?

As an example, you could compare the factors in terms of their duration and their impact. A conclusion that follows this advice should be capable of reaching a high level (if written in full, with appropriate details) because it reaches an overall judgement that is supported through evaluating the relative significance of different factors in the light of valid criteria.

Having written an introduction and the main body of an essay for question 1, a concluding paragraph that aims to meet the exacting criteria for reaching a complex judgement could look like this:

Thus, the reasons for the conciliatory and peaceful period in Europe 1925–9 were complex and interrelated. The Locarno Treaty undoubtedly helped create this new mood. At a stroke it broke the deadlock between Germany and France over the evacuation of the Rhineland, but it did not immediately remove all the differences between France and Germany. Stresemann's refusal to extend the agreement to Germany's borders with Poland indicated that Germany had not accepted much of the Versailles settlement in eastern Europe. At the same time, Stresemann was under intense pressure from the German Nationalists to achieve more, so he had to keep up the pressure on France to make further concessions. On the other hand, the Locarno Agreements ensured that France, Germany and Britain could attempt to solve their differences through negotiation rather than confrontation.

Sources guidance

Whether you are taking the AS exam or the full A level exam for AQA Component 2: Depth Study: International Relations and Global Conflict, *c*.1890–1941, Section A presents you with sources and a question which involves evaluation of their utility or value.

AS exam	A level exam
Section A: answer question 1 based on two primary sources. (25 marks)	Section A: answer question 1, based on three primary sources. (30 marks)
Question focus: with reference to these sources and your understanding of the historical context, which of these two sources is more valuable in explaining … ?	Question focus: with reference to these sources and your understanding of the historical context, assess the value of these three sources to an historian studying …

Sources and sample questions

Study the sources. They are all concerned with the causes of the First World War.

SOURCE 1

From a dispatch to the Austrian Foreign Minister by the German Chancellor Bethmann-Hollweg, 10 February 1913, quoted in M. Hewitson, *Germany and the Causes of the First World War*, Berg, 2004, p. 204.

As far as I can judge the situation in Russia, on the basis of information which I have cause to believe is reliable, we can reckon with certainty that the forces which stand behind the Pan-Slavist agitation will win the upper hand if Austria should get involved in a conflict with Serbia. One must arrive at the conclusion, after objective enquiry that it is almost impossible for Russia without an enormous loss of prestige, given its traditional relations with the Balkan states to look on without acting during a military advance against Serbia by Austria-Hungary. The consequences of Russian involvement, however, are plain for all to see. It would turn into an armed conflict of the Triple Alliance – predictably not supported by Italy with great enthusiasm – against the powers of the Triple Entente in which Germany would have to bear the entire heavy burden of a French and English attack.

SOURCE 2

From a report to the British Foreign Secretary from Sir Fairfax Cartwright, British ambassador to Vienna, January 1913, quoted in Joachim Remak, 'The Third Balkan War', D.E. Lee, editor, *The Outbreak of the First World War*, D.C. Heath & Co., 1975, p. 146.

[Serbia] will some day set Europe by the ears and bring a universal war on the Continent … I cannot tell you how exasperated people are getting here at the continual worry which that little country causes to Austria under encouragement from Russia. It may be compared to a certain extent to the trouble we had to suffer through the hostile attitude formerly assumed against us by the Transvaal Republic under the guiding hand of Germany. It will be lucky if Europe succeeds in avoiding war as a result of the present crisis. The next time a [Serbian] crisis arises … I feel sure that Austria-Hungary will refuse to admit of any Russian interference in the dispute and that she will proceed to settle her differences with her little neighbour by herself. …

SOURCE 3

From the Franco-Russian Treaty 1892, quoted in Yale Law School, The Avalon Project, Documents in Law, History and Diplomacy, http://avalon.law.yale.edu/19th_century/frrumil.asp.

1. If France is attacked by Germany, or by Italy supported by Germany, Russia shall employ all her available forces to attack Germany.

If Russia is attacked by Germany, or by Austria supported by Germany, France shall employ all her available forces to attack Germany.

2. In case the forces of the Triple Alliance, or of any one of the Powers belonging to it, should be mobilized, France and Russia, at the first news of this event and without previous agreement being necessary, shall mobilize immediately and simultaneously the whole of their forces, and shall transport them as far as possible to their frontiers.

3. The available forces to be employed against Germany shall be, on the part of France, 1,300,000 men, on the part of Russia, 700,000 or 800,000 men.

AS style question

With reference to Sources 1 and 2, and your understanding of the historical context, which of these sources is more valuable in explaining why the state of Austro-Russian relations was a threat to the peace of Europe to a historian studying the causes of the First World War?

A level style question

With reference to Sources 1, 2 and 3 and your understanding of the historical context, assess the value of these sources to a historian studying the causes of the First World War.

AS mark scheme

See the AQA website for the full mark scheme. This summary of the AS mark scheme shows how it rewards analysis and evaluation of the source material within the historical context.

Level 1	Describing the source content or offering generic phrases.
Level 2	Some relevant but limited comments on the value of one source or some limited comment on both.
Level 3	Some relevant comments on the value of the sources and some explicit reference to the issue identified in the question.
Level 4	Relevant well-supported comments on the value and a supported conclusion, but with limited judgement.
Level 5	Very good understanding of the value in relation to the issue identified. Sources evaluated thoroughly and with a well-substantiated conclusion related to which is more valuable.

A level mark scheme

This summary of the A level mark scheme shows how it is similar to the AS one, but covers three sources. Also, the wording of the question means that there is no explicit requirement to decide which of the three sources is the most valuable. Concentrate instead on a very thorough analysis of the content and evaluation of the provenance of each source, using contextual knowledge.

Level 1	Some limited comment on the value of at least one source.
Level 2	Some limited comments on the value of the sources or on content or provenance or comments all three sources but no reference to the value of the sources.
Level 3	Some understanding of all three sources in relation to both content and provenance, with some historical context; but analysis limited.
Level 4	Good understanding of all three sources in relation to content, provenance and historical context to give a balanced argument on their value for the purpose specified in the question.
Level 5	As Level 4, but with a substantiated judgement.

Working towards an answer

It is important that knowledge is used to show an understanding of the relationship between the sources and the issue raised in the question. Answers should be concerned with the following:

- provenance
- arguments used (and you can agree/disagree)
- tone and emphasis of the sources.

The sources

The two or three sources used each time will be contemporary – probably of varying types (for example, diaries, newspaper accounts, government reports). The sources will all be on the same broad topic area. Each source will have value: your task is to evaluate how much in terms of its content and its provenance.

You will need to assess the *value of the content* by using your own knowledge. Is the information accurate? Is it giving only part of the evidence and ignoring other aspects? Is the tone of the writing significant?

You will need to evaluate the *provenance* of the source by considering who wrote it, and when, where and why. What was its purpose? Was it produced to express an opinion; to record facts; to influence the opinion of others? Even if it was intended to be accurate, the writer may have been biased – either deliberately or unconsciously. The writer, for example, might have only known part of the situation and reached a judgement solely based on that.

Here is a guide to analysing the provenance, content and tone for Sources 1, 2 and 3.

Analysing the sources

To answer the question effectively, you need to read the sources carefully and pull out the relevant points as well as add your own knowledge. You must remember to keep the focus on the question at all times.

Source 1 (page 225)
Provenance:

- The source is an extract from a dispatch from the German Chancellor, Bethmann-Hollweg, after the Balkan wars of 1912–13. As Chancellor, he is the most powerful figure in the German government and will have well-informed views on Austro-Russian relations.
- The extract is taken from his letter to the Austrian Foreign Minister. He is therefore writing to a politician, who, as he is responsible for Austrian foreign policy, has a detailed grasp of Austria's relations with Serbia and how they impact on Russia.

Content and argument:

- The source argues that if Austria goes to war with Serbia, Pan-Slav influence will increase in Russia.
- Russia will not, without an enormous loss of prestige, be able to remain neutral.
- The consequences of Russian involvement will be a European war involving the Triple Entente.

Tone and emphasis:

- The tone is analytical and realistic. Bethmann-Hollweg is warning Austria of the consequences of a conflict with Serbia.

Own knowledge:

- Use your knowledge to agree/disagree with the source, for example details about why Russia was concerned about the Balkans and why, through the Triple Alliance, France and Britain might become involved.

Source 2 (page 225)
Provenance:

- The source is from a report made by the British ambassador to Vienna.
- It provides the opinion of a professional diplomat on Austro-Serbian relations.

Content and argument:

- The source warns that Serbian actions encouraged by Russia will one day trigger a European war.
- The source argues that the Austrians are becoming exasperated by the Serbs' hostile attitude and may consider military intervention against Serbia.

Tone and emphasis:

- The tone shows sympathy with Austria in the face of Serbian provocation and a belief that this will lead to European war.

Own knowledge:

- Use your knowledge to agree/disagree with the source, for example: Serbian gains from the Second Balkan War and Austria's reaction to this.

Source 3 (page 226)

Provenance:

- The source is an extract from the Franco-Russian Treaty of 1892.
- It is part of the official wording of the treaty agreed by both countries.

Content and argument:

- The source contains the key clauses of the Franco-Russian Treaty.
- It spells out under what conditions each country will help the other.

Tone and emphasis:

- The treaty is a legal document spelling out accurately the terms of the treaty.

Own knowledge:

- Use your knowledge to agree/disagree with the source, for example: detailed knowledge about Austro-Serbian relations, Russian support for Serbia and Russia's links with France and Britain.

Answering AS questions

You have 45 minutes to answer the question. It is important that you spend at least one quarter of the time reading and planning your answer. Generally,

when writing an answer, you need to check that you are remaining focused on the issue identified in the question and are relating this to the sources and your knowledge.

- You might decide to write a paragraph on each 'strand' (that is, provenance, content and tone), comparing the two sources, and then write a short concluding paragraph with an explained judgement on which source is more valuable.
- For writing about content, you may find it helpful to adopt a comparative approach, for example when the evidence in one source is contradicted or questioned by the evidence in another source.

At AS level you are asked to provide a judgement on which is more valuable. Make sure that this is based on clear arguments with strong evidence, and not on general assertions.

Planning and writing your answer

- Think how you can best plan an answer.
- Plan in terms of the headings above, perhaps combining 'provenance' with 'tone and emphasis', and compare the two sources.

As an example, here is a comparison of Sources 1 and 2 in terms of provenance, and tone and emphasis:

The two sources have similar viewpoints despite their differing provenance. Source 1 is a balanced and frank assessment from the German Chancellor. His assessment is based on a realistic analysis of the current situation in the Balkans and on how Russia would react to an Austro-Serbian war. He understands why Russia would have to respond by supporting Serbia and thus triggering a European war. Source 2 is reporting on the same problem, but from the British viewpoint, and broadly comes to the same conclusion. Cartwright has considerable sympathy with Austria in the face of Serbian provocation and believes Russia is actively provoking Austria.

Then compare the *content and argument* of each source, by using your knowledge. For example:

Source 1 is arguing that if an Austro-Serbian conflict breaks out, Russia will become involved to save its own prestige. The consequences of this will be a European war in which Germany will have to bear the brunt of the fighting against the Triple Entente. Source 2 also focuses on Austro-Serbian relations. It also realises the danger of the Serbian provocation of Austria, which it believes is actively encouraged by Russia. Like Source 1, it sees that this could result in European war. Source 1 is quite specific that Germany would become involved in such a war and face the combined forces of the Triple Entente. Source 2 merely refers to a European war and says nothing about possible British involvement.

Which is *more valuable*? This can be judged in terms of which is likely to be more valuable in terms of where the source came from; or in terms of the accuracy of its content. However, remember the focus of the question – in this case, Austro-Russian relations as a threat to the peace of Europe.

With these sources, you could argue that Source 1 is the more valuable because it was written by the Chancellor of Austria's only ally, Germany, which would have to bear the main brunt of the fighting if war broke out. It is a sober assessment, which understands Russia's position and why it might go to war. Whereas Source 1, while valuable in itself, does not provide so good an analysis of the situation. It is also the opinion an ambassador rather than a head of government.

Then check the following:

- Have you covered the 'provenance' and 'content' strands?
- Have you included sufficient knowledge to show understanding of the historical context?

Answering A level questions

The same general points for answering AS questions (see 'Answering AS questions') apply to A level questions, although of course here there are three sources and you need to assess the value of each of the three, rather than choose which is most valuable. Make sure that you remain focused on the question and that when you use your knowledge it is used to substantiate (add to) an argument relating to the content or provenance of the source.

If you are answering the A level question with Sources 1, 2 and 3 above:

- Keep the different 'strands' explained above in your mind when working out how best to plan an answer.
- Follow the guidance about 'provenance' and 'content' (see the AS guidance).
- Here you are *not* asked to explain which is the most valuable of the three sources. You can deal with each of the three sources in turn if you wish.
- However, you can build in comparisons if it is helpful – but it is not essential. It will depend to some extent on the three sources.
- You need to include sufficient knowledge to show understanding of the historical context. This might encourage cross-referencing of the content of the three sources, mixed with your own knowledge.
- Each paragraph needs to show clarity of argument in terms of the issue identified by the question.

Glossary of terms

Adjutant   Military assistant.

Anatolia   The core territory of the Turkish Empire, covering most of the modern Turkish republic.

Anglo-French colonial *entente*   An understanding reached by Britain and France on colonial issues, sometimes called the *Entente cordiale* because it led to the restoration of good Anglo-French relations.

Anschluss   The union of Austria with Germany.

Anzac   Australian and New Zealand Army Corps.

Appeasement   The conciliation of a potential enemy by making concessions. The term is particularly applied to Neville Chamberlain's policy towards Nazi Germany.

Associated power   The USA was not bound by any treaties with Britain and France in 1917–19, and was free, if necessary, to pursue its own policies.

Atlantic Charter   Statement of basic principles issued jointly by Roosevelt and Churchill in 1941.

Autarchy   Economic self-sufficiency.

Autocratic   Absolute government by one person.

Balfour Declaration   A communication of November 1917 to the Zionists by A.J. Balfour, British foreign secretary, declaring British support for establishing a national home for the Jews in Palestine.

'Balkan Prussia'   Bulgaria was compared to Prussia, which in the eyes of the Allies had an aggressive and militarist reputation.

Balkanisation   Breaking up of empires into small and often hostile states, as was done with Austria-Hungary.

Benevolent neutrality   Favouring one side while not officially supporting them.

Black Hand   This secret terrorist organisation was founded in May 1911 and by 1914 probably had about 2500 members. They included a considerable number of the army officers who had taken part in the Serbian revolution of 1903. Its aim was to work for the union of the Serbs living in the Austrian and Turkish Empires with Serbia.

Blank cheque   A free hand, unconditional support.

Boers   Descendants of Dutch settlers who had originally colonised South Africa.

Bolshevism   The ideology of the Russian Communist (Bolshevik) Party. It was based on the theories of Karl Marx and Lenin, which predicted the overthrow of capitalism and the creation of socialism.

Bonds   Certificates issued by a government or large company promising to repay borrowed money at a fixed rate of interest by a specified date.

Buffer state   A small state positioned between two much larger ones.

Carnegie Endowment for International Peace   An organisation founded by industrialist Andrew Carnegie. It describes itself as being dedicated to advancing co-operation between nations.

Carthaginian peace   A peace aimed at destroying the enemy. The term derives from the peace imposed on Carthage by Rome in 146BC.

Central Powers   The wartime alliance of Germany, Austria, Turkey and Bulgaria.

Charismatic   Commanding magnetic charm which inspires enthusiasm and loyalty in others.

China Squadron   Units of the German navy used for protecting their possessions in the Far East.

Chinese Civil War   Initially fought between the Nationalists and Communists under Mao Zedong in 1927–37. It flared up again in 1946, ending in the defeat of the Nationalists in 1949.

Collateral security   Bonds or property pledged as a guarantee for the repayment of a loan.

Collective security   Security gained through joining an alliance or signing an agreement where the security of each state is guaranteed by the others.

Comintern   The Communist international movement set up in 1919 to organise worldwide revolution.

Comity of nations   Nations which respect each other's laws and instituions.

Condominium   Joint control of a territory by two states.

Confederation   A grouping of states in which each state retains its sovereignty.

Conference of Ambassadors   Standing committee set up to supervise the carrying out of the Treaty of Versailles.

Congress   The US parliament.

Congressional elections   The elections to the US Senate and House of Representatives took place on 5 November 1918. The Republicans secured an overall majority of two seats in the Senate and 50 in the House.

Conscription   Compulsory military service.

Convoy system   Group of ships travelling together under escort.

Counter-revolutionary   Person who opposes a revolution and wants to reverse its results.

Covenant   Rules and constitution of the League of Nations.

Creditor nation   A state which lends or invests surplus capital abroad.

Creeping barrage   A moving curtain of artillery fire aimed to eliminate opposition in front of advancing troops.

Curzon line   The proposed demarcation line between Bolshevik Russia and Poland, as suggested by the British foreign secretary, Lord Curzon.

Customs union   An economic bloc, the members of which trade freely with each other.

Defensive alliance   An agreement between two states whereby each will come to the defence of the other if attacked.

Deliberative chamber   An assembly appointed to debate or discuss issues.

Demilitarised   Having all military defences removed.

Détente   A process of lessened tension or growing relaxation between two states.

Diplomatic revolution   A complete change in alliances and relations between states.

Dominions   The British Dominions of Australia, Canada, New Zealand and South Africa were self-governing, but part of the British Empire and the Commonwealth, of which to this day they are still members.

Dreadnought   A class of battleship of 17,900 tons compared to the conventional size of 16,000, its speed was 21 knots rather than 16, and it was much better armed than its predecessors.

Dunkirk   In May 1940 the British Expeditionary Force in France was compelled to retreat to Dunkirk and was only rescued by a risky sea evacuation.

Economic integration   Mutual dependence and the coming together of national economies.

Élites   The ruling classes.

Entente   A friendly understanding between states, rather than a formal alliance.

Executive committee   A committee which can take key decisions.

Fait accompli   A French phrase meaning an accomplished fact or deed.

Fascism   The Fascist Party was formed in Italy by Mussolini in 1919. Its programme combined social reforms and a tax on war profits with an intensely nationalist foreign policy.

Fatherland's Party   The party was founded close to the end of 1917 and represented political circles supporting the war. By the summer of 1918 it had around 1,250,000 members.

Federation   A system of government in which several countries or regions form a unity but still manage to remain self-governing in internal affairs.

Fixed ratio   A scheme whereby Germany would agree not to increase the number of ships beyond a certain percentage of the British fleet.

Formal annexation   Taking over full control of a territory by another power.

Free trade   Trade between nations unimpeded by tariffs.

Free-trade zone   An area where countries can trade freely without restrictions.

Fulfilment   A policy by Germany aimed at extracting concessions from Britain and France by at least temporarily accepting the main demands of the Treaty of Versailles.

Furnishing   Provision.

General staff   A group of officers which plans operations and administrates an army.

German satellite   A state completely dominated by Germany.

Gold standard   A system by which the value of a currency is defined in terms of gold. The value of the pound was linked to gold. On 20 September 1931 the pound was forced off the gold standard and its value fell from $4.86 to $3.49.

Great Depression   The world economic slump from 1929 to 1933.

Greater Asia Co-Prosperity Sphere   A bloc of territory dominated and exploited by Japan which embraced Manchuria, China and parts of South-east Asia. Japan's aim was to create a self-sufficient bloc free of the Western powers and under its own control.

Guerrilla war   An irregular war fought by small groups of troops acting independently.

Honest broker   Impartial mediator.

Howitzer   A gun for firing shells at relatively high trajectories, with a steep angle of descent.

Hyperinflation   Massive daily increases in the prices of goods and in the amount of money being printed.

Ice-free port   A seaport that can be used throughout the year.

Imperial War Cabinet   A cabinet made up of prime ministers of the self-governing Commonwealth countries.

Imperialism   The policy of acquiring and controlling dependent territories carried out by a state.

Inter-Allied commissions   Allied committees set up to deal with particular tasks.

Inter-Allied consensus   Agreement between the Allies.

International civil service   A permanent administration made up of officials from all the member states.

Inviolability   Not to be changed or violated.

Isolationist   Remaining aloof from international politics.

Isolationists   US politicians who were opposed to any US commitments or entanglements in Europe or elsewhere.

Jameson raid   Armed intervention in the Transvaal led by the British politician in Cape Colony, Leander Starr Jameson, over the New Year weekend of 1895–6.

Khedive   The title used by the governor and ruler of Egypt and the Sudan.

Kiaochow   In 1897 the Germans seized Kiachow in revenge for the murder of two missionaries. They also secured mining rights in the neighbouring province of Shantung.

League of Patriots   The French far-right league, founded by the nationalist poet Paul Déroulède in 1882.

Lebensraum   Literally 'living space', which Hitler hoped to acquire in Russia for German settlement.

Left   Term used to denote parties stretching from Social Democrat to Communist.

Liberal ideology   Belief in constitutional government and individual and economic freedom.

Locarno spirit   The optimistic mood of reconciliation and compromise that swept through Europe after the signing of the Locarno Treaties.

Luftwaffe   The German air force.

Maginot line   A line of concrete fortifications, which France constructed along its borders with Germany. It was named after André Maginot, the French minister of defence.

Magyar   Ethnic Hungarians.

Mandates   Ex-German or Turkish territories entrusted by the League of Nations to one of the Allied powers to govern in accordance with the interests of the local population.

Marshall Plan   Programme of financial support by the US government to western Europe announced in 1948.

Mesopotamia   An ancient Greek term literally meaning 'the land between two rivers': the Tigris and Euphrates. Today this area consists of Iraq, as well as some parts of north-eastern Syria, south-eastern Turkey and south-western Iran.

Militarism   Excessive emphasis on military ideals and strength. The supremacy of military values such as discipline, obedience and courage in a society.

Milliard   One thousand million; now largely superseded by the term billion.

Mitteleuropa   A German-controlled central Europe.

Mobilisation   Preparing the armed forces for war.

Moratorium   Temporary suspension of payments.

Multilateral commitments   Membership of international organisations.

Mutilated victory   A victory which was scarred by the refusal of the Allies to give Italy what it had been promised.

Nation-state   A state consisting of an ethnically and culturally united population.

National Service League   A British pressure group founded in February 1902 to alert the country to the inability of the army to fight a major war and to propose the solution of national service.

National Socialism   German National Socialism had many similarities with Fascism, but its driving force was race, and in particular anti-Semitism.

Nationalism   A patriotic belief by a people in the virtues and power of their nation.

Neutral zone   A belt of territory which would be occupied by neither German nor Allied troops.

Non-aggression pact   An agreement between two or more countries not to resort to force.

Nuremberg trials   The trials of war criminals in Nuremberg after the Second World War.

Official historian   A historian appointed by the government to write the history of the war.

Opportunism   Seizing the opportunity when it occurs.

Pan Slavs   Russian nationalists who believed that the Slavs in central and south-eastern Europe should be liberated by their fellow Slavs in Russia.

Panacea   Remedy supposed to cure every problem.

Pandemic   An epidemic on a global scale.

Parliamentary government   A government that is responsible to a parliament elected by the people.

Passive resistance   Refusal to co-operate, stopping short of actual violence.

Peace bloc   A group of states committed to opposing aggressor powers.

People's war   Popular war fought by the mass of the people.

Permanent Court of International Justice   An institution set up at The Hague, in the Netherlands, by Article 14 of the Covenant of the League of Nations in 1920.

Philanthropy   The desire to help humanity.

Phoney war   The period from October 1939 to March 1940 when there was no fighting in western Europe.

Plan 17   The French plan to make a frontal attack on Germany if war broke out.

Plebiscite   A referendum, or vote, by the electorate on a single issue.

Pressure group   An association formed to promote a particular interest by influencing government policy.

Programme school   Historians who believe that Hitler had a specific programme to carry out.

Proletarian nation   A nation that lacked an empire and raw materials. Like the proletariat (workers), it was poor.

Protection   Stopping foreign goods by levying tariffs or taxes on imports.

Protectorate   A territory that is controlled and protected by another state.

Provisional Government   A government in power until the holding of elections.

Prussia   An independent state until German unification in 1871.

The purges   The elimination of about 7 million people alleged to be traitors in the USSR in 1936–8.

Putsch   Takeover of power.

Pyrrhic victory   A victory won at such a high cost that it damages the victor.

Quadruple alliance   An alliance of four powers.

Ratified   Having received formal approval from parliament.

Red Army   The Soviet army.

Reich   The German Empire or state.

Reichsbank   The national bank of Germany.

Reichstag   German parliament.

Reichswehr   The German army 1919–35.

Reparations   Compensation paid by a defeated power to make good the damage it caused in a war.

Rhineland separatism   A movement supporting separation of the Rhineland from Germany.

Right   Term used to denote parties stretching from Conservative to Nazi or Fascist (extreme right).

Rump Bulgaria   What was left of Bulgaria after its partition at the Berlin Congress.

Schlieffen Plan   Planned a two-front war against France and Russia. France was to be defeated within a month by a flanking movement through Belgium, the Netherlands and Luxembourg and then the mass of the German army would move eastwards to deal with Russia. The plan was later revised to omit the Netherlands.

Second industrial revolution   The development of electrical, chemical and engineering industries beginning at the end of the nineteenth century.

Secret annex   Secret addition to a treaty.

Secret diplomacy   Diplomatic contacts, meetings and decisions which are not made public.

Self-governing principality   A semi-independent state ruled by a prince.

Slavs   An ethnic group in central and eastern Europe, of which the Russians are the largest component.

Social cohesion   The social unity of a country.

Social Darwinism   The application of Darwin's theory of the survival of the fittest to international relations, justifying the absorption of smaller, weaker states by more powerful ones.

Social imperialism   A policy aimed at uniting all social classes behind plans for creating and expanding an empire.

Socialism   A belief that the community as a whole rather than individuals should control the economy.

Soviets   Elected councils.

SPD   Social Democratic Party of Germany. Its leaders were hostile to Bolshevism and believed in parliamentary government.

Stabilise the mark   In November 1924 the devalued German currency was replaced temporarily by the *Rentenmark* and then, in August 1924, by the new *Reichsmark*, which was put on the gold standard. Theoretically, this meant that banknotes could be converted into agreed, fixed quantities of gold.

State visit   Ceremonial visit by a head of state.

Status quo   A Latin term to denote the state of affairs as it exists at the moment.

Straits zone   The shores along the Straits of Dardanelles were occupied by Allied troops.

Strategy   The military planning and management of war.

Stresa Powers   The powers who attended the Stresa Conference in 1935.

Successor states   States that were created after the collapse of Austria-Hungary.

Sudeten Germans   Ethnic Germans who had been settled in the Sudetenland since the thirteenth century.

Superpower   A state much larger in size and possessing much larger armed forces than most of the other powers.

Supreme Economic Council   Allied body with the power to deal with economic issues.

Synthetic materials   Objects imitating a natural product but made chemically.

Tariffs   Taxes placed on imported goods to protect the home economy.

Total war   A war waged by a state in which the whole population is involved and every resource is used to further the war.

Trade monopoly   Exclusive control of trade.

Transvaal   This was an independent state, although by agreement with the British in 1884 it could not conclude treaties with foreign powers without their agreement.

Triad   A group of three.

Triple *Entente*   The name often applied to the co-operation of Britain, France and Russia in 1907–17.

Two-front war   A war in which fighting takes place on two geographically separate fronts.

Unrestricted submarine warfare   Sinking by German submarines (called U-boats) of all merchant ships, Allied or neutral, engaged in carrying goods to or from Allied states.

USSR   The Union of Soviet Socialist Republics. The new Bolshevik name for Russia and its satellite states.

Vacuum of power   Territories left undominated by another state after the withdrawal or collapse of the original ruling power.

Volte-face   An about-turn; a sudden and complete change of policy.

Wall Street Crash   The 1929 collapse of share prices in the US stock exchange, located in Wall Street, New York.

War guilt   Carrying the blame for starting the war.

War party   A group of ministers supporting Britain's entry into the war.

Waterloo   In 1815 the British and Prussian armies defeated Napoleon in the Battle of Waterloo.

Wehrverein   Literally 'defence league'. This pressure group was founded in Germany in 1912 to press for an increase in the size of the army.

Weltpolitik   Literally 'world policy' or a policy that attempted to make Germany a global power.

White Russians   The name given to members and supporters of the counter-revolutionary 'White' armies, which fought against the Bolshevik Red Army in the Russian Civil War (1918–21).

Young Turk Movement   The name given to a reform movement in the Turkish Empire. Its members were originally exiles in western Europe.

Yugoslavs   A term for the South Slav inhabitants of Austro-Hungary.

Zionists   Supporters of Zionism, a movement for re-establishing the Jewish state.

Further reading

General texts

M. Kitchen, *Europe Between the Wars: A Political History* **(Longman, 1988)**

Useful survey of Europe 1919–39

A.J.P. Taylor, *The Struggle for Mastery in Europe, 1848–1918* **(Oxford University Press, 1971)**

An interesting and lively study, particularly good on eastern Europe and imperialism

Chapters 1 and 2

J. Joll, *First World War,* **second edition (Longman, 1992)**

Helpful assessments of contemporary militarism and imperialism

J. Lowe and R. Pearce, *Rivalry and Accord: International Relations, 1870–1914,* **second edition (Hodder, 1998)**

A good introduction to Great Power diplomacy during this period

N. Rich, *Great Power Diplomacy, 1814–1914* **(McGraw-Hill, 1992)**

Contains excellent analyses of the period 1870–1914

J. Steinberg, *Bismarck: A Life* **(Oxford University Press, 2011)**

Contains a detailed account of Bismarck's foreign policy

D.G. Williamson, *Bismarck and Germany 1862–1890,* **third edition (Pearson, 2011)**

Succinct analysis of Bismarckian diplomacy

Chapter 3

M. Hastings, *Catastrophe: Europe goes to War* **(HarperCollins, 2014)**

A detailed blockbuster on the outbreak of war

R. Henig, *The Origins of The First World War,* **second edition (Routledge, 1993)**

A brief but scholarly study

M. Hewitson, *Germany and the Causes of the First World War 1914* **(Berg, 2004)**

A helpful study of why Germany went to war in 1914

W.L. Langer, *The Diplomacy of Imperialism, 1890–1902,* **revised edition (Knopf, 1951)**

The classic study on the complexities of imperial rivalries at the end of the nineteenth century

M. MacMillan, *The War that Ended Peace* **(Profile Books, 2014)**

A well-written and thought-provoking book

A. Mombauer, *The Origins of the First World War* **(Pearson, 2002)**

Excellent on the controversies and debates about the war's causes

Chapter 4

R. Chickering, *Imperial Germany and the Great War, 1914–1918* **(Cambridge University Press, 1998)**

Excellent survey of Germany at war

N. Ferguson, *The Pity of War* **(Penguin Books, 1999)**

An interesting and thoughtful account of the causes and course of the First World War

D. Stevenson, *The First World War and International Politics* **(Oxford University Press, 1998)**

An invaluable analysis of international politics 1914–18

N. Stone, *World War One: A Short History* **(Allen Lane, 2010)**

A good up-to-date account of the war

Chapter 5

R. Henig, *Versailles and After, 1919–33,* **second edition (Routledge, 1995)**

A clear summary of the facts and the controversies surrounding the peace treaties

M. MacMillan, *Peacemakers* **(John Murray, 2001)**

Readable and a mine of information on the peace treaties

A.J. Mayer, *Politics and Diplomacy in Peacemaking: Containment and Counterrevolution at Versailles* **(Weidenfeld & Nicolson, 1968)**

Good for detail on 'the new diplomacy' as represented by the USA and revolutionary Russia

G. Schulz, *Revolutions and Peace Treaties, 1917–20* (Methuen, 1972)

A survey of the peace treaties with particular emphasis on Germany and Russia

Alan Sharp, editor, *Makers of the Modern World: The Paris Peace Conferences 1919–23* (Haus, 2009)

Helpful for biographies of the main statesmen at the Paris conferences and also for the international consequences of the treaties

Chapter 6

R. Henig, *The League of Nations* (Haus, 2010)

A helpful analysis and study

M. Housden, *League of Nations and the Organization of Peace* (Pearson, 2011)

A good review of the League with an interesting collection of sources

C.S. Maier, *Recasting Bourgeois Europe* (Princeton University Press, 1988)

A study of the economic and stabilisation policies of post-war Europe 1919–29

Z. Steiner, *The Lights That Failed: European International History 1919–1933* (Oxford University Press, 2005)

A good study of the 1920s and the impact of the Great Depression

A. Tooze, *The Deluge. The Great War and the Remaking of Global Order, 1916–1931* (Allen Lane, 2014)

A study of the emergence of the USA as a financial superpower dominating the global financial system and its impact on the other powers

J. Wright, *Gustav Stresemann: Weimar's Greatest Statesman* (Oxford University Press, 2002)

Contains useful chapters on Stresemann as chancellor and foreign minister

Chapter 7

R. Boyce, 'World depression, world war: some economic origins of the Second World War' in R. Boyce and E.M. Robertson, editors, *Paths to War: New Essays on the Origins of the Second World War* (Macmillan, 1989)

An informative analysis of the impact of the Great Depression

A. Bullock, 'Hitler and the origins of the Second World War' in E.M. Robertson, editor, *The Origins of the Second World War* (Macmillan, 1971)

Still very useful for understanding the motives behind Hitler's foreign policy

G. Roberts, *The Soviet Union and the Origins of the Second World War, 1933–41* (Macmillan, 1995)

A good guide to Stalin's foreign policy

E. Robertson, *Mussolini as Empire-Builder: Europe and Africa, 1932–1936* (Macmillan, 1979)

An important book for understanding the Abyssinian crisis

Chapter 8

A. Adamthwaite, *France and the Coming of the Second World War* (Frank Cass, 1977)

Excellent book on French foreign policy on the eve of the Second World War

W.M. Carr, *Arms, Autarky and Aggression: A Study in German Foreign Policy 1933–39* (Arnold, 1979)

A clear and incisive analysis of Hitler's foreign policy

'Cato', *Guilty Men* (Penguin Books, 1998)

A reprint of the 1940 classic indictment of appeasement

D. Dutton, *Neville Chamberlain* (Hodder, 2001)

A revisionist assessment of Chamberlain and his role in appeasement

R.J. Overy, *The Origins of the Second World War* (Longman, 1987)

A brief but authoritative study

R.A.C. Parker, *Chamberlain and Appeasement: British Policy and the Coming of the Second World War* (Macmillan, 1993) and *Churchill and Appeasement* (Palgrave, 2000)

Both books take a critical line towards Chamberlain's foreign policy

R. Shay, *British Rearmament in the Thirties: Politics and Profits* (Princeton University Press, 1977)

An important study of the progress made in rearming Britain in the 1930s

A.J.P. Taylor, *The Origins of the Second World War* (Penguin Books, 1991)

Originally published in 1961 but still an important and stimulating book

G. Weinberg, *The Foreign Policy of Hitler's Germany*, volume I, *Diplomatic Revolution in Europe, 1933–36* and volume II, *Starting World War II* (University of Chicago Press, 1970, 1980)

A detailed study of Hitler's foreign policy in two volumes

J. Wright, *Germany and the Origins of the Second World War* (Palgrave, 2007)

A clear, brief and authoritative account of Hitler's foreign policy and motives

Chapter 9

W.G. Beasley, *The Rise of Modern Japan* (Weidenfeld & Nicolson, 1990)

Chapters 10 and 11 are useful for Japan's role in Manchuria and the Far East 1931–45

M. Hannemann, *Japan Faces the World, 1925–1952* (Longman, 2001)

Helpful for understanding Japanese foreign policy and expansion 1919–45

M. Lamb and N. Tarling, *From Versailles to Pearl Harbor* (Palgrave, 2001)

Especially useful for the Japanese and Far Eastern perspective

S. Wilson, *The Manchurian Crisis and Japanese Society 1931–33* (Routledge, 2002)

Puts the crisis into the context of Japanese society and economy

Internet sources

Fordham University's Modern Internet History Sourcebook: www.fordham.edu/halsall/mod.modsbook.asp

A mine of source material including treaties, speeches, and so on

Michael Duff's First World War.com: www.firstworldwar.com

Contains a vast amount of material relevant to the causes, course and consequences of the First World War

British National Archives: www.nationalarchives.gov.uk

US National Archives: www.archives.gov

Both the British and the US National Archives contain an enormous volume of material

Yale Law School. The Avalon Project, Documents in Law, History and Diplomacy: http://avalon.law.Yale.edu/

Useful for treaties and other historical documents covering the period of this book

Index

Acknowledgements:

Allen & Unwin, *Bismarck: The White Revolutionary* by L. Gall, 1986; *The Making of the Second World War* by A.P. Adamthwaite, 1979. Berg, *Germany and the Causes of the First World War* by M. Hewitson, 2004. Cambridge University Press, 'Hitler's "Programme" and the Genesis of Operation "Barbarossa"' by H.W. Koch, *The Historical Journal*, volume 26, no. 4, December 1983; *The New Cambridge Modern History: The Shifting Balance of World Forces* by C.L. Mowat, editor, 1968. Chatto & Windus, *Germany's War Aims* by Fritz Fischer, 1967 . Constable, *King George the Fifth: His Life and Reign* by H. Nicolson, 1952. D.C. Heath, 'Third Balkan War' by Joachim Remak in D.E. Lee, editor, *The Outbreak of the First World War*, 1975. Frank Cass, *France and the Coming of the Second World War* by A. Adamthwaite, 1977; *Great Britain, France and the German Problem, 1918–1939* by W.A. Jordan, 1971. Fromm International, *Mussolini as Diplomat* by R. Lamb, 1999. Hamish Hamilton, *The Origins of the Second World War* by A.J.P. Taylor, 1961. HMSO, *Documents on British Foreign Policy*, third series, volume 4, 1951; *Documents on German Foreign Policy*, series D, volume 1, 1957–66; *Documents on German Foreign*, series D, volume VI, 1957–66. House of Commons, *House of Commons Debates*, volume 141, fifth session, cols 2382–5; *House of Commons Debates*, volume 333, cols 1399–407. John Murray, *Peacemakers* by Margaret MacMillan, 2002. Leicester University Press, *The League of Nations, Its Life and Times, 1920–1946* by F.S. Northedge, 1986; *The League of Nations* by F.S. Northedge, 1988. Liverpool University Press, *Nazism, 1919–1945*, volume 2 by J. Noakes and G. Pridham, editors, 2000; *Nazism, 1919–1945*, volume 3 by J. Noakes and G. Pridham, editors, 2001. Longman, *Imperial Germany* by I. Porter and I. Armour, 1991; *Republican and Fascist Italy* by J. Hiden, 1996; *The Origins of the Second World War* by R. Overy, 1987. Macmillan, *Gustav Stresemann: His Diaries, Letters and Papers*, volume 3 by E. Sutton, editor, 1937; *Paths to War* by R. Boyce and E. Robertson, editors, 1989; *The Eastern Question* by M.S. Anderson, 1966. Methuen, *Revolutions and Peace Treaties, 1917–1921* by G. Schutz, 1972. Odhams, *War Memoirs* by David Lloyd George, 1938. Oxford University Press, *Britain and Europe* by J. Joll, 1967; *Hungary and Her Successors: The Treaty of Trianon and its Consequences* by C.A. Macartney, 1937; *Imperial Germany: The Birth of the German Republic* by A. Rosenberg, 1970; *Speeches and Documents in American History, 1914–1939*, volume IV by R. Birley, editor, 1951. Palgrave, *Germany Since 1815* by D.G. Williamson, 2005. Palgrave Macmillan, *Austria-Hungary and the Origins of the First World War* by Samuel Williamson, 1999. Papermac, *The First World War, 1914–1918* by John Terraine, 1984. Pearson, *Japan Faces the World, 1925–1952* by M.L. Hanneman, 2001. Penguin, *The Pity of War* by Niall Ferguson, 1999; *The Wages of Destruction: The Making and Breaking of the Nazi Economy* by A. Tooze, 2007. Profile Books, *The War that Ended Peace* by M. MacMillan, 2014. Routledge, *The Foreign Policy of France* by J. Néré, 2002. Ullstein, *Denkwürdigkeiten*, volume 3 by Bernhard Fürst von Bülow, 1931. Weidenfeld & Nicolson, *The Roots of Appeasement* by M. Gilbert, 1966. Yale Law School, The Avalon Project, Documents in Law, History and Diplomacy.